CAMBRIDGE ECONOMI

Edited by

C. W. GUILLEBAUD, *St. John's College, Cambridge*

and

MILTON FRIEDMAN, *University of Chicago*

Initiated by the late John Maynard Keynes and continued under the successive editorships of D. H. Robertson and C. W. Guillebaud, the Cambridge Economic Handbooks are, in Lord Keynes's words, "intended to convey to the ordinary reader and to the uninitiated student some conception of the general principles of thought which economists now apply to economic problems." The series is now edited jointly by Mr. Guillebaud and Mr. Friedman in order to bring the best American as well as British economic thinking to bear on the major problems of economics in both countries.

The Economics of Under-developed Countries
By PETER T. BAUER *and* BASIL S. YAMEY

International Economics
By ROY F. HARROD

Supply and Demand
By HUBERT HENDERSON

The Business Cycle
By R. C. O. MATTHEWS

Money
By D. H. ROBERTSON

The Structure of Competitive Industry
By E. A. G. ROBINSON

CAMBRIDGE ECONOMIC HANDBOOKS

Edited by

C. W. GUILLEBAUD, St. John's College, Cambridge

and

MILTON FRIEDMAN, University of Chicago

Inaugurated by the late John Maynard Keynes and continued under the successive editorships of D. H. Robertson and C. W. Guillebaud, the Cambridge Economic Handbooks are, in Lord Keynes's words, "intended to convey to the ordinary reader and to the uninitiated student some conception of the general principles of thought which economists now apply to economic problems." The series is now edited jointly by Mr. Guillebaud and Mr. Friedman in order to bring the best American as well as British economic thinking to bear on the major problems of economics in both countries.

BY PETER T. BAUER AND BASIL S. YAMEY

THE ECONOMICS
of
UNDER-DEVELOPED
COUNTRIES

The University of Chicago Press, Chicago 60637

THE UNIVERSITY OF CHICAGO PRESS

Library of Congress Catalog Card Number: 57-11204

The University of Chicago Press, Chicago 60637
James Nisbet & Co. Ltd., Digswell Place, Welwyn, England
The Macmillan Company of Canada, Toronto 2

Published 1957 by The University of Chicago Press in association with
James Nisbet & Co. Ltd. and The Cambridge University Press

INTRODUCTION

TO THE CAMBRIDGE ECONOMIC HANDBOOKS
BY THE GENERAL EDITORS

SOON after the war of 1914–18 there seemed to be a place for a series of short introductory handbooks, 'intended to convey to the ordinary reader and to the uninitiated student some conception of the general principles of thought which economists now apply to economic problems'.

This Series was planned and edited by the late Lord Keynes under the title 'Cambridge Economic Handbooks' and he wrote for it a General Editorial Introduction of which the words quoted above formed part. In 1936 Keynes handed over the editorship of the Series to Mr. D. H. Robertson, who held it till 1946, when he was succeeded by Mr. C. W. Guillebaud.

It was symptomatic of the changes which had been taking place in the inter-war period in the development of economics, changes associated in a considerable measure with the work and influence of Keynes himself, that within a few years the text of part of the Editorial Introduction should have needed revision. In its original version the last paragraph of the Introduction ran as follows:

'Even on matters of principle there is not yet a complete unanimity of opinion amongst professional economists. Generally speaking, the writers of these volumes believe themselves to be orthodox members of the Cambridge School of Economics. At any rate, most of their ideas about the subject, and even their prejudices, are traceable to the contact they have enjoyed with the writings and lectures of the two economists who have chiefly influenced Cambridge thought for the past fifty years, Dr. Marshall and Professor Pigou.'

Keynes later amended this concluding paragraph to read:

'Even on matters of principle there is not yet a complete unanimity of opinion amongst professional students of the subject. Immediately after the war (of 1914–18) daily economic events were of such a startling character as to divert attention from theoretical complexities. But today, economic science has recovered its wind. Traditional treatments and traditional solutions are being questioned, improved and revised. In the end this activity of research should clear up controversy. But for the moment controversy and doubt are increased. The writers of this Series must apologize to the general reader and to the beginner if many parts of their subject have not yet reached to a degree of certainty and lucidity which would make them easy and straightforward reading.'

Many though by no means all the controversies which Keynes had in mind when he penned these words have since been resolved. The new ideas and new criticisms, which then seemed to threaten to overturn the old orthodoxy, have, in the outcome, been absorbed within it and have served rather to strengthen and deepen it, by adding needed modifications and changing emphasis, and by introducing an altered and on the whole more precise terminology. The undergrowth which for a time concealed that main stream of economic thought to which Keynes referred in his initial comment and to which he contributed so greatly has by now been largely cleared away so that there is again a large measure of agreement among economists of all countries on the fundamental theoretical aspects of their subject.

Conclusion

This agreement on economic analysis is accompanied by wide divergence of views on questions of economic policy. These reflect both different estimates of the quantitative importance of one or another of the conflicting forces involved in any prediction about the consequences of a policy measure and different value judgments about the desirability of the predicted outcome. It still remains as true today as it was when Keynes wrote that—to quote once more from his Introduction:

> 'The Theory of Economics does not furnish a body of settled conclusions immediately applicable to policy. It is a method rather than a doctrine, an apparatus of the mind, a technique of thinking, which helps its possessor to draw correct conclusions.'

This method, while in one sense eternally the same, is in another ever changing. It is continually being applied to new problems raised by the continual shifts in policy views. This is reflected in the wide range of topics covered by the Cambridge Economic Handbooks already published, and in the continual emergence of new topics demanding coverage. Such a series as this should accordingly itself be a living entity, growing and adapting to the changing interests of the times, rather than a fixed number of essays on a set plan.

The wide welcome given to the Series has amply justified the judgment of its founder. Apart from its circulation in the British Empire, it has been published from the start in the United States of America, and translations of the principal volumes have appeared in a number of foreign languages.

The present change to joint Anglo-American editorship is designed to increase still further the usefulness of the Series by expanding the range of potential topics, authors and readers alike. It will succeed in its aim if it enables us to bring to a wider audience on both sides of the Atlantic lucid explanations and significant applications of 'that technique of thinking' which is the hallmark of economics as a science.

C. W. GUILLEBAUD
MILTON FRIEDMAN

CONTENTS

PART I—DESCRIPTIVE AND ANALYTICAL

CHAPTER I

THE RELEVANCE OF ECONOMICS TO UNDER-DEVELOPED COUNTRIES

CHAPTER II

SOME PROBLEMS OF ECONOMIC MEASUREMENT: NATIONAL INCOME AND CAPITAL

CHAPTER III

SOME PROBLEMS OF ECONOMIC MEASUREMENT: LABOUR AND ITS DISTRIBUTION

CHAPTER IV

NATURAL RESOURCES

CHAPTER V

HUMAN RESOURCES:
POPULATION; INSTITUTIONS

CHAPTER VI

HUMAN RESOURCES:
UNEMPLOYMENT AND UNDER-EMPLOYMENT

CHAPTER VII

HUMAN RESOURCES:
REMUNERATION, WANTS AND EFFORTS

CHAPTER VIII

HUMAN RESOURCES: ENTREPRENEURSHIP

CHAPTER IX

CAPITAL: LEVEL AND UTILISATION

CHAPTER X

CAPITAL AND ECONOMIC GROWTH

PART II—GOVERNMENT AND ECONOMIC DEVELOPMENT

CHAPTER XI

GENERAL APPRAISAL OF THE ROLE OF GOVERNMENT

CONTENTS

CHAPTER XII

FUNCTIONS OF GOVERNMENT

CHAPTER XIII

ACCELERATED CAPITAL FORMATION

CHAPTER XIV

SPECIFIC POLICY MEASURES AFFECTING AGRICULTURE

CHAPTER XV

SPECIFIC POLICY MEASURES AFFECTING MANUFACTURING INDUSTRY

PART I

DESCRIPTIVE AND ANALYTICAL

CHAPTER I

THE RELEVANCE OF ECONOMICS TO UNDER-DEVELOPED COUNTRIES

§ 1. **Diversity in the Under-developed Countries.** (The term *under-developed countries* usually refers loosely to countries or regions with levels of real income and capital per head of population which are low by the standards of North America, Western Europe and Australasia.[1] In under-developed countries there is no large-scale application of the fruits of scientific and technological advance to agriculture and industry; subsistence production is generally important and markets comparatively narrow; and manufacturing industry is usually comparatively unimportant. As generally used, the term covers the whole of Asia (with the possible exception of Japan), Africa, Latin-America (with Argentina sometimes omitted) and parts of Eastern and Southern Europe. Defined in this way, the under-developed areas contain about three-quarters of the population of the world.[2]

The under-developed world comprises a very diverse collection of countries.) Although in our view this great diversity of circumstances does not preclude systematic and worthwhile analysis of the economic landscape of under-developed countries, we think it important that the heterogeneity of the under-developed world should be borne in mind throughout

[1] 'Backward' is sometimes used as a synonym for 'under-developed'. The adjective 'poor', in the sense of low income per head of population by Western standards, is perhaps the most descriptive term, but it does not avoid the difficulties of definition which are considered in the text.

[2] Well-known statistics for 1949 compiled by the Statistical Office of the United Nations suggest that about two-thirds of the population of the world lived in countries which together produced less than one-sixth of the income of the world. Average annual income per head in these countries was about 50 dollars as compared with an average of over 900 dollars in the remaining group of the richest countries.

our discussion. The characteristics which are common to these countries are specified by the definition itself: poverty in income and accumulated capital and backwardness in technique by the standards of North America, Western Europe and Australasia. But even in respect of these characteristics there are great differences between the various under-developed countries, and, of course, the richest under-developed country is close to the poorest advanced country. The dividing-line is arbitrary, and no analytical significance can be attached to it; this is independent of the serious difficulties which surround attempts to measure real income or capital and *a fortiori* to make international comparisons of these magnitudes.

There are also great differences in the rate of growth both of total real income and of income per head in different under-developed countries; on these criteria some under-developed countries have progressed much more rapidly than others in recent decades. There generally are considerable differences in the wealth, rate of progress and technical advancement of different parts of a particular country, whether it falls within the classification of under-developed or otherwise. Even to-day some of the rural areas of North America exhibit many features characteristic of the so-called under-developed areas, and this was true to an even greater extent in the 1920's and 1930's. In many under-developed countries there are cities and mining and manufacturing districts with the standards of living, technical achievements and commercial sophistication characteristic of North America and Western Europe. The range of internal regional differences is indeed likely to be greater in under-developed than in more advanced countries: the backwardness of communications, an ubiquitous feature of under-developed economies, hinders economic and cultural intercourse even between towns or regions which are geographically close and subject to the same government and monetary system.

Thus under-developed countries differ from each other even in respect of the features which provide the basis for the distinction between under-developed and advanced; and the different regions within each of them exhibit a similar range of variation. But their heterogeneity does not end here. (The poverty and technical backwardness which unite them, however imperfectly, for purposes of broad classification, are but two economic features among many which are relevant to the studies of the economist.) It is when one turns to some of these other features that the difficulties and dangers of generalisation become even more apparent. We cannot consider them all here; but it is necessary to use some of our limited space to illustrate the wide diversity often masked in the use of the omnibus term, under-developed countries.

(Under-development refers simply to a low level of economic and technical achievement; it does not refer to other achievements or qualities.) Some under-developed countries, including the two largest, China and India, have cultures and civilisations which go back over 2,000 years.) Again, settled government and the sway of law and order have obtained for many years in some of the poorer countries of the world; in others the achievement or restoration of law and order is today the most essential pre-requisite for economic growth.

The under-developed world includes areas where settled methods of agriculture have been practised for many centuries, and others where the inhabitants have not yet passed, or have only recently passed, the stage of shifting cultivation and nomadic economic activity. In some areas land is held under communal tenure of one sort or another, whereas individual tenure is practised in others. (In Burma there is a battle to keep at bay the vigorous growth of natural vegetation; in parts of North Africa and the Middle East the problem is to clothe the barren earth with some vegetation. And the qualities, attitudes and scale of values of the people differ as markedly as the terrain they inhabit.)

Demographically there are also important differences. It seems (though the evidence is conflicting) that even in comparatively recent times the population of China did not increase greatly over long periods. In India population has increased greatly since the beginning of the nineteenth century, but in recent decades the rates of increase have been comparatively small. In parts of Latin-America, the West Indies, Ceylon and in a number of other countries the rate of increase has been very high in recent decades. Just as there are differences in the rate of growth of population, so there are differences in the density of population. Some of the Latin-American and African countries are sparsely populated, while population is dense in China, India and Java. Population has been growing rapidly in some densely inhabited areas, and also in some sparsely settled areas. And the various demographic differences are again associated with quite different rates of growth both of total real income and of income per head.

⟨Under-developed countries show as much variation in their ripeness or suitability for economic development or promise of profitable returns to capital investment in the near future as they do in other respects.⟩ And these differences may reflect differences in institutional arrangements or in natural resources, or in the attitudes and aptitudes of the population. Though the word under-developed, or its occasional synonym, undeveloped, may suggest the contrary, it is wrong to infer that all or even most of the countries in question are particularly suitable for early development on economic terms or at an otherwise reasonable cost. Some parts of Africa or South America have no difficulty in attracting large-scale investments on commercial terms without direct government assistance or encouragement. In other countries, for instance Indonesia, Malaya and Burma, sufficient productive resources may be available or accessible to attract external capital profitably but for the presence of political and institutional barriers. Yet other regions, for instance east and central Africa, might prove suitable for development in the reasonably near future if certain changes are effected in the method of land tenure and in certain official policies, and also perhaps if certain basic services are provided by the government. On the other hand, no one would think of Greenland or of much of the Sahara as promising material for experiments in economic development. Moreover, the real returns on additional capital investment will not necessarily be higher in under-developed economies than in the more advanced ones. In terms of potentiality for further growth and of attractiveness for further investment the United States may well be the most 'under-developed' area of the world.

The under-developed areas also differ greatly in the rate at which they have developed economically in recent decades. Some have stagnated or even stepped back, and have not been caught up in the stream of material progress. But not all have stagnated, and 'stagnant' is not an appropriate synonym for under-developed. In several under-developed countries some of the current social, political and economic problems and tensions arise not from stagnation but from the rapid and unequal rate of development—unequal both in the sense that economic development is far more rapid in some geographical or occupational sectors than in others, and in the sense that changes in incomes and economic structure or the economic relationships of the inhabitants have been more rapid and drastic than changes in other facets of social and political life.

The very rapid and unequal rate of development, together with retarded systems of communications and education, helps to explain the extreme differences and contrasts which may be encountered in parts of Africa, South America and the Far East. In Brazil the city and state of Sao Paulo contain rapidly-growing modern communities, while other parts of the country are primitive and stagnating. Port Harcourt is a thriving and expanding port in Nigeria, in which several Africans operate modern wholesaling enterprises on a large scale; thirty miles from Port Harcourt the sale of meat without the hide has been prohibited to prevent the sale of human flesh for human consumption. Indeed, the anachronistic co-existence of the primitive and the modern and of the tribal and the individual-istic is a conspicuous feature of many under-developed economies.

§ 2. **The Relevance of Economics.** We have emphasised at some length the diversity of under-developed countries.

Such heterogeneity, however, does not prevent the establishment of worthwhile generalisations. The discernment of uniformities underlying diversity of circumstances is the primary task of scientific enquiry and, indeed, of all systematic enquiry into phenomena. We think that it is possible to advance propositions of some generality and depth about these countries. But we feel that many of the relevant differences between under-developed countries are so deep and far-reaching that generalisations about their economies are often of limited applicability only, and this is likely to be so especially when we consider factors influencing the growth of resources, and also the effects of different measures and policies on the growth of resources. We shall throughout try to indicate the basis of our conclusions and the width of generality with which they might be applied.

Although many of the differences between the different parts of the under-developed world are very deep seated, some of the basic tools and concepts of economics apply widely to under-developed countries. This is true, for instance, of the basic elements of supply and demand analysis. Similarly, the theory of inflation, the concepts of substitution at the margin, and of the complementary or competitive relationship between factors of production, are equally enlightening whether used to elucidate events and circumstances in advanced or in under-developed countries.

There are no special economic theories or methods of analysis fashioned uniquely for the study of the under-developed world. But while the tools of analysis are of wide relevance, in a study of under-developed countries the situations to which they must be applied vary greatly. The data which have to be considered and elucidated differ in degree and may differ in kind. The economist, although equipped with versatile general-purpose tools, must proceed with caution both in the way in which he uses them and in the identification of the relevant data in a situation or problem to which he is applying them. For example, subsistence production is generally of greater relative importance in under-developed than in advanced economies. It is true that this refers to a difference of degree rather than of kind; but the difference may sometimes be important analytically or operationally. The results of an analysis which is appropriate to an economy in which the subsistence sector is negligible may have to be modified materially when applied to an economy in which exchange is peripheral or not pervasive. We shall in several parts of the book illustrate the relevance of this difference.

Although we think that a substantial measure of generality can be claimed for much of economic theory and of its methods of analysis, we feel equally that some of the main developments in economics over the last half-century or so are of little use for the study of under-developed countries.

In the half-century before the Second World War the advances in economic theory were largely in fields of equilibrium analysis and in subjects related to it.[1] The principal concern of economic theorists of this period (sometimes conveniently known as post-classical economics) was with the theory of value, the theory of the firm and the theory of income distribution which were explored by the method of equilibrium analysis. The writers were concerned with the formal conditions of equilibrium situations, defined as situations which continue unchanged in the absence of external disturbances. Trade cycle theory and the theory of employment also were concerned with movements away from and towards equilibrium, the emphasis being on short-period oscillations in economic activity and employment about an assumed trend. In these fields important advances were made, and the applied economist cannot complain that economic theory has not enough to offer in these fields. Indeed, he is more likely to be confused by an embarrassment of riches and the difficulty of distinguishing the relevant and apposite from what is merely fascinating or ingenious. On the other hand he will find, especially if he is interested in under-developed countries, that some problems that are central to his enquiries

[1] Apart from advances in specialised fields such as econometrics and economic statistics.

were more or less completely left out of the purview of economics for about half a century. The analysis of the factors affecting the level, efficiency and growth of resources in a economy was outside the scope of the deliberations of economic theorists. The discussion was generally at a high level of abstraction, so much, indeed, that the principal long-term determinants of income and wealth, such as the factors underlying the growth of capital, the size of population, the attitude towards work, saving and risk-bearing, the quality of entrepreneurship and the extent of markets, were considered as institutional forces or facts given, as data, to the economist. In his technical or professional capacity he was not directly concerned with the data as such, or with the causes and course of changes in the data. Such studies of these forces and facts as were made by some economists were largely outside the main stream of the subject.

In recent years there has been a reaction to these self-imposed restrictions on the subject matter of economic theory. There seem to be several reasons for the growing dissatisfaction with the customary methods of enquiry. The distinction between the problems of the allocation of given resources and those of the growth of resources is sometimes not quite so clear as is implied; for instance, more efficient utilisation of capital and labour can be seen as a re-allocation of available resources and also as a growth of resources. Further, the problems of the growth and change of resources often raise issues which are of much greater practical significance than those of the allocation of given resources. They are intellectually as interesting and, to some extent, as amenable to treatment by some of the traditional methods of economics as those other problems which in fact attracted most attention. Again, it has come to be realised that the high level of simplification adopted in economic theory in the decades before the recent war abstracted from so many major factors that the variables retained for examination were not always or usually sufficiently important to help substantially with the fullest possible understanding and interpretation of phenomena, and particularly with the establishment of functional relationships. Though the analysis may have been logically correct and formally elegant, it dealt with too few of the influences affecting the situation, so that the results were of limited intellectual or practical interest. Increased preoccupation with the practical problems, especially of the so-called under-developed world, may also have contributed to the reaction against the methods of post-classical economics. In general, preoccupation with immediate issues of policy is often rather detrimental to the advance of systematic enquiry and especially of the methodology of a subject; but in this case it may have had some beneficial effects.

In some of the more recent literature, especially in some (though by no means all) discussions on under-developed countries and on economic development, greater attention has been paid to factors disregarded until recently in the main themes of post-classical economics. In particular economists have come to consider factors and influences which previously had been relegated to institutional literature or left to other disciplines. We shall follow this example in this book and consider such factors and influences. We do so because some of these greatly influence the economic situation in under-developed countries, and also because we think that economic propositions of some generality and depth can be established about them and their interaction with the variables and influences usually studied by economists.[1]

Many of the topics now considered in discussions on under-developed countries and economic development are not new to the literature of economics. Many were treated at length by the classical economists and tended to drop out of the treatises only towards the end of the nineteenth century. The tables of contents of some of the recent writings on under-developed countries resemble those of the works of economists from Adam Smith to Alfred Marshall more than they do those

---

[1] Examples include the effects of different systems of land tenure, or of family obligations, on agricultural productivity and on the supply of labour in non-agricultural occupations; and the influences affecting the emergence and effectiveness of restrictive tendencies.

of the text books and treatises of the inter-war period. The change in interest and emphasis is in a sense the resumption of an earlier practice rather than a complete break with the traditions of the subject; this strengthens the presumption that the current preoccupation with the economic problems of under-developed countries is not likely to be a passing whim, and that the range of topics is at least partly within the traditional scope of economics.

The return to some of the traditional topics of economic enquiry is, however, comparatively recent. We have already emphasised the diversity of under-developed countries and suggested that this is at all times likely to limit the scope of successful generalisation. But the comparatively recent change in interest may also partly explain the paucity of successfully established generalisations in this field. The great emphasis on more or less immediate practical issues may also have contributed to this comparative barrenness.

The shift of interest among economists to the study of the growth of resources would be unfortunate if it led to the neglect of the study of the best use of available resources, on the analysis of which so much attention has been lavished during the last half-century. Such neglect would be particularly serious in investigations into the problems of poor countries. Improvements in the use of available resources and the removal of man-made restrictions on their use are likely to release new productive energies, to stimulate the increase of resources, and to provide part of the means for sustaining growth. Policies and measures purporting to promote economic growth in the long run should be scrutinised for their effects on the use of given resources in the shorter run. For example, uniform railway rates designed to assist in the opening up of new farming areas and the enlargement of the economy should be considered in the light of their effects on established farming areas and the deployment of scarce transport resources. The problems of the allocation of resources and of their long-term growth are inter-related, and this should be recognised in their economic analysis.

§ **3. Scope of this Book.** The aim of our book is not to pro-pose a theory of development, nor to present a bird's-eye view of the under-developed world, nor yet primarily to present a set of proposals for the acceleration of economic growth. Our purpose in Part I is to illumine certain features of the economic landscape of the under-developed world. The topics treated have been selected partly with an eye to their susceptibility to economic analysis and partly for their general interest. We are concerned with what is or tends to be, rather than with what ought to be; that is, we are concerned with positive rather than with normative propositions.

In Part II we turn to certain aspects of the role of govern-ment in promoting economic development.[1] Here much of the emphasis is on normative propositions, and the discussion ranges beyond the confines of economics. Political judgment and political attitudes and preferences have a prominent role, which we recognise explicitly. Nevertheless, economic analy-sis is relevant for the assessment of particular measures of policy, and many of the topics considered in Part I bear directly on broad issues of development policy.

It is, of course, arguable that one's political outlook so colours one's judgment that even propositions which purport to be purely positive are chosen, possibly subconsciously, in accordance with one's political bias, so that even apparently positive propositions have a normative colouring. We try as far as we can to draw the distinction between normative and positive propositions and, further, to indicate or to suggest the basis of our observations; where propositions are depen-dent on conjecture and on a political position, we try to make this clear. But we do not accept the view that because political opinions influence one's choice of topics as well as the weight attached to different influences, therefore the reasoning and the propositions even of positive economics

[1] For convenience of exposition and in order to avoid repetition, in one or two instances we deal briefly with some aspects of government policy also in Part I. The reader will have no difficulty in distinguishing the relevant passages.

are essentially subjective and political and in this way of only very limited value. Reference to its political and psychological origins does not in itself affect the validity of a proposition or argument. Thus an economist who is critical of the capitalist system may concentrate on supposed defects of the system to the exclusion of its achievements or of the defects of alternative systems; but the value and validity of his observations on his chosen topics would be independent of his preconceptions and choice of subject.

In our discussion we use statistics only sparingly. The scarcity of reliable data is not the main reason for this. Many of the most significant features of economic life in under-developed countries and many of the influences conditioning economic growth are not susceptible to meaningful measurement or numerical expression. Some of the difficulties of quantification are illustrated in Chapters II and III. However, the difficulties of statistical measurement need not obstruct the investigation of the economics of under-developed areas or the implications of their economic growth. The difficulty or impossibility of submitting certain economic phenomena to quantitative treatment, or the insufficiency of statistical information, does not mean that the phenomena cannot be understood and analysed. Quantitative analysis and measurement are not always more precise and meaningful than qualitative analysis and assessment, and it would be misleading if discussion and analysis were confined to that part of the data which can conveniently be expressed in quantitative terms.

In Part I the topics with which we are concerned are grouped in terms of productive resources rather than of economic activities; this is largely a matter of convenience. In Part II, after discussing the role of government in economic life generally, we turn to particular topics in agriculture and manufacturing industry respectively; at this stage when considering particular measures of policy it is more appropriate to group them in terms of major classifications of activity. We have no separate discussion of government policy and trading activities. This omission does not reflect a disregard of the importance of these activities.   We indicate in many parts of the discussion the pervasive influence of trade on the distribution and growth of resources and its role in widening people's access to alternatives; this seems to us a more appropriate indication of its influence than treatment under a more restricted or specialised heading.

CHAPTER II

SOME PROBLEMS OF ECONOMIC MEASURE-
MENT: NATIONAL INCOME AND CAPITAL

In the first chapter we referred briefly to economic statistics
in under-developed countries. In the present chapter we give
more detailed consideration to the problems of measurement
of the important economic magnitudes of income and capital.
These two concepts are frequently encountered in modern
economic analysis, and estimates of the relevant magnitudes
for particular economies often figure in discussions of policy
measures. In Chapter III we take further examples to illustrate the conceptual and practical difficulties of economic
measurement; these are drawn from the field of labour statistics. Several facets of economic life in many under-developed
countries are examined in the course of the discussion of
problems of quantification.

§ 1. The National Income and its Measurement. The calculation of the national income in any country is surrounded by
conceptual and practical difficulties even if the country has
well-developed statistical services and sources of information.[1]
The appropriate treatment (that is inclusion or exclusion) of
entire classes and categories of goods and services is often a
matter of doubt, admitting of no unambiguous answer; and
the need to express the flow of goods and services in money

[1] There is a large literature on the definition and measurement of the
national income. Those most helpful include J. R. Hicks, *The Social
Framework*, 2nd ed., Oxford, 1952; J. R. N. Stone, 'Definition and Mea-
surement of the National Income and Related Totals', in *Measurement of
National Income and the Construction of Social Accounts*, United Nations,
Geneva, 1947; H. C. Edey and A. T. Peacock, *National Income and Social
Accounting*, London, 1954; and A. R. Prest and I. G. Stewart, *The National
Income of Nigeria, 1950–51*, London, 1953.

terms presents additional problems. The inclusion or exclusion of certain items and the selection of the basis for valuation involve choices which are often necessarily arbitrary. Thus it is the usual practice to exclude the services rendered by a person to himself or to members of his family but to include the goods produced and consumed within the family circle. Again, it is the common but debatable procedure to value farm produce consumed by the farmer and his family at its realisable value ex-farm, and not at its retail value.

There are even more acute difficulties in distinguishing in border-line instances between payments for services (to be included) and payments which reflect mere transfers of income between individuals or between individuals and government. Serious problems of definition and measurement also arise because it is difficult to distinguish between final and intermediate goods and services, that is, to decide whether a particular type of commodity should be considered part of the net flow of goods and services produced or part of the necessary cost of producing that flow. A significant proportion of the flow of goods and services conventionally included in calculations of the national income is quite as much part of the cost of producing the national income as of the national income itself. While the difficulties apply to many of the component elements of the national income, they are especially acute in the treatment of government services, and expert opinion is divided on the question of the extent to which government services should be included in the net national income. There are further problems in the treatment of government services because they are not usually bought and sold in markets but are paid for out of the proceeds of taxation imposed by government; there are no market prices at which they can be valued to measure the intensity of demand for them.

In every calculation or estimate of the national income decisions must be made on each of several points on which there are differences of opinion stemming from conceptual and practical difficulties. There is no simple and unambiguously correct course to follow; decisions are necessarily a matter of preference or convenience, and hence are arbitrary. This gives rise to the possibility that national income computations for different countries may not be based on identical definitions or on identical treatment of economically similar items. Moreover, even if estimates for a number of countries are standardised in the sense that different categories of goods and services are treated similarly, it does not follow that they are strictly comparable; for example, uniformity of treatment may go hand in hand with non-comparability and unconscious bias if the categories of services which are excluded uniformly are relatively more important in some countries than in others or in some stages of development than in others. The quest for uniformity of treatment to yield strictly comparable results is inherently self-defeating where the organisation of production and consumption is essentially different in the countries in question.

The difficulties of placing estimates on a strictly comparable basis and of avoiding bias are probably quite minor when comparisons of national income estimates are made between advanced economies, for example, the leading industrial countries. But even these comparisons are often much affected by differences in the magnitude and content of government expenditure, and by the arbitrariness of the distinction between final and intermediate goods. Moreover, in international income comparisons problems are posed by the need to translate the basic statistics, which are expressed in different national currencies, into a common currency.

The sources of bias and the obstacles in the way of achieving comparability are more significant when comparisons are made between estimates for under-developed economies and those for more advanced economies. This is so because the categories of items which present difficulties differ in their relative importance in poor and in rich countries. On balance it is almost certain that these categories are generally more important in poor countries. This is true of services produced for consumption by producers and their families, of expenditures which are difficult to classify unequivocally either as payments for services or as transfers of income, and of goods produced and consumed in the subsistence sector of the economy. However, it may be that those types of goods and services, the allocation of which between final and intermediate goods is especially difficult, are relatively more important in richer countries.

The exclusion of intra-family services from calculations of the national income affects international comparisons markedly. In many under-developed countries the concept of the family is much wider than in the West; other things being the same this means that services produced by members of the so-called extended family or family group for consumption within the family occupy a more important place in economic activity. Moreover, whereas the intra-family performance of services in the West are predominantly of a non-commercial character and therefore may be left out of account with more reason, many of the transactions between members of the so-called extended family in parts of Africa do not differ in character from business dealings with outsiders in the market. For example, in West Africa women's services to the rest of the family are often paid for; their earnings from some activities cannot be touched by other members of the family, and wives often sue their husbands for debt arising from intra-family transactions. Again, services rendered by an individual for his own use, or for use within the family circle in the more restricted sense of the term, also tend to be relatively more important in under-developed than in economically advanced countries or regions.[1]

We have already noted that the distinction between transfer payments and payments for services is often difficult to draw. Here again in under-developed countries the amount and range of activities and transactions affected are relatively more important than in the West, and the conceptual problems raised are more acute. Not only does a much wider range of

[1] But we show in the next chapter that people in richer countries are apt to provide for themselves certain categories of services which are bought and sold in poorer countries. In practice, however, the statistician may find it difficult to collect reliable data on the volume or value of these services in under-developed countries.

economic activity take place within the family or clan, but there are also multifarious obligations or payments between members, sometimes unaccompanied by the rendering of any service but often in return for nominal or small services the value of which is not related directly to the payment. This lack of correspondence between service and payment applies also to payments and donations to chiefs, priests and so on. There are whole classes of people in some countries the bulk of whose income is on the shadowy borderline dividing receipts for services rendered from receipts from unilateral transfers. Gratuities are a significant part of the income of lower-paid government servants, minor chiefs and so on in many under-developed countries. The position of beggars, a numerous class in many under-developed countries, deserves a passing mention. Beggary is often a distinct occupation, entry into which may be restricted to certain persons; as is well known, it is sometimes, as in parts of India, reserved for certain clearly defined groups. To confuse the picture still more, beggars often perform some economic activity; in some Middle Eastern countries they sort and clean the food given to them and re-sell it as food or feedingstuffs.

We have noted that it is the convention to include the value of subsistence production of commodities in calculations of the national income. This gives rise to two difficulties: statistics of the output of food and other goods which do not reach the market may be inadequate and inaccurate, and the valuation of commodities which are not bought and sold poses special problems. These difficulties complicate the work of economic statisticians in advanced countries; in under-developed areas they are far more serious. Subsistence production particularly of food is relatively more important; many under-developed countries have only in recent decades begun to be drawn into the orbit of a money economy. The subsistence sector is still important in most under-developed countries. Moreover, the statistics of the volume of this production are generally very imperfect.

In the valuation of subsistence production the choice lies

essentially between prices at the farm and prices paid by consumers in the retail market. A case can be made for each of the bases, and naturally the value imputed to the output depends upon the particular choice which is made. The difference is not likely to be significant when the difference between ex-farm and retail prices is comparatively small. In underdeveloped countries these differences are generally wide because of poor communications. The narrowness of markets in under-developed countries is also reflected in wider price fluctuations within a season and between seasons, as well as in larger regional price differences; it may be difficult for the computer to arrive at a typical price, let alone at an appropriate price for his purposes. In view of all the complexities, it is not surprising to find that a calculation of the national income of Northern Rhodesia is qualified by the statement that 'the figures for subsistence output in the national accounts are purely token figures and it is important to remember that a revised scheme of evaluation would alter the results radically'.[1]

The preceding discussion, which is not intended to be exhaustive, should serve to show that the element of conjecture is far greater in national income calculations for underdeveloped than for advanced economies, and that differences in economic features make it difficult to place national income calculations on a strictly comparable basis. It is probable that the conventions used in the calculation of the national income overstate the rate of growth of real income in a backward country experiencing economic development; this is so mainly because the subsistence sector generally diminishes and occupational specialisation and exchange increase. Thus with economic development many of the services previously performed by individuals or families for themselves are bought increasingly in the market from specialised individuals or firms. As the output bought from outside sources is always included in the national income, while services produced in the subsistence sector are generally excluded or included only in part, the transfer of activities from the subsistence to the exchange

[1] Phyllis Deane, *Colonial Social Accounting*, Cambridge, 1953, p. 129.

sector leads to an increase in the national income as calculated which is bound to overstate the net increase in activity or in the value of the output.[1] For the same reasons national income estimates almost certainly overstate differences between the levels of real income in advanced and in under-developed countries. The tendency for the extended family to shrink with economic development, changes in social structure and habits, and increased urbanisation work in the same direction. Comparisons of the national incomes of different under-developed countries are also affected by these difficulties.[2] The relative importance of the subsistence sector and the nature and extent of intra-family services may be quite different in countries which may seem to be in roughly the same category. Improvements in statistical services and sources also tend to exaggerate the improvement in real incomes which accompanies the development of an economy. Additional sectors of the economy and additional types of activity come under statistical review, and, with better and more reliable sources of information, the statistician is likely to be less conservative in his estimates.[3]

[1] The omission of certain services, however, does not necessarily affect the accuracy of an estimate of the (net) national income. The omission is unimportant where the service is used in the production of other goods or services which are included in the estimate; the value of the intermediate service is then included in the value of the final product, provided the proper basis of valuation is used. Thus it does not matter if the marketing service performed by a farmer who markets his own crops is not included separately, provided the value of the output is based on its value at the point at which he markets it. This is also true of similar services performed by other members of the household, even where, as is sometimes the case, specific payments are made for them. A practical difficulty is that not all farmers undertake marketing operations to the same extent, so that a uniform basis for valuing output is not appropriate, and any other basis is impracticable. The exclusion of other services which are not intermediate services does, of course, mean an understatement of the national income. As we have explained, the distinction between intermediate and final goods (or services) often presents difficulties.

[2] Some important problems of the concept and meaning of the national income in different societies are discussed in S. H. Frankel, *The Economic Impact on Under-developed Societies*, Oxford, 1953, especially Chapter III.

[3] The discussion in the text refers to some factors which tend to overstate the increase in the national income of a growing economy. On the

In international comparisons of national incomes it is necessary to employ conversion rates between national currencies
in order to place the estimates on a common currency basis.
The rates of exchange generally used for this purpose reflect
the purchasing power of the individual currencies over internationally traded goods and services; transactions in these
goods and services affect the balance of payments and hence
the rates of exchange.[1]   The use of these rates neglects the
relative purchasing power of different national currencies over
commodities and services not entering international trade.
This is an important issue because of the large volume of goods
and services (especially the latter) which does not enter into
international trade.   As it is likely that these goods and services are relatively cheaper (that is, relatively to the prices
of internationally-traded goods) in poorer than in richer
countries,[2] rates of exchange tend to understate the relative

other hand national income calculations do not include certain categories
of economic improvement stemming from economic growth.   Perhaps
the most important examples relate to the growth of population, and they
are considered briefly in Chapter V, section 2.

[1] If some exchange rates are pegged by means of exchange controls,
they obviously cannot serve as reliable bases for international comparisons
of real national income.

[2] This may be explained as follows.   Little or no capital is required in
the production of many goods and, more particularly, services not entering
into international trade.   Capital is scarcer, relatively to labour, in poor
than in rich countries.   Hence labour-intensive goods and services are
cheaper (relatively to capital-intensive goods and services) in poor than
in rich countries.   The disparity persists because many labour-intensive
goods and services (notably personal services not embodied in goods)
cannot be exported.   (It helps to explain why visitors to under-developed
countries are apt to find services uncommonly cheap.)   This is an apparent
contradiction to the classical theory of international trade, which would
suggest that the lower wages would be matched by correspondingly lower
efficiency.   But there need be no lower efficiency in the production of
personal services.   This is quite compatible with lower efficiency in the
production of capital-intensive goods, which by itself would be sufficient
to account for the postulated relative scarcity of capital even if there were
no restrictions on the international movement of capital.   The relative
cheapness of some personal services persists because of the cost of, and
the barriers to, migration.   Of course, some personal services are relatively more expensive, e.g. where a long period of training is required;
but this does not affect the main conclusion, since quantitatively they are
less important.

purchasing power of money in under-developed countries; if used for purposes of placing national income estimates on a common basis, they therefore tend to understate the real national incomes of these countries in comparison with those of richer countries.

The foregoing recital of the hazards of national income estimates should not obscure the fact that differences in the standard of living of the poor and the rich countries are real enough; but it should be borne in mind that national income estimates give a spurious definition to these differences. The estimates should be treated with much reserve and comparisons should not be pressed too far, particularly when they purport to refer to differences between countries with different social and economic institutions or at different stages of economic development.

The arbitrary elements in national income calculations do not invalidate their use in under-developed countries. When their limitations are realised, the calculations can be useful. They can indicate the importance of the money sector and the rate and direction of change. Again, estimates of the prospective flows of income in the money sector can at times be made with reasonable accuracy, and they can be set against estimates of the prospective flow of goods and services, and thus indicate broadly the likelihood of inflationary or deflationary pressures in that sector. In the sphere of public finance more narrowly defined the estimates also have their use, especially in assessing the level and burden of taxation generally and in different regions or for different groups within a country.

§ 2. The Measurement of Capital.   By capital is meant the accumulated stock of resources which contributes to a larger flow of goods and services through time, or which serves as a reserve sustaining a higher level of consumption at a time of more urgent demand or need than would otherwise be possible. The value of a stock of capital necessarily derives from the future output of goods or services or the delayed consumption which it makes possible. An attempt to measure the amount of capital in an economy involves an assessment of the present sum which is regarded as equivalent in value to the future flow of goods or services or the delayed consumption which capital assets make possible. In principle the process involves the forecasting of the magnitude of the flow of future goods and services and of the values of these goods and services, and their summation in terms of present values by a process of discounting. The calculation is unavoidably subjective and based on highly conjectural forecasts of the physical productivity of capital assets in facilitating the output of goods and services in coming years, and of the prices they will command when they are enjoyed; it also requires the use of a rate or rates of interest for translating future values into present ones. It follows that any estimate of capital is neither simple nor objective; this is so even if a large volume of statistical data is available on the number and age of specific assets or on the expenditures of governments, firms and individuals on capital account.

It may be thought that the difficulties of estimating the value of future flows of goods and services in calculating the magnitude of capital accumulations can be avoided by working instead from the cost of assets. This may appear to give a more solid basis for the calculation. But the apparently greater objectivity in the calculation may be largely illusory. In the case of assets with long lives, such as roads, bridges and many types of machinery, it is necessary to estimate the length of their prospective useful lives, which is in large measure conjectural.

But more serious drawbacks attach to the cost basis for measuring capital. Investment involves the commitment of money or effort for a more or less specific purpose over a period of time in conditions of uncertainty about prospective supply and demand. A given investment which seemed justified and profitable at the moment when it was made may turn out to be mistaken if expectations about supply and demand conditions are falsified. Conversely, improvements in market conditions may raise the value of capital assets far above

their costs.   The equation of cost and value may seem to
give the economic statistician a firmer footing, but to the
extent that it does so it takes the calculation further away from
the economic reality of the situation.   The procedure is in
principle capable of yielding exact results only in a stationary
state, that is, an economy in which population, preferences
and methods of production remain unchanged.   It is incapable
of yielding exact results in the world as we know it, in which
one of the few certainties is the fact of change, largely un-
predictable change.

The difficulties of valuation are inherent whether the calculation of capital refers to an economically advanced or to a
backward economy.   Further problems arise in determining
which categories of assets are to be included in the stock of
capital and which are to be excluded.   In principle any asset
which is capable of yielding benefits in a future period or
periods forms part of the capital stock; in practice it is necessary to draw a line between included and excluded categories
to make statistical enumeration at all feasible.   These difficulties of classification are also present in attempts to measure
the gross capital formation in a period, that is the value of
current output added to the stock of capital;[1] for it is the
essence of this measurement to identify those expenditures and
activities during the period which issue in new capital assets
or in improvements to existing ones.   The line of demarcation
is necessarily arbitrary between included and excluded items,
and the choice is dictated largely by considerations of statistical
convenience and the accessibility of data.[2]

[1] The problem of valuation is also serious in the estimation of net capital formation, because it is necessary to estimate the loss in value of
existing assets.   The difficulties of valuation are less serious in the measurement of gross capital formation, because the outlay on a new asset acquired
during a period, say, of a year, generally provides a fairly close approxima-
tion to its value at the end of the period.   Cost as a basis of valuation
becomes progressively less reliable the longer is the period between the
acquisition of the asset and the date of the valuation.

[2] Some of the difficulties of deciding where to draw the line are illustrated in the following quotation from A. R. Prest and I. G. Stewart,
op. cit., p. 18: 'Is there not a strong case for regarding education expenditure in Nigeria as a form of capital investment?   Is not the expenditure

The composition and content of capital is not the same every-where, and what is properly regarded as capital depends significantly on the social and economic context.   The validity of international comparisons of capital and of rates of accumu-lation is much affected by these differences.   Distinctions be-tween capital and consumption expenditure valid in the cir-cumstances of one country may seriously mislead if applied to another country.

The types of assets which the people in a country regard as necessary or useful for facilitating future production or for helping to cope with emergencies depend largely upon their techniques of production and their social habits.   These are naturally not the same in rich and in poor countries.   Con-ventions which may give satisfactory results in one case need not be appropriate in another; this can be illustrated by the treatment of durable consumer goods and simple farming or household tools in statistical calculations of capital.   In advanced countries expenditures on acquiring such assets are usually counted as consumption expenditures, and this treat-ment has much to commend it on grounds of practical con-venience.   But in under-developed countries they may be better regarded as capital expenditures.   Household or per-sonal durable goods are often put to commercial or near-commercial use.   Bicycles are often used as taxis for carrying people or for the collection and delivery of goods even over long distances.   Moreover, assets tend to be kept in use for longer periods by having labour lavished on them for repairs.   Similar considerations also apply to textiles in some under-developed countries.   They too are bought with the fruit of

on the studies necessary to obtain a degree in Birmingham just as much a capital asset, both to the individual and to the country, as the purchase of a machine from Birmingham?   This is a very real choice for Nigeria and obviously the pace of one of these forms of "investment" will be regulated by the other; more degrees will mean less machines, and vice versa.   De-spite a good deal of sympathy with this view, we decided not to include education expenditure in our formal estimates of capital expenditure.   The major reason for this decision was that once one leaves the *terra firma* of material capital and branches out into the upper aether of human capital there is endless difficulty in finding a resting place.'

much time and toil, and they are kept in use longer than in countries with higher per capita incomes; they often serve as an emergency reserve or as a form of saving, for which functions they are not required in countries with well-developed banking and other financial institutions. Again, certain durable goods which still have useful life in them may be destroyed in an act of conspicuous consumption. The best known example of this is the pot-latches of certain Indian tribes; in a somewhat spectacular way these demonstrate both the problems of defining capital and the relevance of the social context.

Livestock and especially cattle constitute an important category of capital asset in many under-developed areas. In advanced countries livestock is simply a form of agricultural capital, and is among the most important forms or parts of agricultural capital; but its significance in many under-developed countries is very different, and its role is not the same in all of them. In some of these countries also cattle may provide a source of meat or be used as draught animals. In Argentina and Uruguay, for example, animal husbandry is practised at an advanced level and is a mainstay of their economies. In China pigs and poultry make a material contribution to the food supplies of a vast population. But in some countries cattle are frequently kept mainly as a source of social distinction or of aesthetic pleasure, or are maintained as the object of religious veneration. Their valuation as a form of capital in these circumstances raises nice questions of concept and measurement. For instance, how should the huge cattle population of India be valued, bearing in mind that a large proportion of the total has a negative productivity in the sense that it consumes more than it adds to the value of agricultural output? The accumulation of cattle largely to achieve social distinction or to discharge obligations (for example, to pay the bride-price) in parts of Africa poses similar questions for the economic statistician. Such an interest in numbers rather than in quality gives rise to a quasi-Malthusian situation in which the cattle population grows to the limit of the carrying capacity of the land unless checked by natural calamities such as disease. More serious than the statistical difficulties, of course, is the tendency towards soil erosion and deterioration of pasture, and the conflicts that arise when traditional values, social institutions and social relationships begin to give way with the growth of a money and market economy.

This discussion, which is not meant to be exhaustive, should make it clear that calculations of capital and of rates of capital accumulation are necessarily arbitrary and based on a series of estimates and assumptions. In practice there are also gaps in the statistical material which, if it were more adequate, would at least simplify the task of the economic statistician. Of course the deficiencies are generally greater in poor countries. This is only partly because statistical services in these countries tend to be less developed. The gaps are also more numerous because in under-developed countries important categories of capital are in forms for which it would be difficult to have reliable data even in countries with comprehensive statistical services.

§ 3. **Direct Investment in Agriculture.** We now turn to an issue of much practical importance which illustrates some of the problems discussed in the preceding section. In the conventional estimates of capital resources and of capital formation in under-developed countries the results of the expenditure of time, effort and money in the creation, extension, improvement and upkeep of agricultural holdings are often disregarded. This seems to be the common practice in dealing both with holdings producing for the subsistence sector and local markets and with those producing cash crops for export markets. This omission is serious.

In under-developed countries agriculture plays a large part in total activity and output, and in many of them much effort is spent on the establishment, extension and improvement of agricultural holdings. Much of the effort and resources devoted to these ends does not yield a return in the form of an increase in output until several years after it has been expended. The millions of acres of smallholdings under rubber, cocoa, kola nuts, cotton, rice, groundnuts and millet are obvious examples of investments (large-scale in total) made by peasants in the expectation of profitable returns which often occur only several seasons later or extend over a number of seasons. The failure to include this form of investment in estimates of capital formation is no doubt partly responsible for the erroneous notion that the indigenous population of under-developed countries, such as the African peasant or the Malay smallholder, are unable and unwilling to take a long view in economic matters.

Disregard of investment of effort and resources by individual cultivators in agricultural capital must in these societies give gravely misleading statistical results. The reason for the neglect may be the fact that much agricultural production is subsistence production which is often for no good reason not regarded as economic activity at all. Or it may reflect the contemporary habit of regarding economic development as synonymous with industrialisation, which diverts attention from the non-industrial sectors. Moreover, there can be little doubt that the statistical and conceptual difficulties of attempting to isolate and measure capital-forming activities in agriculture, and particularly in agriculture producing crops for local consumption, are likely to discourage even those observers who are aware of the importance of investment in peasant holdings. One example of the difficulties may be mentioned. Very different results would be obtained if one valued, say, the cocoa acreage in the Gold Coast, the rubber smallholdings in Sumatra, or the padi fields of South-east Asia on the basis of the cost of establishing the holdings rather than on the basis of the discounted value of the net returns yielded by the investment. Moreover, either basis involves the computer in estimates: in the former case the main element of cost may not be money outlays but opportunities for more immediate returns or for leisure forgone; in the latter case the usual estimates of physical yields, future prices and discount rates have to be made.

These difficulties may incline statisticians to the easy way out, that is to disregard the awkward items altogether. But this means that support is given to superficial and erroneous views about capital formation in under-developed territories and particularly in their farming areas. The calculations are particularly misleading when estimates of capital formation are related to estimates of the national income in the form of a ratio. The estimates of capital and capital formation exclude important investments while the national income statistics include estimates of the value of the annual returns derived from these excluded investments. The capital–income ratio is therefore lower than the facts warrant, and conclusions drawn from these ratios need to be treated with scepticism. The misleading nature of the estimates can be illustrated in another way. If the mass of peasant holdings, aggregated, were in the hands of plantation companies, then the investment would almost certainly be included in estimates of capital formation. For instance, the expenditure incurred by British, Dutch and French plantation companies in the establishment of rubber estates is included in the foreign investment of these countries. But the establishment of rubber smallholdings is not generally included in estimates of capital formation in South-east Asian territories. It is also anomalous that the expenditure on a government-sponsored agricultural scheme, like the groundnut scheme in East Africa, is treated as capital formation even if the results of the scheme fall far short of the original budget, while the expenditures in effort and money of peasant producers in extending areas under cultivation are excluded even though they make possible a rise in the standard of living or enable larger populations to be sustained. The statistical omission of capital formation in peasant agriculture is particularly unfortunate in that the development of the production of cash crops is a vital element in economic development, and is generally a necessary prerequisite for, or concomitant of, urbanisation and industrialisation.

§ 1] SOME PROBLEMS OF ECONOMIC MEASUREMENT 31

CHAPTER III

SOME PROBLEMS OF ECONOMIC MEASURE-MENT: LABOUR AND ITS DISTRIBUTION

§ 1. **Measurement of the Labour Force.** There are many obstacles in the way of measuring the occupied or employed population or labour force in many under-developed countries. This is not merely a matter of the inadequacy or absence of basic statistical data the availability of which is taken for granted in the more advanced countries. The identification, and hence the enumeration, of the gainfully employed population is a difficult task where large parts of the economy are not fully drawn into the money and exchange system and where subsistence production is widespread. In subsistence agriculture in particular, as well as in many other farming pursuits, the demands on labour vary greatly with the seasons. Labour which appears to be idle during one season may be indispensable at times of planting or harvesting. There is thus a large element of part-time or seasonal employment which complicates the definition and measurement of the employed labour force. The important contributions to economic activities by wives and children, again often on a part-time or discontinuous basis, raise further difficulties if one attempts to define employment meaningfully, and to gather statistics consonant with the selected definition.

It follows that it is not easy to measure the volume of involuntary unemployment in a backward economy, or to estimate accurately the number of people whose removal from the areas would not lead to any reduction in agricultural output. We have noted that the labour required for farming operations varies markedly from one time of year to another. Labour which seems to be performing no economic function during some months may in effect be supplying the service of availability; a machine is not necessarily redundant if it is not used in production all the time. Agricultural production in some cases may be greatly reduced if the necessary supply is not on hand in times of peak demand for labour. It may, of course, be true that an economic system in which agriculture relies on a pool of partly-employed labour is less productive than one in which it uses the available labour regularly throughout the year. But it may nevertheless be the most economically efficient system in many circumstances, particularly where there are few alternative opportunities for the employment of labour. As a corollary, the emergence of alternative opportunities may require reorganisation of farming operations, possibly with a reduction of agricultural output at least in the period of transition.

Moreover, in the complex and (to a foreigner) unfamiliar economic and social structure of many under-developed countries it may be difficult to appreciate the economic contribution that an apparently idle or redundant individual may be making to the family or community of which he is a member. It may also be very difficult to distinguish the involuntary idle from those with a strong preference for leisure, for a subsistence way of life, or for casual or intermittent employment. In sum, one must be cautious of estimates purporting to show the number of unemployed in these countries and of specific plans based implicitly or explicitly on such estimates. This does not imply that there are not in fact large numbers of involuntary unemployed in certain under-developed countries or that nothing can or should be done about them. We shall return to the economic aspects of these matters in several parts of this book. But it is well to remember that here, as in other connections, statistical concepts and categories which are valid and useful in certain contexts may be inappropriate and misleading in other settings.

§ 2. Statistics of Occupational Distribution. The same general conclusion applies to statistics showing the occupational distribution of the labour force, which are sometimes summarised to show the proportions of the total engaged in each of three main categories of primary, secondary and tertiary employment. (Broadly, primary generally includes agricultural production, secondary covers manufacture and mining, and tertiary the balance consisting mainly of the production of services such as trading, transport and personal services.) The statistics which have been compiled generally indicate that in under-developed countries the great bulk of employment is in primary production, with very small percentages in the other two categories.

Statistics of the occupational composition of the labour force are meaningful and useful in economies in which labour is specialised. In these economies the worker is engaged full-time in his listed occupation, and also he does not normally change from one occupation to another. To describe a man as a welder gives a useful picture of the type of contribution he can make to production and which, when employed, he does make. In a specialised economy the economic activities of a welder outside his trade are likely to be small, and their neglect unimportant.[1] However, the meaning and economic significance of occupational statistics are much affected when occupational specialisation is imperfect and when large numbers of people can and do move easily from one type of activity to another. The imperfect specialisation of labour and, perhaps to a lesser extent, the greater occupational fluidity of labour in many under-developed countries, greatly affect the meaning and significance of occupational statistics.

The weakness of such statistics is apparent when one considers that in most under-developed countries many of the so-called farmers spend a large part of their time in small-scale transport, porterage and trade both during the farming season and much more so outside the season. They may trade not only in the goods they themselves have produced,

[1] But high marginal rates of taxation as well as shorter hours of factory work may raise the importance of unpaid activities or of income earned outside the principal activity.

but also in goods purchased by them for resale. Members of the cultivator's family, including children, may also be engaged in trade intermittently or continually during the year, while also at times helping on the farm or holding. The imperfect specialisation may extend to other classes as well. In West Africa, for example, many African doctors and lawyers and almost all the leading chiefs have trading interests, which are sometimes extensive. Government employees and servants of the European population often trade part-time, either in imported goods or in goods and food bought locally. The economic activity of many people in under-developed countries is better described as the performance of a number of different tasks than as the pursuit of a definite occupation.

Yet almost inevitably, if an occupational census were taken, the so-called farmers would be listed as farmers, and the professional people in their respective professions. The subsidiary activities, which are significant in total, are left out. Moreover, the trading activities of children and of many wives are not likely to find their way into the statistical tabulations. Alternatively, if it were desired to give a more accurate picture of economic activity, the statistician would be up against formidable problems of investigation and measurement. Many Africans who engage in part-time trade, and not only in the marketing of their own produce, are not likely to regard trade as an occupation, because they regard it as part of economic existence and not as a distinct set of tasks; they are not likely to refer to these activities when describing their work. Again, it would be very difficult to distinguish between the social and commercial activities of a group of women traders in a market-place.[1]

[1] The foregoing discussion, and some of the points made later, may be illustrated with extracts from Sol Tax, *Penny Capitalism—A Guatemalan Indian Economy*, Washington, 1953, a fascinatingly detailed and graphic account of economic life in a district (Panajachel) containing 155 Indian 'agricultural' households. Of the 155 households, 142 are 'represented by sellers more or less regularly vending [produce] in the local market . . .'. With rare exceptions 'these families are represented in the [local] market only by their womenfolk. . . . Needless to say, selling in

The imperfect occupational specialisation is largely a reflection of limited markets, since the division of labour is limited by the extent of the market. Narrowness of markets is a very general characteristic of under-developed countries; indeed it may be described as one of the few really general features found in practically all under-developed countries. This is a consequence of high transport costs, the lack of capital for storage which in effect is transport through time, and the poverty of consumers. The narrowness of the markets does not affect labour and small-scale farming and trading only. Even large heavily-capitalised business undertakings in under-developed countries are apt to spread their activities in a number of different directions, in trade, manufacturing and mining. The expensive and productive combination of capital, skill and experience cannot be specialised to serve one or a few markets, since they are too narrow to produce economic returns. Hence there develops a network of a number of different but related economic activities: different in that they may include mining, transport, import and export trade, wholesale and retail trade, and manufacture of a number of products, and related in that they refer to the same economy concerning which the firm has specialised skills, knowledge and commercial contacts. However, it may be noted in passing that the diversification of business activities may sometimes also reflect at least partly the endeavour of the

the market has its social and pleasurable aspects. . . . Most of the produce of Panajachel reaches markets in other towns . . .'. Apart from the activities of other merchants, 'most Panajachel Indians themselves market their produce in other towns, close and far . . . 110 [households] regularly sell local produce in markets of other towns. . . . The more distant markets are frequented by individual men, a man and his son, or two or three brothers of the household. But also, while certain members of the family patronise one series of markets, others as regularly attend others. . . . In general it may be said that the rich sell only their own goods, and the poor, not having much of their own, have to buy at least some of what they sell. . . . Wealthy families do not sell in distant places both because they have much to do at home and because they do not need to travel for a living.' (pp. 122–6.)

J. E. de Young, *Village Life in Modern Thailand*, Berkeley and Los Angeles, 1955, pp. 103–5, briefly describes the widespread marketing activities by Thai villagers.

established firms to limit the prospects of new competing firms.[1]

The fluidity of labour between certain occupations arises largely from the fact that only a low level of skill and of capital is required in these occupations in under-developed countries. People can generally move with little sacrifice or difficulty within a wide range of occupations in accordance with changes in prospective net advantages. These activities include various forms of small-scale trading, the supply of the less-mechanised forms of transport service, and the provision of personal services generally.[2] Many farmers are at no disadvantage in small-scale trading provided they have the small amount of capital which is required in this relatively unskilled activity. They will be willing to undertake the sale of their own produce unless they can spend their time more profitably in some other way, or unless they prefer more leisure.

When the economy develops occupational specialisation generally becomes more marked, and at the same time the fluidity of labour between occupations is reduced. Markets are extended with improvements in transport and increased purchasing power, so that specialisation becomes more profitable. Moreover, the increase in capital requirements and the improvements in techniques of production limit the movement of people between economic activities.

But economic progress cannot be accelerated simply by imposing restraints either on employers or employees to force them to specialise. Enforced specialisation may in fact be a serious obstacle to economic development. In parts of India a person's economic activities are often defined and limited by his membership of a particular caste. Even if the market or

[1] The principal reasons for the diversification of the activities of the merchant firms in West Africa are discussed in P. T. Bauer, *West African Trade*, Cambridge, 1954, pp. 111–14 and 126–9.

[2] R. Firth, *Malay Fishermen: Their Peasant Economy*, London, 1946, Chapter VII, describes in detail the ease of entry into even wholesale trading in fish, the movement of individuals between a number of different activities, and the participation of fishermen in trade; the study refers to the east coast of Malaya.

demand for his services may not be adequate to occupy his time fully, he nevertheless cannot take part in other activities because of the restrictions of caste.[1]   Such restrictions conduce to a less efficient deployment of available labour resources; they also prevent the most economic use of capital accumulated by members of a particular caste.   Again, the enforced division of work between the members of different trade unions or categories of labour, whether in the United Kingdom or in Southern Africa, increases occupational specialisation but reduces productivity.

Though imperfect occupational specialisation is a dominant feature of many under-developed countries, it should not be over-emphasised. Even in simple societies there may be scope for a handful of specialists in activities requiring some special skill (such as thatching, plastering or smithing) or special recognition (such as witch-doctoring);[2] but even then the specialised activity may not be a full-time occupation.

In many under-developed countries narrowness of markets, which discourages occupational specialisation, is found together with a more elaborate or minute division of labour in certain economic activities than is usual in richer countries. Some services which in richer countries are usually performed by consumers for themselves are in under-developed countries provided commercially, often in large volume in the aggregate. Various factors are responsible for this seeming contradiction.[3]

[1] In some parts of India the customary connection between caste and occupation is being weakened. This is discussed and illustrated in M. Marriott (ed.), *Village India*, Menasha, 1955, pp. 2 and 157.

[2] F. Chalmers Wright writes of conditions in Nyasaland and Tanganyika: 'The African boy doubtless is taught the proper way to thatch a roof or make a hoe or weave a mat or tip his arrow with poison; but each peasant community produces its *fundi*, whose special skill will be sought out by his neighbours. Knowledge of beer-brewing may be possessed by every African woman; but it is to the women who make the best beer that customers will flock.'   *African Consumers in Nyasaland and Tanganyika*, London, 1955, p. 10.

J. E. de Young records that there are some 'specialists' in all Thai villages, 'although nearly all of these "specialists" are also part-time farmers'. *Op. cit.*, p. 102.

[3] The contradiction is only apparent and not real, as an illustration will

The low level of capital, the scarcity of certain skills and, sometimes, the lack of opportunities in wage-earning employment,
are among the main factors which create markets for certain
services which tend to be provided by people for themselves in
richer countries. The holding of stocks is one of these services
or activities. Very poor consumers or producers may have
very little storage space or funds to hold stocks. Hence as
consumers they may be able to buy their requirements only in
small quantities on a hand-to-mouth basis, and as producers,
unless they act as their own distributors, they may require the
services of small-scale traders to collect small lots of farm
produce at frequent intervals. Among large sections of the
population there may have to be a number of traders catering
for their needs by dealing in small quantities. The West
African petty retailer selling perfume by the drop or cigarettes
by the piece, the woman spending a full day selling a dozen
mangoes in a Caribbean market, and the woman selling
paraffin in small quantities from door to door in a Thai
village, are examples of an intermediary performing the functions of proximate stockholder, which in a wealthier country
would be performed by each consumer for himself.

Where alternative opportunities for employment are relatively restricted, there will be many people willing to enter
small-scale trading for low rewards which in turn will extend
the demand for their services. Again, where some item of
equipment is necessary, the very poor consumers are not able
to buy the item and have to buy its services from an intermediary who can afford one. Thus in India there are intermediaries who sell the services of a bicycle pump to bicycle
owners who do not have a pump, and the hiring of bicycles
itself is more common in poor than in richer countries. The
possession of certain skills and training by a relatively small
number of people in under-developed countries has a somewhat

make clear. There may be a longer chain of separate independent firms
or persons involved in distributing merchandise in an under-developed
than in a richer country; but many of the traders will also be engaged in
other activities such as farming and transport.

similar effect. Literacy is one example. In some poor countries the illiterate poor may use the services of a letter-reader or writer, and sometimes have to pay for them. Lastly, since personal services are likely to be relatively cheaper in poor than in rich countries (cheaper, that is, in relation to other goods and services), the better-off people of the poor country are likely to buy more of these services than their counterparts in richer countries. This applies to the demand, for example, for boot-blacks and domestic servants, which latter in some under-developed countries fall within the category of conventional necessaries for all but the poorest.[1]

§ 3. Occupational Distribution and Economic Progress. The distribution of labour in primary, secondary and tertiary categories of employment, and the changes in the distribution accompanying economic progress, have been considered at some length in the writings of Mr. Colin Clark and Professor A. G. B. Fisher. Their thesis is that with economic development and rising incomes there is a progressive shift from primary to secondary and subsequently to tertiary employment. The thesis has been supported by reference to statistics of occupational distribution in different countries; it is also supported by an appeal to the propositions that as people grow wealthier they spend relatively less on food and more on manufactured goods and even more on services, and that the productivity of labour increases more rapidly in manufacturing industry than in the production of services (tertiary production).

We cannot examine this thesis in detail here.[2] We have

[1] The lack of servants in more advanced economies is well known. It is interesting that this phenomenon should have been noted by Liudprand, Bishop of Cremona, on his visit to Byzantium in 969. 'He noted with disgust that the bishops of the Greek church were rich in gold, but poor in servants. Their coffers, he says, were full of gold; but in the midst of this plenty, they were their own stewards and their own masters of horse, they opened the door for their guests, and they did their own shopping.' R. W. Southern, *The Making of the Middle Ages*, London, 1953, p. 47.

[2] We discuss it in two articles in *Economic Journal*, December 1951 and March 1954. It is also considered by A. L. Minkes, 'Statistical Evidence and the Concept of Tertiary Industry', in *Economic Development and Cultural Change*, July 1955.

already indicated that the statistical or empirical support for the generalisation is necessarily weak, because statistics of occupational distribution are misleading as a portrayal of the distribution of labour between economic activities. International (and inter-temporal) comparisons of occupational distribution are especially affected by the limitations of occupational statistics, because the degree of specialisation or fluidity of labour is not necessarily the same even in two countries with roughly the same national income per head. Statistical comparisons are vitiated both because of differences and changes in the imperfection of specialisation, and also because of shifts of labour between unpaid and paid activities.

There is much qualitative evidence of the quantitative significance of so-called tertiary production in under-developed economies.[1] This production takes the form mainly of household services and of trading and transport activities. The

[1] 'In Mexico City a visitor gets the impression that everyone is engaged in selling. . . . In front of practically all the stores in the downtown section the sidewalks are lined with peddlers spreading their merchandise on the sidewalks or on portable stands. . . . Block after city block is completely devoted to small shops and portable display stands.' E. R. Barlow, *Management of Foreign Manufacturing Subsidiaries*, Boston, Mass., 1953, p. 27.

In the Caribbean region 'a high proportion of the employed population is engaged in the production of services. Market places and streets are filled with ambulant vendors; there is a proliferation of tiny shops, which break packaged goods and make very small unit sales; self-employed small truckers and sellers of passenger transport services are present in large numbers; and full-time domestic servants are hired by even lower-middle income families.' S. Rottenberg, 'Note on "Economic Progress and Occupational Distribution"', *Review of Economics and Statistics*, May 1953, p. 168.

T. S. Ashton writes of eighteenth-century England: 'The worker [in textiles] had to do his own fetching and carrying. . . . On the roads of the north large numbers of weavers were to be seen bearing yarn in packs on their backs, or heavy rolls of cloth under their arms. The distances covered were often as great as most men would care to traverse in a day. . . . It is said that in the hosiery trade of the east Midlands as much as two and a half days a week might be taken up in getting orders and materials, returning finished work, and collecting wages.' T. S. Ashton, *An Economic History of England: The Eighteenth Century*, London, 1955, p. 102.

crucial role of trade and transport in quickening the process of economic growth and in extending the money economy is a well-known theme in economic history. In under-developed countries these activities tend to be labour-intensive because of the low level of capital and poor communications; small-scale activity in trade and transport also tends to attract many people when there are few opportunities for paid employment.

We may conclude that the thesis connecting changes in occupational distribution and economic progress is not established, and that occupational statistics are an infirm foundation for any generalisation.[1] Moreover, neither the concept of a tripartite classification of productive activities nor a general thesis linking occupational distribution and economic progress is necessary for the study of the economics of under-developed countries in general or any one country in particular. It should not be inferred from this that economic development and change do not require shifts in the distribution of labour in different occupations. Such shifts are both a prerequisite and a necessary consequence of economic change and growth. But there is no simple guide to indicate the direction in which the change will take place, or whether a given distribution of labour is the optimum in a given situation.

[1] One specific example of a reduction of labour in tertiary activity associated with economic development may be noted. S. Tax (*op. cit.*, p. 186) observed that, after the establishment of truck and bus services, peasant producers who had previously 'walked to Guatamala City and consumed a week to sell a load of onions' were able to ride to the city and spend only '2 or 3 days to sell a larger load of onions. . . . The total result for the region was that more time could be spent on the production of wealth than previously, with less required for distribution of goods.' Similar effects of the improvements in transport can be found in many parts of the world.

CHAPTER IV

NATURAL RESOURCES

§ 1. The Concept of Economic Resource. The inherent qualities and attributes of a resource are not sufficient to enable it to participate in production and to acquire value in the process. For this purpose it is also necessary that co-operant or complementary resources (factors of production) should be available, and that there should be a market for the resulting product. Access to co-operant or complementary factors of production and access to the market (or demand) are essential to the concept of an economic resource.

The value of an economic resource depends upon the terms on which the requisite complementary factors of production are available and on the strength of the market demand for its products. Thus its value depends in part on the market for the goods which can be produced with or from it; it also depends in part on the market for other goods which can be produced with the necessary co-operant factors of production. Thus the market, in the widest sense of the term, is crucial. An example may be useful. The value of land suitable for rubber cultivation in Sumatra depends not only on the price of rubber, but also on the remuneration in the alternative employments open to the labour which is required to develop the holdings and to tap the trees, as well as on the cost to labour of moving from one district or island to another. The value of the land therefore is contingent on the price of rubber itself, as well as on the prices of rice, pepper and coconuts both in Sumatra and in other parts of Indonesia, and on the cost of internal migration. The preferences of workers for leisure or for working in particular areas or engaging in particular types of work also affect the supply price of labour and thus the value of land. In short, the value of a resource does not depend upon its physical qualities or technical efficiency alone; a complex network of present and future market influences forms part of the environment in which value is conferred upon resources.

It follows that the value of any one resource is dependent on the value of other resources. It is therefore somewhat misleading and arbitrary to treat particular resources, or categories of resources, in isolation, unless the inter-dependence of resources is kept firmly in mind. Moreover, the productivity and value of labour, capital and material resources are greatly influenced by the state of technology, the methods of organisation or production, the efficiency and policies of governments, and the organisation of societies generally. This once more affects the value of discussing the economics of particular categories of resources in isolation. In practice, too, the distinction between natural resources and produced resources is generally blurred, since human skills and efforts as well as capital (produced resources) are commonly used to improve or increase the economic productivity of natural resources such as farm land or rivers. Improvements in transport and the activities of traders have frequently in effect altered the facts of geography. Agricultural production in many parts of the world depends quite as much on the construction and maintenance of irrigation channels, dykes and drainage as on 'the original and indestructible powers of the soil'. The very soil for farming operations has sometimes had to be gathered together by cultivators, or made productive by clearing, terracing, and the like.[1]

Nevertheless, it is convenient for purposes of exposition to consider successively three broad categories of resources, viz.

[1] Visitors to Malta—an island described by one of them as an 'inhabited quarry'—in the late eighteenth and early nineteenth centuries 'watched the peasant at work, saw the hard rock slowly reduced to small pebbles and then covered with scraps of soil collected laboriously from cracks and crevices all over the islands; observed the unwanted rocks erected into walls to protect each small plot with its valuable topsoil from the ravages of flood and gale...'. C. A. Price, *Malta and the Maltese*, Melbourne, 1954, p. 12.

natural material resources, human resources and produced material resources or capital. The first provides the subject-matter of the rest of this chapter. Chapters V to VIII deal with human resources, and Chapters IX and X with capital and capital formation. This treatment is one of convenience, and the classification is not required for purposes of any of the analysis or discussion which is presented. Each of the three categories is used largely as a peg from which to hang the discussion of topics selected because we believe that their economic analysis may be illuminating, or because they are important in contemporary discussions of economic policy in backward countries.

A methodological point may be noted here. Partial equilibrium analysis, in which a particular sector of the economy is considered in isolation, is a recognised and valuable technique in economic analysis even though it is realised that all markets and prices in an economy are inter-related. Many useful results may be derived from partial equilibrium analysis, even though certain effects of changes in a particular market, or sector, of the economy as well as certain influences coming from outside are implicitly or explicitly ignored. The method is useful because it simplifies and in spite of the fact that it simplifies. No such claim can be made for the treatment of the economics of any one major category of resources taken in isolation. The links between different categories of resources and between their values are too strong and the inter-relationships too significant to be ignored; the neglect of the inter-dependence would vitiate the results of the analysis and the conclusions would be empty of content. We avoid these pitfalls by emphasising accessibility as an attribute or condition which is crucial to the productivity or value of resources; this emphasis is necessary even at the cost of seeming repetition.

§ 2. **The Relation of Natural Resources to Economic Development.** There are some areas where economic development is severely inhibited by very unfavourable natural circumstances. Thus economic development is unlikely in the polar regions, the deserts or the particularly inaccessible and inhospitable parts of Central Asia and perhaps parts of South America, except for such very localised and specialised economic activities as may occur around airports and landing-grounds, or oil-wells and so forth. But over much of the under-developed world there is no such pronounced lack of natural resources, and climatic conditions are not so unfavourable as to present insurmountable barriers to development. It would be an over-simplification to suggest that the under-developed countries in general are ill-favoured with natural resources and have niggardly endowments, especially of minerals and fertile land, and that this is a principal cause or only cause of their poverty which makes it difficult for them to create capital, thus setting up a vicious circle of under-development and poverty. The Creator has not divided the world into two sectors, developed and under-developed, the former being more richly blessed with natural resources than the latter. All developed countries began by being under-developed by modern standards, which are the operative ones; indeed they remained in this state until quite recently. The natural resources in their territories, whether rich or poor, have only been developed within a comparatively short and recent period of history. This is an obvious proposition, which, however, is frequently overlooked.

Throughout recorded history industrial and commercial leadership has passed frequently from one country or region to another, even though they did not differ greatly or obviously in their natural resources. Highly-developed areas or those in the van of economic progress have not been confined to particular climatic zones. Even in recent times countries which had once been in the forefront subsequently lost their economic supremacy and came to join the ranks of the present under-developed countries; parts of southern Europe and of the Mediterranean basin are examples. It is clear from such changes that the availability of naturally-occurring material resources do not immutably determine the economic development of a country. Moreover, since the changing fortunes of

many countries and regions have not been connected with the
discovery or exhaustion of natural resources within their
territories, the fortuitous distribution of these resources certainly
does not provide the only, and probably not even the principal,
explanation of differences in development and prosperity.

It is, of course, the case that prosperous nations either
possess some valuable natural resources in their own territories or are directly concerned in the exploitation of such
resources in other countries or have access to them. But in
most cases they have largely raised the value of these resources
by discovering and developing them through the application of
capital, organising and technical skills and labour. The
necessary and previously lacking co-operant factors of production have been supplied, and the natural resources clothed with,
economic usefulness and value. The vast natural resources
of the United States were *in situ* for many centuries, but that
did not enable the Indians to pass beyond a most primitive
level of economic achievement. The development of these
resources in the nineteenth and twentieth centuries is only one
example of the inter-relationship between production techniques, the size and quality of the population and the value of
material resources; it also indicates clearly that the value
of available natural resources is often a function of the supply of
the former factors. In large measure the prosperity of a
nation as well as the active development of its natural resources
can both be seen as results or aspects of the operation of other
causes, though the presence of the natural resources may serve
to stimulate and reinforce their operation.

The absence of sources of particular natural resources within
its own territory has generally not been a serious impediment
to the prospects of a nation which in other respects has been
capable of initiating and sustaining economic growth. By
means of the export of goods and services a country can buy
the products of natural resources from countries which have
them. So long as they are accessible on economic terms, the
precise location or ownership of the natural resources is a
relatively minor issue. In the nineteenth century coal from

British mines was often used by German industry in preference
to the output of German coalfields which were nearer in
mileage but less accessible economically. Of course, the
accessibility of foreign-owned natural resources may be reduced or destroyed by political action ranging from export
controls to military operations. In this sense the ownership
and location of natural resources may be of vital importance
when international trading and political relations break down.
They assume greatly increased significance when autarky is the
policy chosen by nations or enforced upon them.

§ 3. Accessibility and the Value of Natural Resources. The
economic significance or value of natural resources has been
shown to be affected by access to co-operant resources and
the terms on which these are available, as well as by access to
markets and the strength of demand in them. It follows that
the economic prospects of a country or region cannot be
assessed meaningfully on the sole basis of an enumeration of
its known natural resources. An inventory of a country's
natural resources in physical terms can be compiled readily
enough, and may be of some interest, especially a survey of
natural communications, climatic conditions or ore reserves,
though estimates of the latter are usually subject to a wide
margin of error. But such an inventory cannot be translated
into terms of commercial values or of potential economic
development without importing assumptions about quantities
and prices of complementary resources and about markets
for the products arising from the use of the resources. Any
economic survey of natural resources which does not indicate
these underlying assumptions is of little meaning or usefulness.
Moreover, even if the economic inventory of natural resources
has been drawn up on the basis of the best available knowledge
it is likely to become inaccurate or out-of-date practically as
soon as it is presented, because prices in factor markets and
product markets change, and so does the accessibility of
natural resources both to markets and to the necessary
complementary resources.

It is an understandable temptation for economic survey missions to spend much time on the listing of natural resources and their economic promise. For the reasons given in the preceding paragraph, the usefulness of this activity is doubtful even at the time of their investigations, and much more so after some time has passed. Natural resources, the existence, quantity and technical qualities of which are known, derive their actual or potential value from economic accessibility and the configuration of prices. These are the important but unstable and uncertain factors. Conversely, in appropriate circumstances favourable changes in accessibility and in market prices tend to set in motion activities which lead to the discovery of previously unknown natural resources or of previously unsuspected commercial possibilities in known natural resources.

The same considerations apply to surveys or estimates of cultivable and uncultivable land in different parts of the world. With a given state of farming technique the difference between cultivable and uncultivable land is often, one might almost say generally, a matter of degree, since land classified as uncultivable might become cultivable with the expenditure of additional effort or capital, or with changes in the market prices of agricultural products. Large- and small-scale improvements in irrigation, whether undertaken by statutory authorities, large enterprises or small cultivators, have often greatly extended the area of cultivable land, for example in India and the Middle East. Again, with the rise in the price of rubber in the 1920's large areas in Malaysia were cultivated which had previously been regarded as uncultivable. The boundary beyond which the cultivation of groundnuts as a cash crop in vast expanses of northern Nigeria and the neighbouring French colonies ceases to be worthwhile depends largely upon the level of groundnut prices and the costs of transport. Similar influences determine the ebb and flow in the economic value of land suitable for rubber-planting in the interior of Sumatra.

Accessibility vitally affects the economic position of many

parts of the under-developed world, and changes in accessibility have had striking results in a comparatively short time. Numerous examples could be cited of the rapid growth of production for the market following on the establishment of communications and stable political conditions.   Well-known instances include cocoa production in the Gold Coast, which was greatly stimulated by the building of the railway from Accra to Kumasi.   Production of Nigerian groundnuts for export, and of kola nuts, both for consumption in northern Nigeria and for export overland, sprang up after the construction of the Nigerian railway.   Production of cotton in Uganda was made possible by the construction of the Kenya–Uganda railway.   The building of railways was an essential factor in establishing the accessibility of these producing areas. Another factor was the activities of traders who collected the produce from growers and acted as an indispensable link in the chain of communications.

The recent history of the rubber industry may be cited as one more illustration of the importance of economic accessibility and of the supply of co-operant factors in shaping the fortunes of an industry and of the different producing regions where it is located, and in conferring value on previously valueless natural resources.   Until about 1900 almost all of the few thousand tons of rubber exported annually came from South America.   After the turn of the century there was a large increase in the demand for rubber resulting largely from the development of the motor-car industry and the progress of rubber technology.   The increased demand was met from plantations (both large-scale capitalistic estates and peasant smallholdings) of South-east Asia, chiefly Malaya, Sumatra and Java, while the output of wild rubber from South America declined despite favourable prices.   A principal reason for the migration of the rubber-growing industry is to be found in the access of these countries to large reservoirs of labour in South India, China and Java, as well as to the capital markets of Western Europe; the presence of enterprising European merchant firms and a stable administration also played an indis-

pensable part. It is of special interest that neither Malaya
nor Sumatra, the two main producing territories, had a large
indigenous labour force, a particularly fertile soil, or supplies
of local capital when rubber was first established there. No
survey of their resources carried out, say in 1895, would have
suggested that within a few years these territories would be the
principal producers of the leading tropical plantation crop.

**§ 4. Institutional Barriers to the Efficient Use of Natural Re-
sources.** Institutional arrangements may stand between
natural resources and their most effective development and
exploitation. The accessibility of the resources may be
reduced by measures of official policy. A simple example is
where otherwise suitable land is not made available for particular purposes, or where land in defined areas is not alienated
to members of particular racial groups. In East Africa there
are restrictions on the establishment of trading sites by non-
Africans. This not only restricts the development of land for
trading purposes, but also hinders the development of land
for farming, since the market for farm products is made less
accessible by the curtailment of the activities of traders. The
restrictions on the alienation of land in different regions in
East Africa (notably in Kenya) to members of specified racial
groups are far more serious in their effects. Whatever the
original causes of these restrictions may have been, at present
they prevent new combinations of land, capital, labour and
skills which are essential if the economy as a whole and opportunities for all its inhabitants are to expand. This is a major
theme of the *Report of the Royal Commission on East Africa,
1953–5*, to which the reader is referred for full details and a
thorough and stimulating analysis.[1]

Land tenure systems also may affect the economic accessibility of natural resources. This can be illustrated by a brief
discussion of communal land tenure systems which are a feature, in a variety of forms, of agriculture in many parts of the

[1] *Report of the Royal Commission on East Africa, 1953–5*, London,
1955.

under-developed world. Communal rights prevent the energetic or able individual members of the group from acquiring more land at the expense of the indolent or unproductive. They also make it difficult, if not impossible, for either an individual or the group to borrow on the security of land for such productive purposes as the purchase of fertilisers or of simple equipment. Individuals also are unlikely to spend much effort or money on improving cultivated plots when these are periodically re-allotted by the tribal or village authorities, as often happens.[1] The system tends to encourage uneconomic farming practices in other ways. For example, there is no incentive to the individual to limit the number of cattle he grazes on communal land, since any benefit is likely to be reduced by the over-grazing practised by others. Similarly, the improvement in the quality of cattle is retarded if different herds are grazed together. The system may also discourage economically sound conservation practices; even if the total benefits of such practices should exceed their costs, these may not be incurred if the benefits would be shared by all the communal owners while only some of them would be willing to contribute to the cost of the required improvements. These drawbacks are unimportant when land is plentiful, or when the material aspirations of the group are limited. But they become important when land is conceived of as a productive asset, and when there is a growing desire to maximise the returns to be derived from it. Thus in times of social and economic change land tenure systems become a major issue of public policy; we return to this aspect of the subject in Chapter XII.

§ 5. Unused Natural Resources. The phenomenon of unused resources, and specially of unused land, often puzzles

---

[1] In certain parts of Syria, village land known as *mucha'a* is held in common but cultivated in individual family plots periodically re-allotted among the holders. This gives 'little or no incentive to permanent improvement of the land'. International Bank for Reconstruction and Development, *The Economic Development of Syria*, Baltimore, 1955, p. 353.

visitors and observers in under-developed countries and regions. The idleness of these resources, or their partial or limited use in production, is easily regarded as wasteful and as evidence of maladministration or inefficiency. However, natural resources may be left idle or be used incompletely or inadequately for any one of a number of different reasons. These have to be distinguished for purposes of analysis. Their economic consequences and implications for policy are widely different.

A resource such as land, a mineral deposit, a forest or a river may not be used in production because it is economically inaccessible. A natural resource is valueless when the cost of co-operant resources and the cost of transporting resources and products exceed the price the product can command in the best available market. If a natural resource is valueless, it will not be profitable for anyone to use it, even if the user does not have to pay for it.

There are many instances of known supplies of natural resources in various parts of the under-developed world which depend on improvements in economic accessibility before their utilisation becomes worthwhile; until this happens, they are valueless and unused resources. For instance, it is known that there is a large and rich deposit of iron ore near Lokoja at the confluence of the rivers Niger and Benue in Nigeria, only about 330 miles from the sea and not far from the rivers. But its location is such that the transport costs make its mining uneconomic. In British Guiana as well as in other parts of the tropics there are large numbers of hardwood trees of high quality; their location is well known, but felling is not economic because of high costs of transport to the markets.

It is wasteful to use scarce resources to bring idle valueless natural resources into production. The value of the co-operant resources *ex hypothesi* exceeds the value of the resulting product; that is, the co-operant resources are capable of producing a more valuable output in other productive activities. Their application with previously unused and free natural resources would reduce the value of total output. Thus it is not irrational or uneconomic for some technically fertile or cultivable land to be left unused, even in countries with a low level of food consumption. The diversion of resources with more valuable alternative uses in order to extend the area of cultivation may increase the supply of food, but only at the expense of a net reduction in the value of total production.

The fullest possible use of natural resources is not a sensible aim of economic policy, and the extent of the use of land or other natural resources is not a measure of economic efficiency in the use of total resources. Government measures should not be appraised solely on the basis of whether they have enabled more natural resources such as land to be brought into productive use. An expansion of government services in an outlying area may bring new land under cultivation; though such a geographical extension of the economy may be desirable on other grounds, the policy would not be the most efficient economically if the same expenditure on government services elsewhere would have raised the real national income by an even larger amount.[1] The same considerations apply if railway rates are equalised or otherwise adjusted to subsidise transport to particular areas or regions. This may make it profitable for farmers to bring previously idle land under cultivation or for entrepreneurs to exploit forests or sources of mineral wealth. But to the extent that the reduction of transport costs to some users raises the transport costs of other users, the development of unused natural resources is at the expense of the development of other resources which is burdened with additional costs. The use of natural resources which is made possible only by relieving the users of part of the costs of co-operant resources is uneconomic from the point of view of the economy as a whole, because some resources are not used to the best economic advantage.

However, the idleness of resources does not mean necessarily that they are valueless or economically inaccessible.

---

[1] Where the expenditure is met out of the proceeds of taxation, one should also consider the alternative uses to which the money may have been put if there had been less taxation or none at all.

Natural resources may be left unused as a result of monopolistic action on the part of those controlling them. In such circumstances the value of the output which can be secured by using these resources exceeds the cost of the necessary co-operant factors. Production does not take place because of monopolistic restriction of output, which secures private gains to the monopolists at the cost of social loss through the idleness (or under-employment) of resources which could otherwise make a positive net contribution (or larger contribution) to output and national income. Organised commodity restriction schemes have in the past been among the most important examples of this kind of monopolistic action in underdeveloped countries. There is a clear difference between land left unused because complementary resources are more valuable in other uses, and land kept out of use (or out of the most productive use) by the decisions of a monopoly.[1]

A special situation may be noted which is in some way analogous to non-utilisation of land stemming from monopolistic action. Unused land is often owned by the government which determines the price at which it is alienated to farmers and others or made available for use by them. Land which could make a positive net contribution to output and income will remain unused if the terms are too restrictive or onerous, that is, if the price asked (or the rent charged) is greater than the discounted value of the expected net yields (or the expected annual net yield). This result can occur even when the government is not trying to maximise its receipts from the sale or rental of the land. In Malaya, for example, the 'rents' charged for unalienated state land are often greater

[1] Measures of control, private or public, ostensibly introduced in the interests of conservation of resources (a topic considered in Chapter XIV, section 3, below) may serve as props for the support of monopoly restrictions on output. It is said that measures in certain states of the United States for the conservation of oil deposits were monopolistic in intention and effect, though they were publicly justified as being necessary for the conservation of a wasting national asset. However, monopolistic restriction and conservation are analytically distinct; with the former there is the power and intention to influence the current price of the product, while with the latter the intention, as well as the power, may be absent.

than the net yield of which the land is capable; such charges in excess of the economic rent of the land impede cultivation and development.

Land may be left unused in the commercial sense because its owner prefers to use it for non-commercial purposes, as a private park, game reserve or for sport. Here the commercial idleness of the land is not wasteful; the owner of the resource prefers the pleasure he derives from the private enjoyment of his property to the money income he forgoes by not using the land as a commercial asset. He may do so in full realisation of the income he is able to obtain from using the land in the production of crops, raising of cattle or development of a housing estate. If he himself is ignorant of these possibilities, others with greater knowledge and experience will make him aware of the market value of his land by their bids for the possession or use of it. Moreover, even if owners are mistaken about the most effective economic use of their resources, the resulting loss falls primarily on themselves since, in view of their lower incomes, they will have smaller claims on society's resources. Failure to produce output is essentially a second order effect from the point of view of the economy as a whole.

It would be misleading to consider uneconomic the commercial idleness of land where this is the 'use' preferred by its owner. This would disregard the owner's valuation or use of his own asset; it comes close to saying that a person with great talents uses them uneconomically if he voluntarily indulges in periods of leisure at the expense of a larger value of saleable output. For social and political reasons it may be regarded as undesirable that the owner should continue in possession of land which is not put to the most lucrative commercial use. But this raises issues principally affecting the distribution and redistribution of income and capital which cannot be considered here. In any event these are not significantly affected by the utilisation or idleness of the land.

We have now distinguished three different types of idleness or non-utilisation of natural resources, namely, idleness reflecting the inability of the resource to contribute to profitable production, the withholding of the resource in the interests of monopolistic exploitation of the market, and the employment of the resource for non-commercial or private purposes. A fourth type is the withholding of a natural resource from current production because the owner believes that it will make a more valuable contribution to production at a later date. Thus the owner of a mine may postpone the extraction of the mineral or reduce the current rate of extraction in the expectation that the costs of co-operant factors or the market for the mineral will move favourably in the future. The complete or partial withholding of the resource, and its attendant idleness, is economically desirable if the expectations of greater future returns are likely to be justified. It is speculative in the sense that all economic activities requiring time are necessarily risky in an uncertain world.

Governments often regulate or influence the rate of exploitation of so-called wasting resources by means of one or other of a range of measures, and so alter the flow of income derived from them, both in respect of its distribution through time and its total over time. Measures of official policy in this field are considered in some detail in Chapter XIV, section 3.

CHAPTER V

HUMAN RESOURCES: POPULATION; INSTITUTIONS

§ 1. Scope of Chapters V, VI, VII and VIII. Individuals, communities and nations differ very much in the possession of qualities and characteristics affecting economic efficiency and performance. But the methods of economic theory and analysis are not particularly suitable for discovering uniformities in this sphere, or for generalising about the causes of these differences. It is not for the economist to say to what extent biological, environmental or historical factors account for differences in people and in societies in respect of their ability, desire and willingness to increase their production of goods and services and to promote economic growth. It is easy enough to list the personal qualities which help in the process of economic change and development; such a list would include an interest in material things, responsiveness to new ideas, willingness to learn, perception of economic opportunity, mobility and general ability to adapt to change, ability and willingness to take a long view, resourcefulness, industry and thrift. But the economist is not qualified to pronounce on the cultural, biological, historical, geographical and other factors explaining the distribution and incidence of these qualities in different societies or in the same society at different periods; and there are no general principles of economics directly relevant to these issues.

The more modest purpose of these chapters is to discuss some attitudes and factors bearing on the economic performance of individuals and groups about which economists may have something useful to say, without, however, confining the discussion to so-called economic influences. By limiting our aim to a study of some selected topics, we have been able to steer clear of the danger of confusing causes, effects and symptoms which besets any attempt at a comprehensive survey and analysis of the economics of human resources.

§ 2. Population and Real Income.   The relationship between size of population and real income has interested economists for several centuries.   In the late eighteenth century and first half of the nineteenth century the population problem was central to the enquiries of leading economists.   Interest in it receded partly because the problem seemed to become less intractable, and also because the population question seemed to be less amenable to the techniques of economic analysis. In more recent years interest has revived.   The facts and fears of declining populations in some Western European countries and, later, population pressure in many parts of the under-developed world have attracted attention and provoked enquiry.[1]

The demographic position and trends are not uniform in all under-developed countries.   Countries differ greatly in the density, age-structure and rate of change of population; there is no standard pattern which can be contrasted with that of one or other more advanced economy.   Moreover, the most densely populated countries are not necessarily those with the most rapid rate of population growth; the rate of growth of population in India and Pakistan since 1800 has not been very different from that in several countries in Western Europe in the same period.   The present rate of population growth in India and Pakistan is not significantly greater than that in the United States.   The significant point of contrast is, of course, that in the Far East and in South Asia there is a heavy reliance on a comparatively backward agriculture, so that large areas are over-populated in a sense in which the West is not.

[1] Our discussion of the facts and implications of changes in population in under-developed countries is necessarily brief.   For a fuller discussion the reader is referred to J. J. Spengler, 'Demographic Patterns', in H. F. Williamson and J. A. Buttrick (eds.), *Economic Development: Principles and Patterns*, New York, 1954.

The fact that there is population pressure in many under-developed countries should not lead to hasty generalisation. Though it is fairly evident that some countries are in the position that total output would not fall proportionately if part of the agricultural population were removed, it is also evident that some countries are so sparsely populated that there is insufficient scope for effective division of labour or for the economic installation of technically indivisible productive assets such as harbours and roads.[1] Some countries, indeed, may get the worst of both worlds in that they are very densely populated and yet are too small to justify investment to provide or improve facilities which would widen the market; some Caribbean islands seem to be in this position.

The general ideas behind the terms 'over-population' and 'under-population' are fairly clear. Thus the term over-population serves to indicate a state of affairs in which, with given techniques and natural resources, real income per head would be substantially higher if the population were smaller; and under-population has the converse meaning. These simple considerations are, however, rather remote from the idea of an optimum population, the numbers of which exactly maximise real income per head. This concept is fanciful; and, even if it were desirable, it would not be possible to govern the size of the population by reference to it. It is impossible to ascertain the optimum number in given circumstances, and the very concept is doubtful. It is linked to a given technique and a given governmental or institutional organisation; yet these might be different if numbers were different. With different numbers the methods of cultivation and the crops produced, as well as the cost of transport, might differ so greatly as to make it impossible to measure optimum density. The optimum would also be affected by the time over which adjustments were made and the way in which the

---

[1] The assets in question are those the products (services) of which cannot be transported at all or only at disproportionate cost. They would include harbours, roads and electricity-generating plant, but not steel-making plants or universities.

population change would be affected: the change in numbers, which always affects the age composition, necessarily affects the optimum.

The most fundamental weakness of the concept of optimum population, which is of special relevance in the context of under-developed countries, is the underlying idea that, with given natural resources, output per head is a function of numbers alone. In fact, however, real income is vitally affected by the quality of the population, and the theoretical optimum would depend on the skill, resourcefulness and thriftiness of the population. It is a familiar phenomenon that Chinese, Lebanese and Indians arrive in what appear to be hopelessly over-populated countries such as the West Indies, make a living there, create capital and provide opportunities for the employment of others as well. Thus the quality and attitudes of the population affect not only the level of real income but also the numbers at which the income per head is likely to be maximised.

In those under-developed countries in which contact with the outside world is absent or only peripheral, a Malthusian situation often prevails, with birth and death rates balancing at high levels. The causes of the high death rate include such factors as famine, endemic and epidemic diseases, high infant mortality, tribal warfare, and various social customs. It is conceivable that such a system might be raised to a higher level by some improvement in agricultural methods bringing about an improvement in the standard of living, which would then be followed by a fall both in the birth and death rates, so that the increase in production would not be absorbed by an increase in population.

A more likely course of events is that the principal improvements stemming from closer contacts with more advanced economies are such as to affect death rates in the first instance before a significant increase in total output can take place. In such circumstances population is likely to increase at about the same rate as the volume of output. There may be no marked improvement in the standard of living, the increased output being taken out largely in the form of increased numbers. This, for instance, seems to have occurred in India where the improvement in communications, especially the construction of railways and canals, has transformed the facts of food supply and of famine. Up to about the second half of the nineteenth century a failure of the monsoon generally caused large numbers to starve to death in the afflicted areas, since food could not be brought to them from areas where it was available, whether from stocks or from current production, because of the inadequacy of communications. After the building of railways and canals local crop failures, even if they affected large areas, no longer resulted in mass starvation. The very meaning of the word famine has undergone a change; while in the nineteenth century it referred to conditions in which large numbers died from hunger, nowadays in India it denotes a state of affairs in which large numbers are totally unemployed through the failure of a harvest. The reduction in deaths from famine has been reinforced by the suppression of both endemic and epidemic diseases, a decrease in infant mortality, and the suppression of practices such as widow-burning and infanticide. Thus progress has taken a form first affecting the death rate. Much the same has happened in parts of Africa. Although population density and trends differ greatly in many under-developed countries, this broad sequence of events has been fairly common in the early stages of economic development. As a result population has tended to increase before there has been a substantial increase in real income per head (as measured conventionally).

It has been a common experience in the under-developed world for increased output to be accompanied by increased numbers; but it has been unusual for the sustained rate of change in population to be as great as the rate of change in output, particularly where the growth in output has come after contact with the West. There is ample evidence of an increase in the level of real consumption per head in many parts of the under-developed world. Even in India there has been over the last half-century an appreciable increase in real income per head, which is reflected for instance in the improvement in diets, with the substitution of wheat for lower-grade cereals and the increased consumption of fruit and vegetables.   There is little evidence that, save in the most primitive and isolated communities, the supply of labour (population) is approximately perfectly elastic at a real wage (real income per head) equal to some fixed subsistence level.   Where the volume of production has risen, it has usually been taken out partly in larger numbers and partly in higher real incomes per head. Even where present standards of living are still low, they are higher than they had been before self-sufficiency gave way with growing economic and social contacts, and they represent a more varied consumption.

There is an important point to be noted about the customary emphasis on real income per head as a criterion of economic well-being and development.   The increase in population in under-developed countries generally reflects a fall in the death rate and thus a longer life expectation.   This implies a psychic income, the value of which is clear from people's readiness to pay for the satisfaction of the postponement of death, both their own death and that of their relatives, especially their children.   Satisfactions or incomes of this kind are not included in estimates of national income, and hence in estimates of real income per head; and to that extent the results and implications of population growth and economic development are obscured.

In India and Pakistan the rate of population increase is at present approximately 1–1½ per cent per annum; the very large absolute numbers involved tend to obscure the fact that the percentage rate of increase is not exceptional, and not much higher than in a number of Western countries, including the United States.   But when poor countries are densely populated and have large absolute increases in numbers they are in a vulnerable position even if the proportionate increase is small, since a harvest failure may mean a large external deficit with a balance of payments crisis, and may even turn the terms of trade against the afflicted country. Of course, if such a country not only has a large absolute increase in numbers but also a large percentage increase, its position is even more vulnerable.

Although economic development is often accompanied initially by a fall in the death rate, so that part of an increase in total output is absorbed by larger numbers, the birth rate often falls subsequently, especially when it had previously been high. But this is not an inevitable development. The improved status of women and the greater variety of ways in which leisure can be used are among the forces which often serve to reduce the birth rate.

Other economic and social problems arise when economic advance is accompanied by a reduction in death rates. The economy may have to bear a heavier burden of dependency. This is likely to be particularly acute in the transitional stage, for improved levels of consumption and health services are likely subsequently to lengthen the effective working life of members of a population with a longer average expectation of life. The difficulties of transition may be increased by the need to find resources for the education of the larger number of children. The burden of dependents is once more increased, and a source of labour is diminished. Changes in the age structure of the population and in its social structure may have as important consequences as changes in absolute numbers or in rates of increase.

§ 3. The Extended Family: the Economic Implications of a Social Institution.

Certain social institutions which are appropriate to a subsistence or near-subsistence economy may impede economic growth directly by reducing the rewards of individuals who take advantage of the opportunities presented by wider markets and the improved availability of co-operant resources. The extended family, sometimes known as the joint family, is an example of an institution which has many advantages in one stage of economic achievement but which may later become a drag on economic development.

In many parts of Africa and Asia the term family has a different and wider connotation than that which is customary in more industrialised societies. The term includes many more distant relatives and kinsmen than in Western Europe, and in many ways refers to a group more akin to a clan than a family in the narrower sense. It is a feature of the economic and social life of the countries in which the concept of the extended family prevails that a man has obligations towards a much larger number of people than in communities in which the concept of the family is more restricted. Even a moderately prosperous man may find that he has scores of relatives and clansmen to provide for; hospitality on a lavish scale to family members and indiscriminate maintenance of distant relatives is a feature of economic life in many parts of Africa, India and China.

The institution of the extended family is a feature of a subsistence or near-subsistence economy. In such a society surpluses cannot be marketed; this partly explains the readiness of people to make gifts of their surpluses and the dictate of custom that they should do so. Moreover, wide personal obligations act as a form of insurance in societies in which most people live at a very low level of income and have little or no reserves. The larger the number of people who have recognised obligations to contribute their surplus as well as rights to share in the surpluses of others, the more effective is the insurance. This is valuable when there is no alternative private or public provision for the relief of distress. The extended family system serves as an insurance fund, as an informal poor law, as a means for pooling and circulating capital within a group, and also as an outlet for charity and generosity. For instance, distant relatives who are mentally or physically sick are often maintained in Chinese or Indian extended family households. In West Africa family resources are often pooled for such purposes as educating a promising child or assisting a member of the family in setting up in trade or in an occupation. The informal extended family system is also a common feature among immigrant communities even in advanced economies, particularly before the immigrants are well integrated into the life of their new country.

We have mentioned the virtues of the family system in appropriate circumstances. But on the negative side it acts as a serious obstacle to economic progress. A man is much less likely to be willing and able to rise in the income scale, and to save and invest, when he knows that, should he succeed in improving his position, he would have to maintain a large number of distant relatives, distant in the sense of having remote blood ties and quite often also in the sense that they normally live far away. At the same time the system, which is largely indiscriminate in its operation, minimises the inducement for people to improve their own position because they can count on being provided with the means of subsistence at a level not very different from that of the majority of their kinsmen, including the more energetic, thrifty and able. The system has other adverse effects which are less obvious. It obstructs the spreading of the banking habit since people are unwilling to have banking accounts the contents of which are likely to be divulged to kinsmen. Generally, it weights the scales against investment in forms which are particularly conspicuous in a largely agricultural society.[1] It also adds to the reluctance of foreign firms to employ members of the local population in positions of trust and responsibility. Indeed, it often discourages men from accepting such posts or similar posts in government service, because increased responsibilities do not necessarily bring with them the personal enjoyment of a proportionately increased reward if the larger income, or part of it, has to go into the family pool.

As the economy develops and becomes increasingly removed

[1] 'Each member of the extended family group may have a more or less effective contingent claim on the use of chattels possessed by other members. . . . A shop being, by definition, a repository of commodities awaiting, as it were, exceptional possession by individuals, the African shopkeeper [in Nyasaland and Tanganyika] is peculiarly exposed to requests of relatives that he should enable them to share with him possession of his stock. . . . The African trader often finds it expedient to establish himself outside his native habitat.' Chalmers Wright, *op. cit.*, pp. 54–5.

from the subsistence stage, the concept of the family narrows, and the number of people to whom individuals recognise family obligations tends to become smaller. Surpluses can be marketed regularly with the growth of specialisation and of wider markets. A larger proportion of the population is raised above the strict subsistence level; and though there is often a time lag, alternative private or public insurance or other arrangements replace the traditional methods for the relief of personal distress and disability. The development of exchange tends to eliminate custom-dominated personal relationships. Relationships become increasingly impersonal, which tends to reduce the number of people who have claims on individuals.[1]

An institution like the extended family does not give way equally easily in all societies. In Africa its disintegration is proceeding apace in areas in which the money economy is advancing rapidly. In India and China it has been a feature of the social landscape for many centuries, during which these countries had at times attained levels of economic achievement far beyond those now current in Africa.

§ 4. Some Implications of Institutional Change.
The disintegration of institutions in the course of economic development is not an unmitigated blessing, even though it may clear the way for more rapid progress and be a necessary consequence of it. Individuals are not equally adaptable to change and able to deal with the challenge presented by changing conditions, relationships and opportunities. The less adaptable may go to the wall; and in the process of change, if it is rapid, those institutions which gave some security and protection to

[1] An anthropologist, examining changes among the Pondo in South Africa, summarises these tendencies in the following terms: 'There is increasing economic individualism. The co-operative economic unit, the *umzi* [local kinship group], is decreasing in size, and more and more families of a man, wife, and minor children, tend to become independent groups. Economic values are becoming dominant. . . . Whereas formerly, a big *umzi*, many adherents, and the giving of many feasts carried prestige; now a man tends to be judged by his house, his clothes, his food.'   M. Hunter, *Reaction to Conquest*, London, 1936, p. 546.

the weak may have disappeared.   Moreover, economic change
and development are not as a rule equally pronounced in all
regions or in all sectors of the economy.   Older institutions
exist side by side with the emerging institutions and customs
of an exchange economy.   Social and political tensions between different areas and different occupational classes result
from this dichotomy, and complicate the difficulties which
confront people when personal relationships based on long-
accepted status and customary rights and duties are replaced
by relationships based on impersonal commercial considerations and contract.

The increased prosperity and influence of individuals who
are most successful, either because they have the special
qualities required by the changing conditions and moving
economic horizons, or because they are less mindful of the old
order of things, are likely to be particularly resented by many
of their fellows; the very qualities which become important
and valuable are almost by definition far removed from those
treasured in the established social structure.   These tensions
are perhaps fully resolved only when economic growth has
permeated the whole country, when the values and habits
appropriate to an advancing or advanced economy have dis-
placed those of an earlier stage, and when new institutions have
replaced those jettisoned in the process of change.   It is a
matter of opinion how thorough-going and pervasive the
change in social ethos and social structure must be.   Some
economic historians have sought for (and sometimes thought
that they have discovered) connections between the religious
reformations of the sixteenth century and the economic
changes experienced in Europe.   On the other hand the
economic history of Japan demonstrates the compatibility of
rapid economic change and growth with the preservation of
traditional attitudes and social relationships, re-cast or re-
emphasised as these may be to suit the needs of a new economic
order.

However, it is clear that economic progress both requires
and causes significant changes in social institutions and

in the people who are served by them. The social structure
becomes transformed, new opportunities appear, the population increases, latent qualities become more valuable and are
brought into use, and new incentives are held out. Just as
the opening up of a railway may raise the value of hitherto
neglected land and reveal unsuspected productive powers, so
the growth of markets and the greater availability of co-operant
resources may raise or otherwise alter the value of the talents
of people in a variety of ways.

In a sense there is a choice between the material benefits of
economic growth and the (temporary) social disruption and
change on the one hand, and the economic backwardness and
established social system on the other. In practice the people
concerned rarely have had this choice, since it has been difficult
in a world of dwindling distances to keep out foreign influences
and to isolate an economy. Moreover, it is somewhat misleading to talk of the population of a country in the aggregate,
since the economic interests and preferences of all individuals
and groups in it are not likely to be the same. Naturally the
passing of a previously established system is regretted by many,
more so as its virtues are nostalgically exaggerated and its
drawbacks, including its economic drawbacks, are forgotten in
the contemplation of the inevitable difficulties of the new or
emergent system.

Some of the difficulties and tensions set up by economic
development are illustrated in a particular context in the
following passage describing the experiences of African workers in the developing industrial society of the town of Jinja
in Uganda:[1]

> 'The African . . . finds it difficult to adjust himself to the
> new economic system and the way of life which goes along
> with it. He has to carry out operations which are un-
> familiar, on new materials and with new implements, in an
> unaccustomed environment in which timing and attention

[1] C. Sofer, 'Working Groups in a Plural Society', *Industrial and
Labour Relations Review*, October 1954, p. 73.

to detail have a previously undreamed of importance. He is expected to work for long stretches every day, at a time and place determined by others, to keep working all the time, and to associate during the working day with Europeans, Asians, and Africans of other tribes whose behaviour bewilders and often antagonizes him. He comes to regard his European and Asian superior as impatient, over-critical, and unjust. They are in an incomprehensible hurry to complete every task.'

It is not surprising that the European or Asian employers or supervisors have to accept the fact that by their standards 'the African worker is unsatisfactory' and that the 'quantity and quality of his output is poor'. The resulting attitudes and tensions are, no doubt, exaggerated by the fact that the employers and supervisors are non-African; but the early history of industrialisation in Britain and elsewhere indicates that the difficulties stem basically from change and not from racial differences. Moreover, British industrial experience also suggests that the economic performance of the Africans is likely to improve over the years as the process of acquiring skill and settling into a changed environment goes ahead, though it is not possible to generalise about the rate of improvement or the level eventually to be reached. In other parts of Central Africa tensions of another kind are already being created precisely because African workers have within a short period become serious competitors for employment in occupations requiring skills which originally were beyond their reach.[1]

It is possible that the process of adaptation of most individuals to a changed social and economic order is shorter and less difficult than is often supposed. Adaptability to change is an attribute which may possibly be more widespread and effective than ability to introduce change. Much depends

[1] According to a recent report American managers of branch factories in Mexico consider the local labour to be about as efficient as their counterparts in the United States, a judgment confirmed in some cases by comparative statistics relating to plants using the same equipment, E. R. Barlow, *op. cit.*, pp. 47–50.

upon the way in which the process of growth and change is set in motion, the speed of the process, and the extent to which it permeates all sectors of the economy. Generally, a slow but steady development is likely to create fewer political, social and economic tensions; and it is likely that an attempt to force the pace too strenuously may also be economically wasteful because the social and personal changes may not take place which are necessary to enable individuals or the society to profit from the development and to sustain it. A serious dilemma is posed by the possible conflict between the desire for rapid growth which is displayed by influential groups in under-developed countries and the difficulties of adaptation to rapid growth.

§ 5. Economic Implications of Restrictive Tendencies.

Restrictions on the movement of people or on the acquisition and exercise of skills prevent the best use of available human resources. Their operation also obstructs the most effective use of other available resources, and thus retards economic growth generally.

There is a strong tendency towards restrictionism in societies based on specialisation and the division of labour. The motive for restrictive measures protecting the members of a particular vocational or occupational group is the desire to increase, or at least to maintain, the value of the services provided by its members by restricting their supply or regulating additions to the supply. Another type of restrictionism stems from, or is connected with, xenophobia, which is often very marked in societies at or near tribal levels. In these societies economic intercourse with people outside the tribe is often discouraged for a variety of reasons, but chiefly because it is believed to be harmful to the cohesion of the group. Restrictive tendencies stemming from these two distinct sources are often found side by side and merge into each other. When the impact of a money economy has been sudden, the type of restrictionism associated with economic specialisation may come into play while the restrictions stemming from village or tribal exclusion still operate.   Governments of under-developed countries often support restrictionism by the encouragement and promotion of trade unions, or the introduction of minimum wage regulation in particular sectors.   This means that there is no appreciable stretch of time during which economic development can take place untrammelled by the obstacles erected by restrictive groups and organisations. The breakdown of earlier economic restraints and the general absence of major or widespread economic restrictionism contributed materially to the growth of the British economy in the eighteenth century and much of the nineteenth century, and of the American and Japanese economies in the nineteenth century.   It seems that many of the present under-developed countries will not have this period of respite unless there is a material change in government attitudes towards restrictionism.

For obvious social, political and administrative reasons restrictive measures are prominently and effectively directed against foreigners in the sense of people of racial, national or tribal origin different from that of the majority of the local population.   But quite often they are directed also against members of the local population.   Such restrictions are a notable feature of West Africa and of many other under-developed countries.   In West Africa the transition has been rapid from the tribal and subsistence to an individualistic exchange economy, and the two sources of restrictionism have reinforced each other.   The narrow economic motive tends to be the dominant one.   An instructive example is provided by the vocal opposition in the Oyo and Ondo provinces of western Nigeria to the operations of produce buyers from Ijebu-Ode.   For some years past Jebu traders from Ijebu-Ode have been operating in the neighbouring districts of Oyo and Ondo purchasing cocoa and palm kernels.   The Jebus are racially closely related to the population of Oyo and Ondo; ethnically and linguistically they are almost identical; moreover, the Jebus frequently engage local agents and lorry drivers to act on their behalf.   These traders have secured supplies by outbidding the local produce buyers, and their activities have aroused opposition which is led by certain influential Yoruba chiefs. It is clearly unconnected with racial animosity and is a straightforward attempt by the local produce buyers to curtail competition which obviously benefits the local farmers. This is a particularly clear-cut example of the economic basis of ostensible xenophobia. In many cases the restrictions on the activities of West Africans have official support, taking the form of official restrictions on the granting of trading plots or market-stalls to Africans from other districts or tribes, restrictions on the leasing or alienation of land even where it is amply available, and restrictions on the employment of strangers and on the movement of commodities.[1]

Official restrictions on the entry or activities of foreigners are common throughout the world. Their effects on development are likely to be particularly serious in the poorer countries. We shall note (in Chapter VIII, section 2) the large and sometimes vital part played by immigrants in economic development. They have supplied missing or scarce resources, attributes and skills, and by their activities they generally have widened the opportunities of the indigenous population. The general failure of the largely inarticulate beneficiaries to understand the significance of the economic contribution of immigrants, allied with the pressure of local sectional groups whose interests may appear to be directly threatened by immigrant competitors, are largely responsible for the popularity of restrictions on the entry and activities of foreigners even in countries in which, in other contexts, a high priority is given to the forcing of economic growth. The fact that the controls and restrictions operate directly against foreigners adds to the popularity of such measures in countries in which the presence of foreigners is resented on various political grounds.[2]

[1] A more detailed analysis of restrictive tendencies will be found in P. T. Bauer, *op. cit.*, Chapters 3 and 12.

[2] These matters are considered in some detail in our article 'Immigration Policy in Nigeria and the Gold Coast', *South African Journal of Economics*, June 1954.

CHAPTER VI

HUMAN RESOURCES: UNEMPLOYMENT AND UNDER-EMPLOYMENT

§ **1. Unemployment and Under-employment in Under-developed Countries.** Widespread unemployment or under-employment of unskilled labour is a notable feature of the economies of many backward countries. Many people are unemployed or under-employed not because they prefer idleness to work, but because there is an insufficiency of co-operant factors of production to set them to work: unskilled or poorly-skilled labour is without work because the supply of other complementary factors of production is inadequate. The factor in insufficient supply may be either land, capital, technical, administrative or entrepreneurial skills, or a combination of all or some of these. Though an insufficiency of any one of these can be the principal reason for the involuntary idleness of unskilled labour, the unemployment generally manifests itself in the form of a surplus population on the land, so that a material proportion of the rural population is largely idle. Cultivators and their families have too little land or insufficient equipment at their disposal to keep them fully occupied, while at the same time there are obvious obstacles in the way of their securing employment outside agriculture.

The best known instances of this rural overcrowding are in parts of India and Pakistan, but it seems to prevail also in China, Java, parts of Eastern and Southern Europe, Egypt and some other countries as well. But though unemployment due to lack of co-operant resources is a feature of many parts of the under-developed world, it is not to be found in all parts of it. There are sparsely-populated countries and regions in Latin America and Africa which are economically backward but do not have to contend with the problems of

74

rural over-population or unemployment. The presence or absence of such unemployment cannot provide a criterion of under-development.

Unemployment of unskilled labour reflecting a lack of co-operant resources was an important theme studied by the classical economists, and is sometimes called classical unemployment. This type of unemployment differs from the periodic unemployment of labour, skilled and unskilled, which has been a feature of more advanced industrialised economies. The latter is the concomitant of an inadequacy in effective demand; and, since effective demand is deficient, the unemployment of labour goes together with unemployment of other complementary factors of production. The remedies for unemployment in advanced economies are therefore not appropriate for dealing with classical unemployment in backward economies. On the other hand, some influences may affect the volume of both types of unemployment; the level of money wages in manufacturing industry is an example.

Classical unemployment in backward economies is among the most important of their problems, and it will be considered in more detail in one or other of its many aspects in other parts of this book. Some general points are noted at this stage.

The problem of unemployment of unskilled labour in various backward economies tends to become more serious as economic growth takes place. This is not because the volume of such unemployment increases, but because its existence becomes more obvious and its implications more acute. In a largely subsistence economy the idleness of labour may be regarded as part of the nature of things; the pooling of economic activities and of its output within a family or more extensive group, which frequently accompanies subsistence or near-subsistence production, provides for the economically redundant members of the community. But with the growth of a money or exchange economy there is a tendency towards a greater individualism, which places the unemployed in a changed and weakened position, with grave social and political consequences. These consequences are more serious if some of the unemployed are literate.[1]

In considering remedies for the removal or alleviation of classical unemployment it is necessary to be discriminating because the lack of employment opportunities is not caused everywhere by the absence or inadequacy of the same type of resources. Nigeria provides a useful illustration of this point. In eastern Nigeria there is an insufficiency of suitable land; in northern Nigeria there is ample land but a dearth of capital and of local technical and clerical skill. Not only are physical resources unequally distributed throughout these territories, but the aptitudes of the different sections of the population differ markedly. In Nigeria the southerners have the advantage in enterprise, thrift, resourcefulness, literacy and ability to perceive economic opportunity; the northerners display greater sense of discipline, endurance and perhaps greater discrimination in the choice or acceptance of leaders. The uneven incidence of different scarce co-operant resources in different regions of the same country points to one general type of policy measure which is likely to alleviate classical unemployment everywhere, that is, the removal of barriers impeding the movement of men and resources.

§ 2. Wage Rates and Unemployment. The economist will ask why the presence of unemployed workers does not force down the rate of wages for unskilled labour and the rates of remuneration in other simple activities which the unemployed can perform. Why do these rates not fall so as to extend the demand for labour and to absorb the unemployed? The answer is complicated, for several influences may operate to cause wage rates for unskilled labour to be inflexible downwards.

[1] Unemployment among the ranks of the white-collar workers or the academically qualified creates similar difficulties, particularly if there is classical unemployment as well. The unemployment of educated people in backward areas often represents the over-supply of particular types of trained labour, that is, it is the result of misdirected investment of capital embodied in human beings.

We have seen that in subsistence economies the extended family system (or analogous arrangements) provides for a form of collective or communal production and consumption. Each member of the family shares in the family income and not necessarily or strictly in relation to the value of his individual contribution.   This system sometimes continues even when the subsistence economy has given way increasingly to the development of a market economy.   The right of the unemployed person to share in the family output secures for him an income the value of which in effect establishes a reserve price for his labour.   Other things being equal, an unemployed person will not be prepared to accept employment which deprives him of the right to share in the family income (for example, employment in the towns or in other regions) unless the wages offered exceed this reserve price.[1]   Thus the presence of unemployed in the rural areas need not cause wage rates to decline in the towns where there are employment opportunities.   Rural unemployment is compatible with equilibrium wage rates in the towns.

It should be noted that the reserve price or opportunity cost which is relevant for the unemployed individual's actions does not represent the value of his output when he is unemployed; by definition he has no output, though in fact many of the so-called unemployed on the land participate in some economic activity.   The value of his output from the point of view of the economy is smaller than it would be if he were fully employed; but the economically-desirable use of his labour is frustrated because when he is unemployed or under-employed his personal income is not directly linked with the value of his personal output.

So far we have considered an inflexibility in wage rates brought about by a force operating from the supply side of the labour market.   This inflexibility may be reinforced by other institutional factors.   In many parts of the world employers

[1] The reserve price will be still higher if the unemployed suffers non-pecuniary disadvantages if he leaves home; and conversely, it will be lower if leaving the family circle is thought desirable.

of labour, especially if they are government departments, official organisations and large-scale or foreign enterprises, are not able to offer employment at wage rates as low as those which would bring about equilibrium in those sectors of the labour market with which they are concerned.[1] Public opinion generally would not tolerate that such low rates be paid by employers who are politically vulnerable; in any case many of these employers like to act as 'good employers'.   Even if there are no minimum wages established by legislation and collective bargaining between organised employers and organised employees, 'there is ... a minimum price [for labour] which is established and enforced by the conscience of the community.   Wage rates may not fall to the point where the community feels that the employer is " exploiting " his workers.'[2] Those who hold these views usually are not aware that their influence serves to contract employment in certain sectors of the economy, to aggravate over-crowding in other activities, and to increase unemployment or under-employment. Finally, minimum wage legislation and trade-union action may raise particular wage rates above the levels which would otherwise be politically acceptable; the effects on employment are intensified.

The wage rates settled by political and social pressure, by legislation or by trade-union action are generally above market equilibrium levels.   The number of workers, whether drawn from the rural unemployed or from the rural employed, who are willing to work at these rates exceeds the number of jobs available at these rates.   Thus employers often know that they can enlarge their labour force quite considerably without raising wages; at the prevailing rates they can obtain more labour than it is economical for them to use.   And large numbers of applicants present themselves whenever large-scale

[1] As has just been shown, this equilibrium rate may be compatible with large numbers of rural unemployed, who, at that rate, prefer to be idle.

[2] S. Rottenberg, 'Note on "Economic Progress and Occupational Distribution"', *Review of Economics and Statistics*, May 1953, p. 169.

employers of unskilled labour advertise vacancies or are known
or thought to be expanding their activities. The relatively
favourable wage rates for those who find employment may
attract work-seekers from the country districts to the towns,
and since employment at these wage rates is limited, pools of
urban unemployed may come into being. These urban unemployed do not enjoy the security of the extended family system, nor are they subject so closely to traditional discipline.
They therefore are apt to constitute a more serious social and
political problem than the rural unemployed.

Such institutionally fixed wages and rates of remuneration
do not apply in all forms of economic activity. The social conscience does not as a rule concern itself with the remuneration
received by self-employed people or by labourers working on
farms or in other rural employment. Hence, where there is
classical unemployment, wages in the farming districts tend to
be particularly low. However, since much of the employment
of labour is connected with the extended family, it is not always
meaningful to discuss the use of hired labour in terms of
specific payments for specific services; a good deal of the
labour is given without receiving specific payment. A further
consequence of rural unemployment is that the ranks of the
self-employed are swelled in all activities which do not require
land and call for little or no skill or capital. Petty trading and
porterage are perhaps the most important of these, though
the provision of all kinds of unskilled personal services represents such overflow occupations.

§ 3. Monopsony in the Labour Market. In the preceding
section we have considered the common situation in under-
developed countries in which some employers can, if they
wish, enlarge their labour force at the current wage rates, but
do not do so because it would not pay them; such wage rates
are above the equilibrium level in that there is an unabsorbed
supply at the ruling rate. We now turn to another situation
in which an employer finds it profitable to employ more labour
at the ruling wage rate than is offered by the market at that

rate; in a sense the wage rate is below the equilibrium level in that there is an unsatisfied demand.

Such a situation arises where the employer exercises monopsony power in the labour market, for example where one firm employs a significant portion of the relevant labour, or where an important group of firms act together in the recruitment of labour. As compared with the situation in which there is effective competition for the labour, wage rates can be kept down, and up to a certain point this will raise the profits of the monopsonist firm or group, even though the quantity of labour employed, and hence the output, is smaller. Fewer workers will be employed at a lower wage than if there were more buying competition in the labour market, the difference depending largely on the elasticity of supply of labour.[1]

Monopsony power seems more likely to be present in labour markets in under-developed countries than in wealthier countries. Competing employment opportunities are more numerous in wealthier countries, and relatively more wage-earners are likely to be members of strong trade unions. But it is nevertheless doubtful whether effective monopsony is common even in poor countries. Labour is less specific, and hence the worker can turn from one employer to another or from one job to another without sacrificing the value of acquired skills or experience; the supply of labour to any one employer tends to be elastic, and there is little scope for monopsonistic exploitation. As has been explained in section 2, there also are forces raising wage rates in some sectors above the equilibrium rates; these sectors often are those in which otherwise some monopsony power may have been present. Nevertheless, it is pos-

---

[1] This is so even if the monopsonist sells his output in a perfectly competitive market; the exercise of monopsony power in the labour market alone provides scope for increased profits.

In technical language, it will be profitable for the monopsonist to employ labour up to the point at which the marginal increment in the wage bill (which will be greater than the wage rate) is equal to the marginal value product of labour; it will be less profitable to employ the larger labour force at which the wage rate is equal to the marginal value product of labour. Cf. Joan Robinson, *The Economics of Imperfect Competition*, London, 1933, Book IX.

sible, particularly in rural employment when hired labour becomes important, that monopsony in the form of tacit adherence to conventional wage rates may have a dampening effect on the speed of adjustment to changing equilibrium levels. However, monopsony power tends to disappear or to be weakened with economic growth and the widening of the range of employment opportunities. Perhaps the most telling example of labour monopsony was that of the co-operative arrangements practised by the South African gold-mining companies in recruiting and rationing African labour; the power of this group to influence wage levels has been limited by the growth of the South African economy over the last two or three decades which has raised the supply price of African labour generally, and which has probably made the supply to the gold-mining industry more elastic.

CHAPTER VII

HUMAN RESOURCES: REMUNERATION, WANTS AND EFFORTS

§ 1. **Remuneration and the Supply of Effort.** People do not give their labour and energies for economically productive purposes unless they think the reward is worthwhile. The reward may take many forms, but generally the direct reward in the form of an income which can buy goods and services is the most important incentive. The lure of larger real incomes, the opportunities for securing higher real incomes, and an increased awareness and valuation of the things that purchasing power can command are important features in economic development. It is therefore of interest to consider in some detail the nature of the response of individuals to higher rewards.[1]

An increase in the rate of remuneration received by a man has two effects on his willingness to work rather than to enjoy leisure. First, he is in a position to maintain his existing standard of living even while working less; to put it differently, he can enjoy a higher standard of living by working as much as before. His real income has increased, and he can spend his increase either wholly by taking more leisure (his money income being unchanged but his real income being higher because he has more leisure), or wholly by buying more goods and services (his leisure being unchanged), or by a combination of more leisure and consumption of more goods and services.

---

[1] We are selecting for special treatment only one of the inducements to participation in productive activity. We believe it is an important inducement, and it is one which is amenable to the tools of economic analysis.

The reader is referred to C. S. Belshaw, *Changing Melanesia*, Melbourne, 1954, Chapter IX, for a useful discussion of the pattern of inducements and deterrents affecting productive activity among the Melanesians of New Caledonia, the New Hebrides and the British Solomons.

The second effect of an increase in the rate of remuneration is that the price of leisure is raised relatively to the prices of all goods and services which an income can buy: an additional hour per day or week per year spent on leisure costs more in terms of goods and services than before because a larger money income is forgone.   The first effect is an income effect, the second a substitution effect.   The two effects generally operate in opposite directions, the former favouring less work and more leisure, the latter more work and less leisure.   Which effect will be the stronger cannot be determined *a priori*.[1]   But it is clear that the extreme case where the person elects to use his

[1] The income effect is associated with changes in total income, the substitution effect with changes in the marginal rate of remuneration. A change which affects the average and marginal rates of remuneration differently emphasises one of the two effects.   Thus doubling the rate of pay for overtime work would not affect the supply of effort in the same way as would the payment of the same total increase in the form of a higher rate without differentiation in favour of additional work.   But in general the net result of a change cannot be determined with certainty even when it affects the marginal and average rates differently.   However, an unambiguous result can be predicted when the change leaves unaffected one of the two rates.   Thus the imposition of a poll tax does not affect marginal remuneration, and therefore has only an income effect.

Certain changes in under-developed countries operate more markedly on marginal incomes, and so strengthen the substitution effect relatively to the income effect.   Indivisibilities in expenditure (of money or effort) to clear land or tend herds or crops may mean that the rate of (net) remuneration at the margin is higher than the average.   Again, where the head of the household has few duties in connection with customary subsistence production, the emergence of opportunities of employment in the exchange sector may operate strongly in favour of a reduction of his leisure.   On the other hand, intensification of effort to produce for the market may, after a certain stage, require the hiring of paid labour; other things being equal, this will reduce the rate of net money remuneration at the margin below the average rate.

The employment of labour on long-term contract (for example various forms of indentured labour) may also affect the amount and duration of labour-effort supplied by the individual worker in response to a given rate of remuneration.   He is prevented by the terms of contract from bringing into equilibrium at the margin his valuation of (or preferences for) money income, other work (for example in his village) and leisure. He either has to reject the offer of indentured employment or to commit his supply of labour for the stated period of months or years; he is not able to reach his most preferred position, if that should be somewhere between these two points, because of the contrived indivisibility of demand for one particular use of his time and work.   The system of indentured

7

improved rate of earnings wholly by having more leisure without increasing his money income is possible only if he has no desire at all for more goods and services which can be bought with money, that is if at the given level of money income the income elasticity of demand is zero for everything except leisure.

The discussion so far has been in terms of the choice between leisure and the money income from productive effort. However, in backward areas particularly the choice is not so simple. Production for one's own or family consumption is another alternative, which is very real when the subsistence sector of an economy is large, and when in some activities (for example in some branches of agriculture) it is not necessarily much less remunerative than production for the developing exchange sector. A policy of keeping down rates of remuneration in the exchange sector, or a fall in these rates, is likely to reduce the supply of labour or of saleable output in that sector, for there would be a tendency to reduce the earning of money incomes and to devote more effort to subsistence production. The products of subsistence production are, of course, not perfect substitutes for the commodities which can be bought in the exchange sector; but the lower is the purchasing power of wages or the lower are product prices for the cultivator's crops, the stronger is the incentive to refrain from entering the money sector, or to withdraw from it after having entered it.

The foregoing suggests that the supply of work and of saleable output in the exchange sector is likely to vary positively with the real rate of reward in that sector. This is so even if individuals have completely fixed wants (which is most unlikely), since they would wish to satisfy these fixed wants by the least effort and would therefore work in the sector in which a given effort yields a higher reward.

labour may increase the supply of labour to the employer(s) in question if workers prefer taking on work under long-term contract rather than going without it altogether—but would prefer even more, if it were possible, to work intermittently or for shorter periods at a time. In other cases, however, it may reduce the supply. In general, the growth of employment opportunities in an economy is likely to make the system of indentured labour less profitable from the point of view of employers.

Differences in the circumstances and desires of individuals reinforce the general conclusion that the supply of effort and of saleable output offered in the exchange sector tends to vary positively with the rates of reward obtainable in that sector. This is so even if each person has fixed wants. Not every producer in the subsistence sector is equally eager or able to transfer his efforts to the money sector to satisfy his (supposedly) fixed wants either wholly or partly out of a money income; and the level and composition of the wants are not the same for all. With the assumed fixity of wants an individual's supply curve of effort to the exchange sector turns back for rates of reward above a certain point; beyond this point the quantity of effort offered varies inversely with the reward per unit. But the slope of the curve and the point at which it turns back will not be the same for all individuals. These differences make it almost certain, even where individual wants are fixed, that, over the range of likely rates of reward or remuneration, the supply curve of effort to the exchange sector from the population as a whole will be of the conventional kind with the quantity supplied increasing with the reward per unit. A series of individual backward-sloping supply curves does not necessarily produce a backward-sloping aggregate supply curve. Moreover, though individual supply curves of effort may be backward-sloping at a particular moment of time, there has been a tendency in large parts of the under-developed world for wants to be elastic through time and for the individual's supply of effort to be responsive to the incentive of improved rates of remuneration.

§ 2. Flexibility of Wants. It is widely believed that many people in the under-developed areas, especially agriculturalists, respond to increases in the rate of earnings by producing or working proportionately less, because they need only a money income sufficient to pay for their fixed and limited requirements. This is sometimes said to be true of the mass of the people, for example, in Africa, India and South-east Asia. But the most cursory examination of changes in the habits of

consumption of many of the people in these territories is sufficient to establish that the wants of large numbers of peasants
and others have not been fixed or static.[1] The facts of consumption and imports demonstrate that increases in the rate of
remuneration and the emergence of more numerous and profitable economic opportunities have not been accompanied by
counterbalancing increases in leisure.[2] At least at present
there appears to be no ceiling to economic development
imposed by inflexibility in habits of consumption in many,
perhaps most, under-developed countries.

If it were true that the whole or a large part of the population
in some under-developed area had the alleged inflexibility of
demand for the things that money can buy, this would weaken
the arguments in favour of its economic development; for few

[1] Thus in a Board of Trade report entitled *The African Native Market in
the Federation of Rhodesia and Nyasaland* (London, 1954) the point is made
that 'the range of goods now advertised in the African press will be found
remarkable by those who still think in terms of "Kaffir truck" and is
clearly indicative of the expansion in the range of goods desired. Adver-
tising of bicycles and bicycle accessories probably takes pride of place,
closely followed by patent medicines, toilet preparations, and cosmetics.
Other goods which are widely advertised are musical instruments, gramo-
phones and records, cameras and films, foodstuffs and non-alcoholic
drinks.' (p. 28.)
This phenomenon is of course not peculiar to Rhodesia and Nyasaland.
Studies by anthropologists often include material illustrating it; for
example, changes in Bechuanaland are cited in I. Schapera, *Migrant
Labour and Tribal Life*, London, 1947, esp. pp. 8, 122–6, and Appendix E.
It is worth noting that the sale of alcoholic drinks, which are among
the most potent incentive goods, is severely restricted by official measures
in many under-developed countries.
[2] S. Tax writes in his study of an Indian community in Guatemala
from which we have previously quoted: 'It is frequently said of Indians in
Guatemala, sometimes as a reason for not improving their work conditions and wages, that if they earn enough money for the week in three days,
they will not work the rest of the week. I doubt if this is true on an
important scale anywhere in the country, but as applied to Panajachel,
nothing seems further from the truth than this dictum which implies that
the Indians work for bare necessities alone and have no desire to improve
their way of life, or attain the security that wealth (especially in land)
gives, or accumulate something for their children. I think that enough
evidence has been presented to make my assertion credible. The Indians
already live above a subsistence level (by their standards); they are certainly working for the luxury of meat as well as for corn, for their church
as well as for their food.' *Op. cit.*, p. 204.

would be prepared to advocate international or other measures for, say, the investment of capital in such an area, if the main result would be the enjoyment of greater leisure or the maintenance of the subsistence economy. Of course, there is nothing immoral or even uneconomic about an unwillingness to increase money incomes to buy goods and services, or, what is the same thing, a strong preference for leisure or self-sufficiency.[1]   Indeed, people and societies differ in the intensity with which they desire the fruits of a larger or growing national income, and in the willingness to make the necessary sacrifices and put up with some of the less agreeable concomitants of the emergence and growth of the money economy. But it is plain that such attitudes run counter to a desire for the results of economic development as they are generally understood.

Wants which are generally tending to increase may at times be static; there may be lulls in the growth of demand for goods and services, and time-lags between increases in rates of remuneration and the upward adjustment of desired standards of living. This phenomenon is not confined to the populations of the present under-developed world. It was a frequent complaint of manufacturers in England in the early nineteenth century that higher wages only brought about more absenteeism or shorter hours of work. More recently, after the Second World War, there were criticisms of the alleged immutability of the wants of mine workers in England with adverse effects on the output of coal.

The speed with which wants are adjusted to a higher attainable level depends on various social and ethnic characteristics. Where people are in contact with foreigners with a higher standard of living, or when they have brought to their notice

---

[1] According to one writer the average Sicilian petty land-owner (as distinct from the farm labourer) has limited wants and a strong preference for leisure. 'Since self-advancement and ambition are not Sicilian characteristics, the man's aim in life is to perform the least possible amount of labour commensurate with a bare subsistence level.' The Sicilian attitude of *dolce far niente* is to be explained not in terms of climate, malnutrition or innate laziness, but 'in a personal choice of one particular way of life in preference to any other'. V. Cronin, *The Golden Honeycomb*, London, 1954, pp. 76–7.

different commodities on which incomes can be spent, wants and the corresponding desire for increased income are likely to be more readily adjusted than when such comparisons are not possible. In stable, rigid and stratified societies with established traditions, wants are generally less responsive than in other societies. For instance, rural communities are perhaps less responsive than town-dwellers, though generalisation would be dangerous. In Nigeria the southerners, especially the Ibo who only a few decades ago were in a backward and barbarous state, seem to be readier to revise their standard of living and more eager to adopt the consumption habits of more advanced societies than the Hausa in the north, who have reached a more advanced and stable social life but who now seem to be falling behind the Ibo in the struggle for material advancement.

Throughout the under-developed world there is ample evidence of the importance of contact with foreigners in bringing about a revision of wants and needs. Indeed, in many parts of the under-developed world, notably in Africa and South-east Asia, what is remarkable is not so much the stability of habits of consumption as the readiness with which the local population accepts the consumer and capital goods brought to their notice and within their means.

Developments in South Africa and elsewhere illustrate both the revision of wants of the local population resulting from the examples set by others and also the possibility that this effect may be delayed. Africans in tribal areas in the nineteenth century were often unwilling to work regularly in the employment of Europeans. Their knowledge of the goods which they could not produce for themselves was limited, and in the early years they saw little to whet their appetites for money incomes. Measures to induce them to leave their subsistence economy to work on the mines or the farms included the imposition of taxes to be paid in money; thus a demand for a money income was created by compulsion. Subsequently the desire to earn money has needed no such kindling; it has been stimulated by the knowledge that the market offers a wide variety of useful or interesting things, and that it can be within the African's means to buy some of them.[1]

§ 3. Relative Prices and the Supply of Particular Products.

In the preceding discussion we have shown that, given the appropriate incentive, the quantity and value of total output in the money sector can be increased at the expense of subsistence output and leisure. *A fortiori*, the supply of any particular product or service in the money sector is responsive to an increase in its price relatively to other prices. The time and effort which are necessary for an increase in the supply of one product can come from the same two sources as before, subsistence activities and leisure; in addition time, effort and money previously devoted to the production of other goods and services in the money sector can be diverted to the production of the more profitable product. Even if there were some substance in the view that backward people have an absolutely limited demand for money income or for real income generally (and this, as we have seen, is a doubtful generalisation), there can be no doubt that they prefer to get the money income, and the things they wish to buy with it, as easily as possible. A relative rise in the price of one product or service is bound to increase its supply if this is physically possible.

There are various technical difficulties in the way of detailed and specific verification of this general proposition. The student of economics is familiar with the general difficulty of empirical proof because of the impossibility of eliminating the disturbing influence of factors other than those under examination, and it is distressingly easy for economists to fall into the error of confusing historical relationships with cause-and-effect relationships. Moreover, the results of the response to an increase in price may be delayed because of obstacles to an immediate increase in the rate of supply. But these and other difficulties do not detract from the validity of

---

[1] Other forces have been at work as well, but these cannot be considered here.

the proposition established from simple general reasoning, which is confirmed by the historical evidence of the increase in the production of export products and other crops, and the extension of capacity for producing these crops by peasant producers in Africa, Asia and elsewhere under the stimulus of attractive prices.   There is a wealth of examples from which to choose for purposes of illustration; here we refer only to a recent one.   The high level of coffee prices in recent years has led to a greatly increased rate of exploitation of coffee trees growing wild in the south-western part of Ethiopia.   People have been attracted to this sparsely populated part of the country and hired labour has been brought in when necessary. Expense and effort have been put into the clearing of the forest to improve yields.   At the same time in other areas in which coffee is *cultivated*, there has been a tendency for producers to change over from the growing of cereals to that of coffee. The high price of coffee has justified this even though cereals for local consumption have had to be transported long distances over bad roads.[1]

Nevertheless, policy measures influencing particular prices are frequently advocated or implemented apparently without regard for the influence of absolute and relative prices on the direction of productive effort and on investment in productive capacity; numerous examples could be cited referring to the imposition of export duties and the price policies of statutory marketing monopolies.   Sometimes it is contended that the price of a certain product has risen so high as to represent the maximum possible incentive to further production.   Such statements tend to neglect the possibility of extending production in outlying areas and of shifting between different activities and crops.   A price which may induce a higher (perhaps even the highest possible) rate of output from a given capacity may still be insufficient to ensure an extension of productive capacity.   Exceptionally high prices may be required to induce producers to establish capacity in remote areas or to switch

---

[1] These developments are described in Z. Siemienski, 'Impact of the Coffee Boom in Ethiopia', *Middle East Journal*, Winter 1955.

capacity from one use to another; and these high prices, even if only temporary, may provide the wherewithal to meet the initial cost.   The very high price of rubber around 1910 and in 1925–6 was largely responsible for the planting of large areas of rubber both by estates and smallholders in remote regions.   Moreover, producers may be able to buy certain desired goods (such as boats, wire fencing, furniture, watches or an expensive education for their children) only if their incomes increase quite substantially, because the goods are expensive per piece; they may only be willing to make the additional effort to acquire the income when the prices of their products are unusually attractive.   Particularly high prices may be necessary to enable and to induce producers to take large strides forward in both production and consumption. Once the producers have acquired new needs and new tastes, the level of effort put forward may remain higher than before even if the high prices for their output do not persist.[1]   Further, some of the goods bought when product prices are unusually high help in subsequent production, that is they are capital goods.   In short, high prices, even though they may not be permanent, play an important part in economic development.

§ **4. Economic Responsiveness.**   It may be thought that the analysis presented in the preceding three sections is unrealistic in assuming that prices and relative prices serve to guide productive effort in under-developed countries.   It may be suggested that because of their illiteracy and lack of commercial sophistication, and because of the poor communications in under-developed countries, peasants and others in these countries cannot take advantage of changes in the relative prices and market prospects of different crops, or of the differences in the prices for the same product offered by different

[1] In technical terms, there may be discontinuities in the demand curve for income in terms of effort because some items of expenditure are significantly indivisible; and a movement along a given demand curve may change the demand curve itself, that is, there may be an irreversible functional relationship between reward and the supply of effort.

buyers or in different markets, or of the rewards in different occupations and employments.

In the early stages of development from a subsistence to an exchange economy ignorance of available economic opportunities may indeed inhibit the most profitable production or disposal of output, particularly when the hand of custom characteristic of a subsistence economy lies heavily on the producers. But once economic development has started, the sharpened interest of producers in maximising the income from their efforts, and the activities of traders in search of business enlarge knowledge of market conditions and prospects in general, and about prices and opportunities for profit in particular. Observation of behaviour in many different parts of the under-developed world suggests strongly that most producers are aware of current opportunities open to them, and are also anxious to use the information that they seek out or is conveyed to them.

All producers are not equally industrious and expert in the collection and interpretation of market information, or conversant with available methods of production and the costs of different methods, or agile in response to particular changes in relative prices. These are merely some of the many differences between individuals which bear on their economic performance. But it is fair to generalise that among producers and others in under-developed countries there is a strong tendency to make the most of economic opportunities and possibilities within the limits imposed by the state of their technical knowledge and the availability of co-operant resources. Some specific examples may be useful here to illustrate the points that the inhabitants of poor countries generally are well-informed as producers and consumers, and that they are responsive to changes in the alternatives open to them; the examples cover the activities of people as producers, processors, sellers and buyers.

The peasant vine producers of Cyprus keep themselves informed of the prices at which they can dispose of their vine produce, namely the prices of grapes sold to wineries for wine production, and the prices of raisins, wine and alcohol (*zivania*) produced by themselves; they are also well aware of the rates at which particular lots of produce can be converted by them into other forms of vine produce (for example, raisins or wine into alcohol). Even comparatively small changes in price ratios bring about large changes in the conversion and disposal of produce. Moreover, in Cyprus as well as elsewhere peasants are known to shift from the production of one crop to another in response to market prices if their land is suitable. Thus one of the difficulties of attempting to improve the earnings of vine producers in the hilly areas, where the land is relatively unsuitable for other production, is the fact that higher relative prices of vine produce tend to induce peasants on the plains to turn part of their land from cereal and other crops to vine production. The long-run elasticity of supply complicates and endangers simple price-support or subsidy schemes.

The ready response of many East African cotton growers to price differences was recognised in an unusual context by an official commission of enquiry into the Uganda cotton-growing industry in 1948. Minimum prices payable to growers had for many years been officially prescribed. The commission recommended that a higher price should be paid to the grower if he brought his cotton to a recognised market than if he and his cotton were transported at the expense of a ginner to his ginnery. The commission considered the possibility that knowledge of the suggested price difference might work to the disadvantage of ginners; it was conceivable that, while growers and their cotton were being transported by ginners, 'growers passing a cotton market might wish to dismount and sell their cotton at the higher price prevailing at the market as compared with their ginnery destination'. If this happened ginners would be providing transport without getting any return. But the commission did not think this would be a serious difficulty, 'as the high rails of the ... lorry would prevent them getting out and the driver who is responsible for getting them to the ginnery would certainly not slow down when passing a store market'.[1]   The physical obstacles and hazards were thus thought to be strong enough to thwart the recognised desire for profit maximisation.

It is well known that Africans in various territories are keen and discriminating buyers, even though many of them are illiterate.   Thus a Board of Trade report observes of the African consumer in Rhodesia and Nyasaland that

> 'for articles which are familiar to him, blankets, clothing, saucepans, etc., he is a very careful and shrewd judge of quality.   In this connection it is important to remember that time is of no object to the African.   If he goes to buy a pair of trousers it is very likely a day's job and moreover he will have the assistance of all his friends.   He will examine the seams, the stitching and the lining and long discussions and comparisons will ensue.   Where articles which he understands are concerned he is a more exacting purchaser than the European.'[2]

In poor countries there are usually some members of the household with time to give to shopping; the low average level of money incomes makes it worthwhile for them to look around for low prices for the goods they buy and for high prices for the goods they sell.

Interesting illustrations of economic discrimination in the choice of methods of production are furnished by the practices of rubber smallholders in Malaya and Indonesia.   Two examples are given, the first relating to planting densities and the second to methods of treating raw rubber.

On the average, rubber trees are planted far more densely on peasant smallholdings than on the large estates.   It is often thought by European observers that the high density of planting by smallholders reflects their ignorance of the harm it does to the yielding capacity of the trees.   But this is not so.   The different planting densities on smallholdings and estates reflect

[1] *Report of the Uganda Cotton Industry Commission*, Entebbe, 1948, pp. 8–9.
[2] *Op. cit.*, p. 11.

differences in their economic basis.   The estates are owned by plantation companies or individuals who command substantial capital and employ much hired labour.   The smallholders have little capital, apart from that represented by the holding itself, and they rarely incur cash wage costs; labour is provided by the owner and his family assisted by outside labour paid on a share basis.   The smallholders try, broadly, to maximise the gross yield per unit of surface area.   On their holdings the trees are of smaller girth and the yield per tree lower than on the estates, but the yield per unit of surface area is higher.   On the other hand, the yield per tree and per tapper is higher on the estates.   The estates, which employ paid tappers, try to maximise the cash profit per acre or the return on capital employed, and so aim at a higher yield per tapper.   It is held that this more than offsets the reduction in gross receipts due to the lower planting density.   Thus the rational course to pursue is not the same for estates and for smallholdings, and differences in technique are rational.

Our second example from South-east Asia concerns the preparation of raw rubber for sale.   It has been the practice for rubber smallholders themselves to convert the liquid latex tapped from their trees into so-called sheets or blankets. This individual small-scale processing may seem wasteful as compared with a system of centralised processing which ostensibly could secure economies of scale and of division of labour. But in fact the practice has normally been economic, primarily because two-thirds of latex is water, a large part of which is extracted in the process of making the sheets or blankets; there is therefore a material saving in transport costs if the process is carried out on or near the individual holdings.   Attempts by private individuals to set up centralised processing depots proved to be unsuccessful.   The responsiveness of smallholders to price differences is illustrated further by their choice of method for smoking rubber sheets, a subsequent stage in the processing of the product.   In Malaya in the 1930's smokehouses were made available to smallholders for their own use; but the smallholders preferred to let Chinese dealers carry out the process unless the charges rose above a level representing their estimate of the cost to them of doing their own processing.

Our last illustration comes from Latin America. The widespread knowledge of market conditions and production costs and the strong desire to maximise returns from productive effort are well illustrated in absorbing detail by an American anthropologist, Professor Tax, in his study of an Indian community in Guatemala; the title he chose for the published account of his researches, *Penny Capitalism*, epitomises his main findings. A few short extracts follow:

'... the purchasers of goods make a choice of markets according to what they want to buy and how much time they are willing to spend to get it more cheaply and closer to its source. Everybody in the region I have studied knows that Tecpan is the place to buy lime. . . . If one wants a few ounces of lime for the weekly cooking of corn, he will not go to Tecpan for it. But if he wants a hundred pounds for the building of a house, it may pay him to take the journey.

'This basic knowledge about markets is known even to a child, and it is consistently acted upon when conditions permit.

'In Panajachel, where merchants come to the farm and bargain for beds of onions even before they are harvested, the farmer calculates his chances of getting more by harvesting the onions, taking them to market, and so selling them at wholesale or retail. In doing so he calculates the value of his time; and in doing so, both he and the buyer also use their knowledge of what market prices are apt to be when the onions are taken to town.

'Since most of the people in the region are illiterate it may be questioned whether they are capable of the mental bookkeeping that is involved if we are to call them economically wise. Are they able to figure their costs of production with some accuracy? I think that in most cases the answer is unequivocably in the affirmative.   In Panajachel where I laboriously calculated costs of production I had frequent occasion to remark the accuracy of the estimates given by the Indian producers themselves.'[1]

Thus it can be concluded that people in under-developed countries are generally well aware of such alternatives as are open to them as sellers or buyers (though these alternatives may be limited) and of the terms on which they are open to them, and that they take advantage of changes in these alternatives, the speed of response naturally varying considerably among individuals.   There is therefore no case for measures which can be justified only on the assumption that peasants and others are incapable of choosing from among available opportunities, and so are unable to make the most of them. Yet their alleged incompetence is the ostensible excuse for measures of compulsion covering the production and marketing of farm produce in many under-developed countries. Moreover, even if producers were ignorant, it is difficult to see how administrators can be aware of the different money costs of each producer, let alone of his preferences and of the alternative opportunities open to him.   Without this knowledge any decision about what he should produce or how he should sell his output is bound to be economically wasteful from the points of view both of the producer and of the economy.

The responsiveness to changes in relative prices is in fact clearly acknowledged in the widespread practice of governments in under-developed countries of protecting or otherwise subsidising the production of agricultural commodities which they wish to encourage, and of taxing those commodities the output or consumption of which they wish to discourage. The payment of premia for certain grades of a product has often succeeded in its purpose of inducing an increase in their supply.   The statutory marketing monopolies in West Africa

[1] *Op. cit.*, pp. 14–15.

have in this way elicited a great increase in the supply of grades of cocoa and oil-palm produce qualifying for the premia.[1]

Although producers and consumers are generally aware of prices and price differences, it may nevertheless be desirable for governments to assemble and disseminate market information, to supplement the information which is gathered by producers and consumers in other ways. But it may well be that economic development is better served by devoting resources to acquainting producers with new methods of production rather than to improving market information. The improvement of market information is generally, though not always, within the competence of producers, consumers and traders, and they can decide readily whether additional effort and expense are worthwhile for their purpose.[2]

---

[1] The payment of premia which are unrelated to differences in commercial values leads to economic waste. This is discussed in sections XI–XIII of our article, 'The Economics of Marketing Reform', *Journal of Political Economy*, June 1954.

[2] In some countries small-scale transactions do not always take place in terms of units of official weights and measures. Purchases and sales may be by the individual lot or piece, or different units may be customary in different regions. This does not hinder the parties concerned in any way. But it does somewhat reduce the usefulness of official price quotations; these would be expressed in terms of official weights and measures, which might not be intelligible to producers, though they would be of assistance to some of them and to traders. It is also more difficult to arrive at a market quotation if actual dealings take place in a variety of units of transaction or in a number and variety of places; of course, this does not point to the desirability of compulsory measures to standardise dealings in terms of quantity, conditions of sale, or place of sale.

The following passage from *Memorials of Alfred Marshall* (ed. A. C. Pigou), London, 1925, p. 356, illustrates the practice of selling goods without reference to standard measures; it also shows the working of competition in what might seem to be unpropitious circumstances: 'Things which are not sold by measure, but by name, are altered quickly in quantity; and since selling by name is the rule in backward districts, retail prices in them are often astonishingly sensitive. For instance, in 1878, when the taxes on salt were readjusted throughout India, being raised in the southern half and lowered in the northern, it was expected by many that the rule of custom and the smallness of retail purchases would prevent the raiyat from feeling the change for a long time to come. But the result was opposite. Salt was retailed by the pinch. And from the day when the new rule came into operation, the pinch was increased in size in the northern, and diminished in the southern half.'

§ **5. Institutions and the Direction of Economic Response.** It does not follow from the preceding discussion and its emphasis on economic discrimination and responsiveness that a desire to maximise money income excludes all other considerations. When deciding what to do, people in under-developed countries, as elsewhere, compare what Marshall called the net advantages of different occupations and lines of production. Earning money in the cities and towns has special attractions for some Africans; to others the pleasures of rural life, the security of proximity to the family and the hazards of a new environment reduce the value of urban cash wages. Moslem vine-growers in Cyprus often prefer to make raisins rather than wine or alcohol even though a given batch of grapes may yield higher cash returns if converted into the latter. The presence of these non-pecuniary incentives and deterrents does not affect our main thesis; but they are clearly relevant for an understanding of the economics of particular situations and developments. For instance, the responsiveness of labour to wage changes in Antigua cannot be understood unless it is known that many workers have a strong dislike for work on sugar-cane estates as compared with other work, and their behaviour has been misinterpreted as evidence of a backward-sloping supply curve of labour.[1]

The institutional framework, including the beliefs and values cherished by people, defines and limits the direction and operation of economic activity; but, however unusual customs, beliefs and social arrangements may seem to the outside observer, they are not incompatible with adjustment to changing economic variables, unless this itself is proscribed. The familiar responses to differences and changes in net advantages and prices are at work in under-developed countries, though the setting may be strange and the manifestations of the forces may be unfamiliar. The refusal of Hindus to slaughter cattle has had far-reaching effects on Indian agriculture; but the Indian who refuses to slaughter cattle or

[1] This is discussed by S. Rottenberg, 'Income and Leisure in an Under-developed Economy', *Journal of Political Economy*, April 1952.

8

contravene other tenets of his religion is still generally found to sell his crops where he can get the best prices. Tibetan belief in reincarnation, with the corollary that one should go to some lengths to avoid taking the lives of animals and insects, increases the effort involved in building operations;[1] peasants in Tibet, however, sell their sheep in markets in northern India when they fetch higher prices than in Tibet. Fulani herdsmen in Nigeria 'spread the . . . salt for cattle on a termite hill . . . the theory being that, as a termite hill is constantly gradually increasing in size, so will the cattle increase in numbers';[2] their ability and desire to increase their incomes, however, are illustrated by the fact that many of them take evasive action with their herds to escape the cattle-tax inspectors.[3] The Bantu of North Kavirondo in East Africa have been eager and enthusiastic in introducing profitable cash crops; but they use cattle-dung reluctantly for manuring, mainly because this use is associated with evil magic, and also partly because of the 'pride taken in the size of the dung-heap in the cattle-kraal' as a 'symbol of the owner's wealth in cattle'.[4]

Both the economic discernment of primitive people and the influence of customs and institutions on the course of economic activity are particularly well illustrated by the practices of the Amba in eastern Uganda.[5] It is the custom for the husband to appropriate 'all the money received from the sale of the cash crops', though he usually spends part of it on gifts to his wife. The woman 'has a relatively strong control over the

[1] H. Harrer, *Seven Years in Tibet*, London, 1953. 'I saw . . . how the coolies used to go through each spadeful of earth and take out anything living' (p. 170).

[2] F. W. de Ste. Croix, *The Fulani of Northern Nigeria*, Lagos, 1944, p. 68.

[3] The evasive action takes many forms, including driving the cattle during the critical period into areas where the collection is less rigorous, or into neighbouring French territories, or into places inaccessible to the inspectors. *Ibid.*, pp. 36–8.

[4] G. Wagner, *The Bantu of North Kavirondo*, vol. II, London, pp. 33–4.

[5] This paragraph is based on E. H. Winter, *Bwamba Economy*, Kampala, 1955, p. 15; the quotations are from this study.

... food crops'. This influences the women against working on the production of cash crops. They feel that 'labour expended upon cash crops enriches their husbands, and that they themselves do not receive returns commensurate with their efforts'. This tendency is strengthened by the prevalence of divorces among the Amba, divorces usually occurring at the instigation of the woman. This impermanence of marriage also affects such work as the women do on the cultivation of cash crops. The wife prefers to work on cotton, an annual crop, rather than on coffee, which produces returns over many years. There is a strong probability that she will still be with her husband when the cotton is harvested and sold, whilst her work on coffee cultivation may continue to yield benefits to him long after she has left him. 'For these reasons it is undoubtedly true that the production of cash crops in Bwamba is much lower than it would be under other institutional arrangements.'

CHAPTER VIII

HUMAN RESOURCES: ENTREPRENEURSHIP

§ 1. **The Uneven Distribution of Entrepreneurial Faculties.**
Knowledge of prices and costs and the ability and desire to use
this knowledge are important as conducing to the most economic use of available resources. They improve the productivity of given resources, and by raising incomes help to make
possible the accumulation of additional resources. They
operate unspectacularly and stealthily, but their influence on
economic development is nevertheless pervasive. Innovation
and the exercise of entrepreneurship in the sense of creating or
taking advantage of hitherto unsuspected opportunities for
profitable economic activity are often more dramatic in their
impact. The material progress of a society is likely to be
assisted greatly when the qualities of entrepreneurship, and
the willingness to engineer change and to depart from customary or traditional methods and practices, are present in high
degree.

The ability of individuals to perceive new opportunities for
profit and the ability and willingness to exploit them are indeed
crucial in economic development. The activities of the innovators or entrepreneurs who introduce new crops or techniques
of production or open new trading routes or areas of cultivation, and of those who appreciate the potentialities of new
ideas and novel methods and adopt or adapt them for local use,
raise the level of the economy. The economy is especially
fortunate when the qualities of the entrepreneur are possessed
by individuals who are also resourceful, thrifty and industrious,
have technical or administrative skills, and are willing to take
a long view. For example, the combination of these qualities
seems to have been present in large measure in the improving
landlords of eighteenth-century England, and in some of the

industrialists, merchants and bankers of Victorian England. The general literature of eighteenth-century England provides many illustrations of the interest of landlords in new ideas and their application, and of their readiness to envisage the fruits of their enterprise and improvements accruing for the benefit of their children and grandchildren.

In economically backward societies there are difficulties in the way of developing and using the entrepreneurial qualities. The force of custom, the rigidity of status, and the distrust of new ideas and of the exercise of intellectual curiosity, combine to create an atmosphere inimical to experiment and innovation. The collectivism of the extended family, the village, the clan or the tribe also inhibits innovation because the rewards, if any, have to be shared widely. The innovator disrupts the established order of things in promoting new activities and is therefore often an object of suspicion. The low level of capital also hampers innovation. But these difficulties should not be exaggerated. The influence of foreigners and contact with a money economy have often elicited a response from the adaptable, energetic or ambitious members of native societies. Whether the foreigners have come in pursuit of commerce or for the propagation of ideas, they have provided models in production and trade for local entrepreneurs to follow. The emergence of a money sector in a backward economy itself tends to encourage those seeking to profit from change; in a pure subsistence economy there is no scope for entrepreneurial qualities.[1]

There are many examples of poor economies in which local entrepreneurs, necessarily operating on a small scale individually, seek out and develop new economic opportunities.

[1] In this context, as in some others in this book, we have for convenience drawn distinctions more sharply than the facts might warrant; this does not affect the analysis or conclusions.

Exchange by barter is often widespread before the emergence of a money economy, and often continues concurrently with a money economy. This barter trade provides scope for entrepreneurial initiative and activity, though its geographical extent is restricted, and it is also circumscribed by tribal customs and other institutional forces.

The more successful individuals are able to enlarge the extent of their operations; the accumulation of experience and capital from earlier profitable ventures helps this process along. In East and West Africa and South-east Asia, areas in which the market economy is not very old, there are substantial firms in trade and transport owned and run by local businessmen.[1] Naturally the number of local entrepreneurs operating on anything but a small scale is likely to be limited at first, and they will be able to earn high incomes.[2]

An observer examining a backward but developing economy is apt to miss a good deal of the activities of the local innovators. The transition from a subsistence to a market economy involves a multiplicity of small changes—introduction of new crops to an area, clearing of land in new regions to extend cultivation, development of trading connections and routes and improvement in transportation—which have to be carried out by individuals with or without complementary government measures, using foresight, adapting ideas and taking risks. Local entrepreneurship necessarily begins in a small way because technical and administrative skills as well as capital are

---

[1] Here is the success story, in brief, of one African entrepreneur. He is a cattle dealer in Accra on the Gold Coast, who operates on a large scale. He began life as a migrant farm worker. Now he administers a large business and imports cattle from as far afield as Duala in the French Cameroons, Lake Chad in French Equatorial Africa and Timbuctoo on the Niger bend. His secondary business interests include dealing in grain and running a transport enterprise serving places as distant as Khartoum. He cannot sign his name, but is said recently to have given a deposit of £50,000 on a government contract.

Another African entrepreneur in Eastern Nigeria has for some years successfully operated a large transport enterprise with a fleet of over thirty lorries in an area where sixty years ago the population had not yet invented the wheel.

In Johannesburg a large passenger bus service is owned and operated by an African businessman, one of several substantial African entrepreneurs in South Africa.

[2] It is said that American companies with branches in Mexico have had difficulty in attracting Mexicans to serve as top executives since a person with the necessary talents 'could make so much more money in a business in which he had a financial interest'. Thus though Mexican personnel for subordinate positions can be secured at salaries below the American equivalent, the reverse is true for recruitment to the senior positions. E. R. Barlow, *op. cit.*, pp. 167–8.

at a low level; its manifestations may easily be overlooked by those who equate entrepreneurship with the launching on a massive scale of a new industry or product, and who forget that large industries and firms have almost invariably sprung from small beginnings. It is worth recalling that the establishment of the cocoa industry in the Gold Coast owed much to the initiative of a few Africans to whom the cocoa plantations in Fernando Po had suggested the possibility of a profitable cash crop.

In some societies or economies entrepreneurial talents and attitudes seem to be particularly widespread; or it may be that their social structure or social values may encourage the exercise of entrepreneurship, or at least do not inhibit it actively.[1] In Nigeria, for example, enterprise and innovation are at present more marked among the Ibo than among the Hausa. Again, in his study of an Indian economy to which we have referred before, Professor Tax has concluded that 'the Indian is perhaps above all else an entrepreneur, a business man, always looking for new means of turning a penny'. He continues:

'I know of boys 8 and 10 years of age who have set themselves up in business, buying and selling independently of their parents. Boys of 12 or 14 are apt to be pretty sophisticated traders. I doubt that I know even one man in the region who is not interested in new ways of making money, who does not have, typically, an iron or two in the fire, and who does not make his living partly as a business enterpriser. His wife is often the brains behind the business, too, and women also independently engage in business enterprises of one kind or other. It is therefore easy to go for descriptions of Panajachel to the writings of classical economists,

[1] It may be asked why higher material levels have not been attained in such economies. The answer may be that the entrepreneurs have little knowledge of Western techniques, or that natural resources are at a low economic level in the given state of local knowledge, or that the supply of capital is low. Again, in some of these economies general restraints on economic growth have been removed or weakened in recent decades only. Willingness to innovate and venture is not enough for economic growth.

for (as Adam Smith says . . .) "Every individual is continually exerting himself to find out the most advantageous employment for whatever capital he can command." [1]

On the other hand, there are societies or economies in which, at present, a lack of entrepreneurial spirit is a serious barrier even to limited change and growth. After a close study of conditions in a native reserve in South Africa, two economists came to this conclusion:

'It is, however, in the matter of entrepreneurial ability that the Bantu peasant shows the greatest deficiency; economic enterprise and initiative are most noticeably lacking. This fact presents the greatest obstacle to any improvement in the situation.' [2]

§ 2. The Foreign Entrepreneur.

We have purposely put much emphasis on native entrepreneurship in under-developed countries because it is so easy to ignore small-scale activities which are nevertheless essential for initiating or sustaining economic growth. However, it is clear that foreign entrepreneurs have been largely responsible for bringing many of these countries progressively more closely in contact with the network of international commerce, and they have introduced some of the fruits of modern organisation, capital, science and technology, and, in the process, they have provided vastly increased means and opportunities for native entrepreneurs.

The important part in economic development played by foreigners is indeed a striking feature in economic history generally; often it has been very large in relation to the small numbers involved. Obvious examples include the role of the Huguenots in the development of British and German industry, and, more recently, of German refugee businessmen in various parts of the world. The general economic effects on backward economies of the entrepreneurial activities of trading, transport,

---

[1] *Op. cit.*, pp. 12 and 18.
[2] D. H. Houghton and E. M. Walton, *The Economy of a Native Reserve*, Pietermaritzburg, 1953, p. 186. The authors discuss some of the factors inhibiting the development and exercise of entrepreneurial ability.

mining, plantation, farming and manufacturing companies financed, directed and largely staffed by people from the more advanced countries are too well known to require elaboration here. In many instances Western-type large-scale economic activities have been established, providing employment for many people and, in appropriate circumstances, affecting the activities of many more by creating markets for products and improving the means of transport.

On a less substantial scale individually, the work of immigrant Chinese in South-east Asia, of Indians in East Africa, of Lebanese and Chinese in the West Indies, and of Lebanese and other Levantines in West Africa has done much to further the growth of the exchange sector of backward economies and to promote their economic growth generally. They have accumulated capital, provided skills and aptitudes not present or developed among the local people, and have pioneered in the development of trade, transport and industries. By permeating the economy more extensively than the establishments and activities of the large-scale European mercantile, industrial, mining or plantation concerns, their influence has generally been more widespread and has affected large numbers of the local people directly. In some cases the number of immigrants has been very small. For example, there are only some two thousand Levantines among the 30 million people of Nigeria; yet this mere handful have acted as a leavening to raise large areas from subsistence production to a more advanced level of economic activity.

The Chinese immigrants and settlers in South-east Asia have been more numerous. Their contribution to economic development has been striking and they play a prominent part in the economic life of Malaya. The economic superiority they generally have over the indigenous Malays is due overwhelmingly to their greater industry, ingenuity, thrift, ambition and resourcefulness. It is not unusual to find a Chinese rubber smallholder and his family cultivating a holding of perhaps twenty acres, and having interests in half-a-dozen other activities such as a transport enterprise, a tailor's business, a tapioca plantation, a rubber dealer's business and a garage, while in the same area a Malay might perhaps cultivate a smallholding of two acres, often with the help of a share-tapper, and look after half an acre of padi. It has been said that modern Malaya is very largely the creation of the Chinese. This does less than justice to the work of the British administration and the European merchants and planters. But it does not greatly exaggerate the comparative roles of the Chinese and of the local population, even though in certain activities, particularly rubber-growing by smallholders, the Malays have played an important part.

The principal reason why emigrants often are economically successful in backward countries (and sometimes in advanced countries as well) is that they have skills, abilities and attitudes which are not possessed to the same degree by the local population; indeed, emigrants tend to go to countries where their qualities are largely complementary with those of the local population, since otherwise their prospects of making a satisfactory living would be slender. In backward areas the relatively scarce qualities may be the possession of technical knowledge or aptitude, perception of economic opportunity, administrative skill, industry, frugality or endurance.

The economic achievements of Chinese and Indian emigrants or settlers in various backward countries raise interesting questions. The original emigrants by and large were unable to prosper or exercise their talents profitably in their own relatively backward home countries. But whilst the Chinese in China have failed to achieve much economic advance and the Malays in Malaya had failed to develop their country, the Chinese emigrants and their descendants in Malaya have contributed signally to the economic growth of that country. The remarkable contribution of migrants to economic development may be explained in various ways. The explanation may lie partly in the fact that only the most enterprising and ambitious section of the population tend to emigrate. It may also lie partly in the stimulating effect of a new environment which so often results in a revision of existing habits, methods and attitudes, and in the removal of the social restraints inhibiting economic change in their country of origin. Further, the emigrants as strangers may not be subject to the institutions and customs inhibiting the more enterprising natives of their adopted country.

Émigré entrepreneurs from poor countries often make a special contribution. Initially, at least, they are accustomed to a low standard of living, so that they are prepared to accept very low incomes and can thus operate—for instance as traders —in regions where the turnover is as yet very small. Their supply price is low, and below that of temporary or permanent immigrants from wealthier countries. The presence of a trader or a few traders at the economic frontiers of a growing economy provides a demand for the output of the local producers and acquaints them with the goods which the market offers. These influences are important in encouraging production for sale and thus the emergence and spread of the exchange economy. The immigrants are also likely to have a high propensity to save, because they tend to value the security provided by the possession of capital. Even when they have entered their country of adoption without capital, immigrants have often contributed greatly to capital formation by spending less than their incomes. The massive capital accumulation by poor immigrants in North America is an obvious historical example; more recently, the capital accumulated by Chinese in Malaya and Jews in South Africa have been important factors in the progress of these economies.

A significant aspect of the activities of foreign entrepreneurs is that they stimulate, intentionally or unintentionally, the exercise of such talents of entrepreneurship as may be available locally. This is not only a matter of the growth of the economy brought about by these activities, though this is obviously important. Foreign entrepreneurs foster local entrepreneurship both directly by providing training and experience to employees who later strike out on their own,[1]

---

[1] 'The more prosperous African shopkeepers of Nyasaland and Tanganyika had usually passed through a period of apprenticeship in a

and indirectly by creating demands for services (for example those of transport and trading intermediaries), since foreign enterprises can rarely be completely self-sufficient and often find it more economical to tap the resources of local enterprise. The role of foreign enterprise and of immigrant businessmen in enlarging the scope for indigenous entrepreneurs is rarely clearly appreciated; instead, in political discussion attention tends to be focused almost exclusively on the indisputable fact that some foreign or immigrant business firms compete with some local enterprises. The complementary nature of their activities with those of the vast majority of the local population is overlooked.

This spontaneous development of entrepreneurship may be contrasted with the emergence of local entrepreneurs as the result of preferential treatment in such matters as taxation or the allocation of licences or of supplies under various trade controls; and it may also be contrasted with the fostering of co-operative societies by financial assistance from the government and the granting of official favours. These methods in force in many under-developed countries often have unfortunate results. They hamstring the more efficient competitors, local as well as foreign, of the preferred individuals, groups and business organisations; they create monopoly or quasi-monopoly situations; and they are apt to mislead actual and potential entrepreneurs among the local population about the nature of business profits, suggesting that these consist primarily in the collection of gains from riskless activity or in the reward of securing privileged positions from the government. They also put a premium on political activity and the search for political and personal contacts as against the acquisition of technical knowledge, capacity for administration and business experience.[1]

non-African shop, whether as counter assistants or as storekeepers in charge of supervised branch establishments; and they had postponed establishing themselves on their own account until they had accumulated a capital sum of not less than £50–£100.' Chalmers Wright, *op. cit.*, p. 56.

[1] In the republic of Panama a nationalist writer wrote in 1928 that 'the Chinese had the retail groceries; Greeks, the fruit trade; Spaniards,

Those who possess and exercise successfully the qualities of entrepreneurship are often unpopular; they are apt to be viewed with particular disfavour in countries undergoing a major economic, social and political transformation. Where, in addition, many of the leading entrepreneurs are foreign or of foreign origin, popular feeling against them is apt to be even more hostile. Their contribution to economic development, the formation of capital, and the increase in employment of labour and in opportunities for other entrepreneurs tend to be neglected. The capital they have accumulated tends to be seen not as a valuable addition to the country's meagre supply of vital resources but as the ill-gotten gains of a process called exploitation, which is neither defined nor its economic meaning understood.[1]   Or, alternatively, attention is focused on that portion of their wealth which they export as remittances or gifts to relatives in their home countries, and which is depicted as a drain on the economies to which they in fact contribute so much.

The foregoing remarks seem to be necessary as a corrective to popular misconceptions and prejudices, and to draw attention to the value, in terms of economic advancement, of the contribution of expatriate communities, large or small. No doubt the immigrant entrepreneur does not always behave impeccably in commercial matters. Opportunities for imperfect behaviour and exploitation in the strict economic sense are

---

French and North Americans, the hotels; Hindus and Chinese, the dry goods; Syrians, Turks and Armenians, the cheap clothing; the Jews, some of everything'. The Panamanians resented this competition and in 1941 President Arias 'by devious means . . . dispossessed most Chinese owners of their shops and handed them to his henchmen or sold them for ridiculous amounts'. The constitution of 1946 also limits the entry of foreigners into retail trade. Nevertheless, it appears that some of the Panamanians have already re-sold their stores to the previous owners or to others, and that the competitive efficiency of the average Panamanian is below that of the foreigners. J. and M. Biesanz, *The People of Panama*, New York, 1955, pp. 102–4.

[1] It is often overlooked that the businessman cannot decide what profit he wants and then go and get it, and that no profit can be made unless there is a demand for services which previously was not met or not met equally efficiently and cheaply.

likely to be found in an emerging economy where distances
may be great and communications poor, and where the ways
of a money and exchange system are not always properly
grasped. However, as we have said before, peasants and
others in poor countries are far better informed on market
matters than might be inferred, in error, from the standards of
formal education, and are neither easily imposed upon nor
backward in taking advantage of those with whom they deal.

CHAPTER IX

CAPITAL: LEVEL AND UTILISATION

§ 1. **Low Level of Capital in Under-developed Countries.** It is inherent in our rough definition that the level of capital is low in under-developed countries, and that, in particular, economic activity in them is carried out without the assistance of large quantities of the capital assets (communications, machinery, equipment and tools) which are commonplace in wealthier and technically more advanced countries. The meaning of a low level of capital can perhaps best be explained with the aid of an illustration. Nigeria, which has a population of over 30 million, is an under-developed territory which has made rapid economic strides in the last few decades. Nevertheless, the total mileage of railway track in 1950 was about 2,000 miles in a country of more than 350,000 square miles in which a large part of its bulky exports comes from regions over 500 miles from the sea. Bituminous roads extended to about 1,000 miles, and there were about 11,000 commercial vehicles, of which almost one-half were over ten years old. There were less than 900 telephone subscribers and about 8,000 instruments. Meagre as this collection of assets appears to be, it is quite lavish when considered from the point of view of countries like Nepal or Afghanistan, for example, which in comparison are even more scantily equipped with produced means of production and transport. In parts of the most under-developed countries the wheel is still virtually unknown.

The low level of capital is also indicated by statistics of consumption of energy for purposes of production. Estimates for the year 1937 suggest that in the United States the consumption of energy provided by sources other than man or beast was of the order of the equivalent of 7,000 kilowatt-hours of electricity per head of the population; in Brazil the corresponding figure was about 230, in India 100, in Egypt 80 and in China 30.[1] These estimates show not only the low levels in under-developed countries relatively to that of the United States, but also the wide spread between different under-developed countries.

The general effects of a low level of capital in under-developed countries tend to be aggravated by factors which reduce the economic effectiveness of a large part of the available capital. Much of it is in the form of agricultural holdings and improvements and of durable consumer goods, and is essentially specific and personal. The effectiveness of available capital assets is also curtailed by the narrowness of markets and poor communications; these bring it about that the capital assets available in one place as well as the products of these assets have a limited geographical impact. The high geographical and personal specificity of capital is sometimes reinforced by institutional obstacles. For instance, capital in the hands of certain people may not be available for use in some activities. Indian caste restrictions provide familiar examples. In Ceylon the official policy of 'favouring peasant development to the exclusion of capitalist development has denied to agricultural expansion an important contribution'.[2] Similarly, foreign capital may be debarred from particular branches of agriculture, industry or trade; in West Africa, for example, for political reasons the expatriate trading enterprises do not take part in the internal trade in local foodstuffs even though it is recognised that there are opportunities for the profitable employment of capital. Again, in East Africa there is legislation which makes it difficult for non-Africans to recover debts from Africans; this impedes the flow of non-African capital to African enterprises.

The general implication of a low level of capital is a low level of output, and its concomitant, a low level of consumption per

[1] U.S. Department of State, *Energy Resources of the World*, Washington, 1949, Table 51.
[2] This is briefly considered in *Report of the Taxation Commission*, Ceylon, 1955, pp. 82–3.

person. This is too obvious to require illustration or discussion. It may be noted, however, that the level of consumption tends to be low not only quantitatively but also qualitatively in that there is little variety in the available consumer goods, and there is often no assurance of reasonable continuity of supply. Transport costs are high because technically efficient transport equipment and good roads are lacking.[1] This limits the availability of perishable or bulky commodities. Moreover, because of the low level of working capital and of storage facilities, local crop failures result in acute shortages.[2] The early stages in economic development almost invariably involve a significant improvement in transport services. The fact that famines have been banished from large parts of the under-developed world during the last century is evidence both of capital formation and of more general economic improvement in these countries.

§ 2. High Rates of Interest in Under-developed Countries. A low level of capital tends to bring about high rates of interest (reflecting its scarcity), and this in turn induces both lenders and borrowers to make the most of the available supply.[3]

[1] '. . . On the best highways [in Japan], even as late as 1884, the cost of transport doubled the price of a bushel of rice in twenty miles. In Germany, by way of contrast, grain could now be hauled 100 miles on turnpikes or 400 miles by rail before its cost was similarly increased.' William W. Lockwood, *The Economic Development of Japan*, London, 1955, p. 105.

[2] Where a substantial part of the capital is in the form of livestock kept for reasons of religion or social prestige, the capital itself may exacerbate rather than relieve the shortage of food.

[3] The low level of indigenous capital, the high rates of interest, and the commercial astuteness of small-scale local entrepreneurs are all illustrated by the practice known in Lagos and the Western Provinces of Nigeria as 'gold-coasting'. The gold-coaster is an established customer of one of the large importers. He buys standard articles of merchandise on credit at the beginning of the month, say, a case of cigarettes at £130. He immediately resells the goods, if necessary at a loss, at, say, £128. With the funds obtained in this way, the entrepreneur can engage in other trading operations or money-lending. It is frequently possible to lend at a rate of interest of 6d. in the pound from one market day to the next, an interval of about five days. The debt to the importer can be paid at the end of the month. In the meantime his capital has been used to

Attempts by legislation to fix the rate of interest below the equilibrum level are likely to be ineffective. But if they are effective they are likely to reduce the supply of capital and lead to its uneconomic use. They reduce the willingness of potential lenders to make their capital available to others, and this may prevent the available capital from going to its economically most productive uses. Those who have access to capital, whether as owners or as borrowers, are encouraged to use some of it in activities which are less productive than it would be in other sectors and activities which have to go without capital.

The relative scarcity of capital in poor countries is the major factor in the high rates of interest prevailing there. In particular sectors of the economy additional factors may serve to raise the rate of interest further. For instance, the risk of illiquidity and of default and the high cost of administering small loans raise the rates charged to small-scale agriculturalists. There are, also, situations in which prospective borrowers may have to deal with monopolist lenders who may be able to secure monopoly profits.

For various reasons the apparent rate of interest charged on loans may misrepresent the effective rate of interest paid by the borrower and received by the lender. Even very high apparent rates of interest need not reflect a high yield on capital in money-lending. The failure of the borrower to meet his obligations is an obvious reason.[1] In parts of Africa there is an equity element in loans to peasant-farmers in that it is understood that the loan need not be repaid if the crop fails even though the borrower may have other assets. Time often

lubricate the workings of the local economy, to the profit of the intermediary and to the advantage of the economy.

It is interesting that the practice of buying on credit and selling for cash at a loss to obtain funds for financial or trading operations was used by Italian wool-buyers operating in medieval England. It was also a device to evade the letter of usury laws.

[1] A study of the economy of a cocoa village in the Gold Coast in the 1930's showed that on the bulk of the debt no interest was collected and the debts were being increased. H. S. Booker, 'Debt in Africa', *African Affairs*, April 1949.

is not of the essence of the contract; the agreed sum of interest is not revised though there may be a substantial delay in the repayment of the loan. On the other hand, the ostensible rate of interest may understate the real rate of interest where the borrower commits himself to sell all or part of his output to the lender at a price below the ruling market price.[1]

In general, the possession and exercise of effective monopoly power in money-lending cannot be deduced from high rates of interest charged, or high yields on the capital used in money-lending, or the frequency of foreclosure on land given as security, or the presence of ancillary obligations on the borrower (for example to sell his crops to the lender). The fact of monopoly and the measure of its use in a particular situation can only be established by examining, principally, the access of individual borrowers to independent alternative sources of supply, the productivity of capital in other activities accessible to the lenders, and the special advantages and disadvantages of money-lending.

§ 3. **The Level of Capital and Methods of Production.** The low level of capital in under-developed countries implies that capital is relatively expensive and unskilled labour cheap compared to the relationship in wealthier countries. Differences in the relative supply of the factors of production affect the economic landscape and the nature and organisation of economic activities. Differences in the relative prices at which capital and labour are available influence the behaviour

---

[1] In his *Report on a Melanau Sago Producing Community in Sarawak*, London, 1953, H. S. Morris writes that the members of only 5 out of a total of 255 work groups were 'completely free to sell their sago for the best price'; the rest were bound to sell their sago to the dealers who had given them credit. However, it should not be inferred that the debtors in such a situation are necessarily at the mercy of their creditors. 'Workers will be unwilling to tie themselves to a trader who is not trusted, and since few people are irretrievably in debt, it is always possible to transfer an allegiance. For the poorer workers this would undoubtedly be difficult, but it can be done. Moreover, if the trader were seriously failing in his business, his rivals would lose their fear of his influence and might help his tied workers to desert.' (pp. 45–7.)

of all who aim at economy in the use of resources.   Thus the methods used in farming, manufacturing, marketing or domestic operations are not usually the same in countries in widely differing economic circumstances.   What is an economic use of resources in one country may be uneconomic in another in which relative factor prices are quite different. A capital-intensive method of production may be most economical and cheapest in an economy in which real wages are high and the rate of interest low; the same method of production need not be economical in another economy in which labour and capital are available in a completely different ratio.   It follows that the *economic* efficiency of methods of production and economic organisation in under-developed countries cannot be judged simply by comparing them with those familiar in North America or Western Europe.   Economic efficiency relates to economy in the use of available resources; it postulates that the various factors of production should be combined in different proportions where the relative quantities of available resources are different.   Tests of performance based on purely physical criteria (for example, physical output per man-hour) are therefore not adequate or reliable as tests of economy.   Technical efficiency is not to be confused with economic efficiency.

In under-developed countries many economic activities are performed with little or no capital; in contrast to the same activities in advanced countries, there is a massive substitution of labour for capital.   Thus in richer countries the supply of water for domestic use involves heavy capital expenditure; in many poor countries the women of the household fetch and carry water in simple containers from natural sources or simple wells often over long distances.   Grain is ground by laborious hand methods; the lack of capital rules out the use of technically more efficient milling operations.   Houses or dwellings are built largely from materials occurring naturally, are not long-lived structures, and a good deal of labour is expended on maintaining them.   A study of the economy of a South African native reserve shows that nearly one-third of the women's time 'is taken up in fetching wood and water for household needs, stamping and grinding mealies [maize] by hand for cooking, and in keeping the thatch, walls and floors of their living huts in a state of repair'. Since in this area, as in some other under-developed economies, women are largely responsible for farming operations, the necessary preoccupation with household duties reduces the amount of labour they are able to devote to their crops and livestock.[1]

In many under-developed countries a large proportion of transport services is performed by porters without any capital equipment at all, or with the aid of simple carts, wagons or rickshaws or beasts of burden, with bicycles becoming more prominent as economic development takes place. The extent of human porterage, if this could be measured, might well provide one of the more illuminating indices of economic development. The latest refinements in the mechanical handling of stores, components and work-in-progress in American factories indicate the extent to which in a wealthy country labour in the movement of goods can be replaced by equipment. It is indeed a feature of backward economies in which capital equipment of all kinds is meagre that much economic activity may consist very largely of fetching and carrying, and of simpler forms of production in which fetching and carrying loom large.

Farming methods also tend to be labour-intensive; the padifields of the East illustrate this type of farming most clearly. The scarcity of capital also affects agriculture in that it is difficult for peasant cultivators to replace producing assets (for example, cocoa or rubber trees, vines or cattle) by technically superior varieties which give larger or better-quality yields. The capital is often lacking to acquire the new stock. Moreover, where several years elapse before the asset begins to yield an income (as is the case with tree crops), the producer often cannot afford the reduction in current income which results

---

[1] D. H. Houghton and E. M. Walton, *op. cit.*, p. 182. It is of interest that only about 10 per cent of women's time is devoted to the cultivation of the fields and the harvesting of crops.

from replanting. He does not have the capital to tide him over, and his rate of time-preference is such that he is not willing or able to forgo a large part of current income in exchange for the higher deferred income which would be available technically.

Marketing is also influenced by the scarcity of capital and the plenitude of labour. There is the obvious effect associated with methods of transport. It is perhaps less obvious that consumers and also producers substitute labour for capital when they spend much time buying or selling small quantities at short intervals because they have little storage space and working capital. The low level of capital in the form of work-ing capital, storage accommodation and communications also affects the structure of market prices; it is primarily responsible for large regional differences in the prices of bulky goods and for wide seasonal variations in prices. Monopoly elements may sometimes be a contributory influence. But the mere fact that there are large price differences and variations does not establish that monopoly power is present and is being used. It also does not establish that the methods of distribution are inefficient.

Labour-intensity in manufacturing activities is vividly and noisily brought home to the visitor to the metal-working quarters of cities in the Middle East. It is illustrated also by the time and effort used for example in the production of textiles and carpets by domestic handicraft methods. Again, in spite of the rapid economic growth of the last seventy or eighty years, mechanisation has been slow in Japan, except in a few manufacturing industries.[1]

In economies in which labour is plentiful and capital scarce much labour is often spent in prolonging the life of capital equipment of all kinds, and capital equipment is kept in use long after it has reached a condition in which it would be scrapped in wealthier countries. The exports of second-hand machinery from advanced to under-developed countries afford a general illustration of this phenomenon. Moreover,

[1] W. W. Lockwood, *op. cit.*, p. 288.

assets such as lorries tend to be used intensively, their useful life being extended by repeated repairs, though their life may nevertheless be shorter than in more advanced economies because of the low level of technical skill both in driving the lorries and in repairing them. Further examples may be found in the treatment of the motor tyre and the petrol can, twin symbols in under-developed countries of the advent of economic change. Rubber tyres are repaired repeatedly, and when finally unfit for use on vehicles they are transformed into the soles of shoes or into other durable objects of utility. We are told that the four-gallon tins in which petrol is delivered to the inland and southern regions of Persia are 'multifarious in the uses to which they are put; they are beaten into trays, into watering cans, into drain pipes, shop counters, and window sills and soldered into any shape that is desired. ... Being the prime source of metal in that region they are much sought after, but nowhere are they elevated to such a position as on the mosque at Kermanshah', which has a covering of beaten-down petrol tins.[1]

Several features of economic activity and conditions in under-developed countries are illustrated by the trade in empty containers such as paraffin, cigarette and soup tins, flour, salt and cement bags, and bottles, which frequently are used for storing or transporting goods or are converted into a variety of semi-durable articles. The traders, often women or children, who seek out, purchase, carry and distribute second-hand containers maintain the stock of capital; they prevent the destruction of the containers, usually improve their condition, distribute them to where they can best be used, and so extend their usefulness and their effective life. Their activities represent a substitution of labour for capital. The substitution is economic as long as six or eight hours of their time are less valuable (in view of the lack of alternatives) than the small profit to be made from the sale of a few

[1] Anthony Smith, *Blind White Fish in Persia*, London, 1953, p. 138. This interesting and amusing book has many penetrating observations, in passing, on the economics of an under-developed area.

empty containers. The system is highly economic in substituting superabundant for scarce resources; within the limits of available technical skill nothing is wasted.

In under-developed countries naturally-occurring materials take the place, on a substantial scale, of some of the products of capital-intensive production in richer countries. These materials are often put to a great variety of uses with a high degree of skill. Thus it is said of the Bemba, in North-eastern Rhodesia, that not only are the trees the 'ultimate source' of their food supply,[1] but more than this, 'they are the means by which all the material equipment of his life is secured. Huts, granaries, fences, beds, stools, drums, canoes—in fact, all the furniture of domestic and village existence—are made of wood. Bark forms the rope used for nets and snares, or the rough strands with which poles are lashed together in building'.[2] In many of the islands of the Indian Ocean and of the South Pacific, as well as in parts of India and Ceylon, the coconut palm fulfils a similar role of universal provider.

§ 4. The Distribution of Capital between Sectors and Activities.
In the preceding section we have analysed and illustrated the effects of the relative scarcity of capital and abundance of labour on the methods of production of goods and services in under-developed countries. It is self-evident that the ratio of capital to labour and other resources used in economic activities is lower in poor countries than in rich countries. However, within a given country the ratio of capital to other resources (that is, the capital intensity) is not the same in each line of production. It is economical to employ available capital in each use up to the point at which the marginal return to the capital in it is equal to that in all alternative uses competing for the limited capital. This optimum distribution of capital will not, save by coincidence, result in identical ratios of

[1] The trees are the source of food supply in that branches are cut, laid on the ground, and burnt—a process which clears the ground, destroys weeds, produces a fine soil and improves its chemical composition.

[2] Audrey I. Richards, *Land, Labour and Diet in Northern Rhodesia*, London, 1939, pp. 230–1.

capital to other resources (or to output) in all economic activities. Labour and other resources are not equally good substitutes for capital in all lines of activity or in all circumstances. Indeed, the ratio need not be the same in all production units performing the same service or producing the same goods in a particular economy;[1] just as there are differences in the capital intensity of techniques of production available in different sectors of an economy, so there are differences in the techniques available to different producers.

Where there is a continuous series of alternative methods for performing a particular activity employing different combinations of capital and labour with variations in physical productivity per unit of input,[2] the particular method best suited to a rich country is more capital-intensive than that best suited to a poor country. However, for the performance of some activities there may not be available a series of alternative methods with a continuous gradation of different combinations of capital and labour; there may be breaks in the range of substitutes. A mechanical bulldozer, for example, may be far superior to even the most capital-intensive man-with-tools in terms of physical productivity. In this situation the bulldozer may well be more economical than pick-and-shovel methods in many countries even though they have quite different combinations of resources. It will be the economical method in a poor country unless the price of labour relatively to that of capital is so low that it can compensate for the (postulated) greatly inferior physical productivity of the manual methods.[3]

---

[1] The example of rubber production in South-east Asia is considered on pp. 94-5, above.

[2] That is, where the technical coefficient is variable.

[3] When constructing an aerodrome runway in Jordan it was found that 'machine construction was far cheaper than hand construction for almost all operations, the one possible exception being that it might be cheaper to break stone by hand rather than by crusher plant'. This was so despite the high costs of carrying equipment to Jordan and maintaining it there and the low price of labour, which, however, it would seem was raised above the equilibrium level by non-commercial considerations. A. R. Macrae and A. F. Smith, 'The Construction of a New Runway at Amman,

This provides a partial explanation of the phenomenon of some examples of the most advanced technology being present in backward countries, outcroppings of scientific and mechanical modernity amidst generally backward production. The choice of method of production may also be influenced by the scarcity of technical and supervisory personnel. It has sometimes been found that cheap unskilled labour can be used economically only if methods are highly mechanised.[1] This enables the scarce and expensive technical skill to be concentrated on the construction and maintenance of the equipment, while unskilled labour, or labour with simple skills which can easily be taught and acquired, is used in operating the equipment. A large investment in technically-advanced capital goods may be a prerequisite to the use of available cheap labour. In this situation the complementarity between expensive capital and cheap labour is more important than the substitution (or competitive) relationship between them. Again, in sparsely populated countries with difficult terrain capital-intensive methods of road-building may be economical despite the apparent cheapness of labour, since it would be expensive to maintain a large labour force for long periods in inaccessible regions.[2]

Jordan', *Proceedings of the Institution of Civil Engineers*, Part II, October 1954, p. 421.

[1] When planning building extensions of Takoradi harbour in the Gold Coast the contractors decided 'to utilise Africans to the utmost on the work in all its phases so as to minimise the number of Europeans who had to be sent from England. . . . To accompany that decision, it had been decided to move very much in the direction of the mechanisation of operations.' A. J. Hill, Discussion on 'Extensions at Takoradi Harbour', *Proceedings of the Institution of Civil Engineers*, Part II, October 1954, p. 444.

[2] A description of road-building in Nepal emphasised that the population 'is not dense enough to substitute man for machine'. It was observed in the same account that the backwardness of communications and transport facilities (i.e. low level of capital) meant that much of the necessary road-building machinery had to be manhandled to the site. Two thousand men had to be harnessed to a steam-roller wheel, 'and they walk over the bridle-path, an extraordinary sight, like ants on a wall pulling a huge crumb'. The contrasts which are so striking a feature of many under-developed economies are illustrated here by the fact that some machinery parts were carried into Nepal by aircraft. Report by T. Zinkin, *Manchester Guardian*, 16 April 1955.

From the discussion it should be clear that it may be economic even in the early stages of economic development to invest heavily in particular sectors of the economy. Thus the construction of an irrigation scheme, a road or a canal may take up a large part of the available capital and yet represent the most effective use of the capital;[1] this may be so even if it gives rise to a large-scale displacement of labour (for example, of labour formerly used in labour-intensive porterage or farming methods).

In practice the distribution of the available capital among competing uses may be affected by institutional factors. Wage rates above the equilibrium level maintained by trade unions or government regulation in some parts of the economy encourage the use in them of more capitalistic methods.[2] Over-valuation of the local currency reduces the local prices of imported machinery and equipment and tilts the scale in favour of more capital-intensive methods, using imported capital goods. Again, governments often lend to certain categories of borrowers on subsidised terms; loans to co-operative credit societies are an example. The distribution of capital may also be influenced by market imperfections reflecting the limited knowledge of prospective lenders and borrowers. Lastly, the subsistence sector of a backward economy is

---

[1] An extreme case should make this quite clear. In some parts of the world a supply of water cannot be obtained without considerable capital investment. The availability of the capital and its use to provide water are then indispensable for all other economic activities and indeed for human settlement. If capital is very limited, a large part of it may have to be applied to this purpose while all other activities are labour-intensive. The construction of underground water channels in some dry countries is an example. However, in the construction of these capital assets labour-intensive methods will be used if they are available. The building and maintenance of these channels, called *quanats*, in parts of Persia, are described by Anthony Smith, *op. cit.*

[2] Trade unions may attempt to resist the substitution of labour by capital; an important example of successful resistance, tending to keep uneconomic methods in being, is provided by the textile industry in Mexico. A. Sturmthal, 'Economic Development, Income Distribution, and Capital Formation in Mexico', *Journal of Political Economy*, June 1955, p. 186, n. 13.

generally cut off from capital available in the exchange sector; indeed, one of the advantages of a decline in the relative importance of subsistence production is that, together with the greater possibilities of specialisation and the enlargement of the range of consumption, it increases the supply of capital to farmers.

CHAPTER X

CAPITAL AND ECONOMIC GROWTH

§ 1. The Relation between Capital and Economic Growth.
Capital per head is high in economically advanced countries
and low in those which are called under-developed. It is
tempting to deduce from this difference in the availability of
capital that the key to the problem of the development of
backward economies is the provision of capital on a large
scale. Indeed, after the Second World War it was fashionable
to diagnose the economic malaise of the under-developed
world in these simple terms. More recent events and developments have made it clear that, even though increased capital
may be a necessary concomitant of economic growth, it is not
a sufficient condition for it. Merely to supply a backward
country with capital funds or with supplies of the most modern
equipment will not ensure economic development even if the
capital is given away.

Many aspects or features of an economy undergo significant
changes as the economy develops. Capital formation takes
place, the physical composition of the stock of capital changes
and the relative prices of capital and labour alter. Economic
development is also accompanied by other economic and social
changes, such as the urbanisation of the population, the
increase in the percentage of trained or skilled personnel,
or the increase in the ton-miles of goods transported by rail
and road. But it would be a confusion of cause, effect and
symptom to argue that economic development can be pro-
moted merely or solely by bringing about any of these changes.

It is often nearer the truth to say that capital is created in
the process of development than that development is a function
of capital accumulation. This is clear not only from the importance of technology, skill, attitudes and so forth for the

process of economic growth, but also from the composition of capital. Housing is almost always a major component of gross investment in advanced countries, and it is essentially an item on which income is spent. The same applies to some other items of construction such as churches and museums, and less obviously to hospitals, schools and government buildings. Investment in increasing inventories is also better regarded as a function of the growth of output than as a condition of it. These important components of investment, especially housing, are dependent rather than independent variables in any functional relationship between capital formation and long-term growth.[1]

Economic development is the result of a combination of social, cultural, political and economic changes which in turn brings about further changes. It has taken place in the dissimilar circumstances of England, the United States, Canada, Japan, Soviet Russia, South Africa and Nigeria. Economists have no special insight enabling them to reduce these different historical experiences into straightforward causal relationships between simple economic magnitudes. At most it can be said that economic development has been accompanied, *inter alia*, by a heightened spirit of enterprise, by capital formation, by improvements in production techniques, and by improvement in the economic qualities and productive capacity of labour. But it seems impossible to isolate any one of these as the inevitable prime mover in the process of economic development and change.[2]

---

[1] Some suggestive remarks on this subject will be found in a summary of a paper by A. K. Cairncross in the *International Social Science Bulletin*, Vol. VI, No. 2, 1954.

[2] 'The rise of productivity [in Japan since 1868] involved much more than the acquisition of machinery and a corps of technicians to supervise its use. . . . To place it [the acquisition of capital and technicians] in the foreground runs the risk of obscuring other conditions of economic progress which are less visible but no less essential. . . . It rested upon much broader changes in economic life, including especially the growth of the market. . . . Historically, then, the development of technology and the development of the market proceeded simultaneously, each reinforcing the other. Each was fostered by the new freedom of occupation, security of property, and stimulus to business enterprise afforded by the political

The productivity of resources depends upon the availability of complementary resources and of a market for the output. This is as true of capital as it is of natural resources. There are at present a number of under-developed countries which cannot use all the capital to which they have access on easy terms; there is an insufficiency of suitable opportunities for the profitable employment of the available funds and of personnel with the required experience and skill. There are countries which would not benefit if large-scale injections of capital in the form of modern equipment were introduced. Indeed, it is not unlikely that inexperience, lack of training and acquired skills in the population and inappropriate social and economic institutions curb the economic development of backward countries more effectively than lack of physical capital assets. As Professor Simon Kuznets has put it, 'the major capital stock of an industrially advanced country is not its physical equipment; it is the body of knowledge amassed from tested findings and the capacity and training of the population to use this knowledge effectively.'[1] Investment in human resources is usually a lengthy process; and to be economically effective it may require far-reaching social changes which are also likely to take much time.[2]

institutions and objectives of the Meiji government. Technical, economic, and political changes were intertwined.' W. W. Lockwood, *op. cit.*, pp. 186-8.

[1] Quoted in United Nations, *Processes and Problems of Industrialisation in Under-Developed Countries*, New York, 1955, p. 5. An aspect of this general thesis is illustrated colourfully by the following incident. In Ethiopia, as in many other parts of the under-developed world, the educated are often unwilling to learn jobs that entail 'putting on overalls'. Once during a display of some agricultural machinery the Emperor was informed that the young man who was sullying his hands in order to demonstrate its performance and maintenance was a university graduate. 'What I need as an exhibit here,' said the Emperor, 'is not that tractor, it is that young man.' *Economist*, 12 March 1955, p. 908.

[2] Professor Ashton, after pointing out the class gradations in eighteenth-century England and the differences in incomes with which they were associated, notes that they were 'the product of centuries of history' and that this is often not sufficiently appreciated by those who look at England's rapid progress in technology and wealth in the eighteenth and nineteenth centuries and lightly assume that the same results can be obtained with equal speed in 'communities of undifferentiated peasants'. *Op. cit.*, pp. 21-2.

It is impossible to state in general terms how much time is likely to be required. This will depend, among other factors, on the aptitudes and attitudes of the population, on the existing social structure, and also on the ability and readiness of the political leaders to effect far-reaching social changes, possibly at very great cost. Capital formation in the ordinary sense of the term cannot shorten this time appreciably: in at least one important sense capital cannot buy time. Capital can be used to finance the education abroad of promising individuals or to build schools and technical colleges; but, important as this may be, it does not get to the root of the difficulties.

In arguing against the mechanistic and over-simplified linking of capital formation and economic development we do not dispute the obviously important role of capital in making possible higher productivity and higher incomes per head. We have already discussed this sufficiently at the beginning of the preceding chapter. However, it must be added by way of necessary qualification that economic development is affected by the forms in which capital is available; the stage of development and the availability of other resources are important influences determining the suitability of different types of capital assets. Capital, once it is invested, ceases to be a homogeneous factor of production. The word capital includes a wide variety of types of productive facilities, equipment and reserves, differing in their specificity and durability and in the demand they make on various complementary resources. The problems of economic investment are not merely those of collecting quantities of capital, but of deciding the forms it should take and the specific uses to which it should be put. The source of the capital and the method of its accumulation and investment affect these forms and uses, and therefore the productivity of capital and its contribution to economic growth.

It is sometimes suggested that the ratio of capital to income or output in an economy is useful in studying economic growth; or that statistics of this ratio in different countries (or for the same country at different periods) are useful in gauging the productivity of additional capital in a particular economy. We do not think this approach is helpful. We have already examined in Chapter II the conceptual as well as practical difficulties involved in the measurement of the two quantities; these make it unwise to erect any theoretical structure or system of prediction on the basis of such estimates. But even if these difficulties were not present there is room for skepticism. Capital, as we have seen, consists of a wide variety of assets in a wide variety of uses, and emphasis on the total rather than on its composition and balance is often misleading. Much of economic growth, whether in an economy in which the state takes a large part in economic life or in one in which its activity is minimal, consists largely of many diverse changes, adjustments and adaptations; and this is one reason for skepticism about the value of the aggregative approach to these problems, that is, the approach in terms of total capital and national income.[1] Finally, as we have seen, even if there were a firm statistical relationship between capital and income in the process of economic growth, it would not necessarily betoken a cause-and-effect relationship, nor, of course, indicate which is the independent and which the dependent variable.

§ 2. Capital Formation in Under-developed Countries.

It is sometimes said that a vicious circle constricts under-developed countries in their attempts to raise their low level of capital: a low national income means a negligible rate of saving and capital formation; a low rate of capital formation means low productivity in agriculture and manufacturing; and low productivity once again means a low national income. There are obvious elements of truth in this statement; but it is a severe and misleading over-simplification.

All the countries which today are economically and technically advanced began as countries which were as poor as some of the under-developed countries are today. Yet internal

[1] The relevance of the heterogeneity of capital and criticism of the aggregative approach in capital theory are central themes in L. M. Lachmann, *Capital and its Structure*, London, 1956.

capital accumulation took place as part of a process of economic development and change; however low the income per head may have been at one time, part of current income was set aside to create and augment a stock of capital. The vicious circle has been broken in the past, provided the general circumstances and opportunities were favourable for economic growth.[1] In examining the prospects for economic development in any country the presence or absence of such circumstances and opportunities is as important as the level of the national income per head; it may sometimes be even more important.

There are numerous impediments to private saving and investment in many under-developed countries. These include the imperfect maintenance of law and order, political instability, unsettled monetary conditions, lack of continuity in economic life, the extended family system with its drain on resources and its stifling of personal initiative, and certain systems of land tenure which inhibit saving and investment. All these impair the ability and willingness of people to look beyond the immediate present and to take a long view, characteristics which are necessary both for decisions to save, that is to defer consumption, and for decisions to use resources in the expectation that their deferred output will be profitable and advantageous. Viewed in the light of the varied and powerful influences restraining economic development in many under-developed countries, it is not surprising that the rate of capital formation is low, and one need not look to the low level of available resources to explain it; indeed, it is more surprising that in unfavourable circumstances many individuals devote as much energy as they do to improving their land, for example, a form of capital formation which, as we have seen, often escapes the attention of economic statisticians.

The willingness and ability to take a long view and interest in material things are not present in equal degree in all individuals and countries. Nevertheless, some measure of private capital accumulation has taken place whenever general ob-

[1] In these circumstances, foreign capital has also often been available.

stacles to saving and the productive use of capital have been
removed or weakened, and opportunities for the profitable
use of capital have been present.   In favourable circumstances
many individuals have contributed to the fund of savings.
Some examples may be in point.   According to Gregory King
in seventeenth century England, though the nobility, gentry
and large merchants were, individually, the largest savers, the
largest contribution to resources came from thrifty freeholders
and farmers who in 1688 made up the bulk of the middle
classes, while 'lawyers, dealers, officials, shopkeepers, and
tradesmen also added to the fund of savings, and even the
artisans and craftsmen contributed their mites'.[1]   In nineteenth-century Japan 'the great bulk of new investment
resources came not from the coffers of the State, but increasingly from personal and business savings.   The critical
function of the new [post-1868] government was to establish
and maintain the framework of political order and legal
security essential to this purpose'.   Professor Lockwood, from
whose book *The Economic Development of Japan* this quotation
is taken, emphasises further that contributions to capital
formation came from numerous individuals, rich and poor,
and that the process of accumulation was spurred on by the
widening of the market and the presence of inducements to
save and invest: 'The decisive difference between Japan and
most of her Asiatic neighbours . . . was not so much a greater
disposition to save on the part of the Japanese as it was the
more effective inducements to a high rate of investment in
productive enterprise.   Everywhere the process of capital
formation has in some degree this boot-strap character.'[2]   In
postwar Syria, to take another example, the rate of private
saving and investment has been high, in spite of political uncertainty and frequent changes of government.   'A substantial part of the profits earned in the postwar expansion of
agriculture, industry and commerce was evidently reinvested.
. . .   Once the profitability of industry was demonstrated,

[1] T. S. Ashton, *op. cit.*, p. 23.
[2] W. W. Lockwood, *op. cit.*, pp. 268–70.

additional capital was attracted. . . . The fact that at least some of the stock [share] ownership [of some companies] became rather widely dispersed testifies to the appeal which industrial investment has made to a growing number of people.'[1]   Considerable capital was also directed to the rapid extension of raw cotton production.   Lastly, in several countries the emergence of a demand for export crops has in appropriate circumstances encouraged peasants to devote resources for improving and extending their holdings, and the growth in the economy has enabled individuals and firms in transport and trade to accumulate capital.

§ 3. Special Aspects of Capital Formation in Under-developed Countries.

Where the general environment is not favourable to productive investment, it is likely that a large part of savings is kept in such forms as trinkets, precious stones and metals, coins or textiles.   Such objects of wealth are more readily concealed in times of trouble than buildings and equipment; they are portable and can easily be turned into purchasing power; they are also useful as insurance against currency inflation.   Economic and political uncertainty also tends to encourage investment in trading rather than in manufacturing operations; the assets in the former are more liquid and they have to be committed for a far shorter average investment period.

This pattern of investment (or of holding of assets) is primarily a reflection of certain economic and political conditions; it is not a major factor retarding economic growth, nor evidence of an inability to take long views in investment decisions.   Investment in industrial and transport enterprises or in plantation agriculture is much more readily undertaken once political conditions become more stable and institutional arrangements more favourable to long-term investment, and when inflation is controlled or removed, and supplies of factors complementary to capital expand.   When

[1] International Bank for Reconstruction and Development, *The Economic Development of Syria*, Baltimore, 1955, pp. 22, 104–5.

these changes take place both the margin of current income which is saved, and some savings previously accumulated in other forms, become available for industrial and commercial investment. For instance, the readiness of traders to invest in manufacturing and transport enterprises when the economy develops, or when they have become more experienced, is familiar in economic history, and is at present observable in several under-developed countries.

In many under-developed countries savers, especially when they are agriculturalists, often buy land with their savings for reasons of prestige or as a hedge against inflation. It is often suggested that if the savers buy land this does not result in capital formation, but affects only the price and distribution of land. This is an error, even if the total quantity of land in use remains unchanged. The savers consume less than their income, that is, they make resources available to the rest of the economy, and there must be corresponding net capital formation unless the rest of the economy dis-saves. This may indeed happen, but it has nothing to do with the type of asset bought by the savers; it would apply equally if the savers bought securities or machinery sold to them by the dis-savers.

We have already referred to unemployment and under-employment in some under-developed countries. This may represent a potential source of saving and investment. Social institutions in these countries often secure for the unemployed and under-employed a level of consumption in excess of the value of their contribution to output.[1] Looked at in another way this means that some people are producing an output in excess of their own consumption and savings, the excess going to sustain the unemployed or under-employed members of their social group, in effect as transfer payments. If the obligation to make these transfers disappeared, then, other things being equal, producers would have available additional resources for consumption or saving. The development of opportunities for employment outside the rural areas and the breakdown

[1] The general implications of this situation are discussed in Chapter VI, section 2, above.

or weakening of traditional systems of group obligations and responsibilities are therefore likely to release resources, part of which becomes available for investment. Apart from the resources set free for saving and investment as a result of the absorption into employment of those previously unemployed or under-employed, the breakdown of the extended family and kindred social institutions is likely to foster saving and invest- ment in other ways as well, since the fruits of thrift and enter- prise accrue more fully to those who save and invest wisely.[1]

We have already discussed briefly direct investment in agri- culture as an important category of investment in the early stages of economic development; the establishment, extension and improvement of agricultural holdings generally constitute the most important component of this category of investment. The resources for this investment usually reflect the sacrifice of leisure or the diversion of resources from activities of lower productivity in which the agriculturalists had previously been engaged, especially subsistence production. When produc- tion for wider exchange becomes possible, people may find it worth while to give up leisure or activity of low productivity to undertake direct investment in agriculture.

Another potential source of capital formation in the early stages of economic development is the improvement in the quality of certain assets, especially roads. This enables manu- facturers, traders and others to reduce working capital rela- tively to the volume of activity undertaken; it becomes possible to reduce, relatively to output, stocks of materials and the

---

[1] Professor R. Nurkse has discussed the relation between disguised un- employment and potential savings in his book *Problems of Capital Forma- tion in Under-developed Countries*, Oxford, 1953, pp. 37–47. He suggests the possibility of converting the 'unproductive consumption' of the under-employed into 'productive consumption' by using them on labour- intensive capital projects; the workers would be fed ('financed') by using the surplus food production which they would have consumed if they had remained on the farms. Professor Nurkse considers some of the practical difficulties; but he does not present a clear statement of the policy measures he considers necessary to translate disguised unemploy- ment into capital formation.

volume of goods in transit. The saving in working capital in effect provides the means for further additions to fixed capital.[1]

Some peoples have customs and practices which work against the accumulation of capital of all kinds; the ritual destruction of assets on death or on other occasions is an example. These practices become less prevalent with economic and social change, and the assets also become less easy to destroy; capital accumulation is made easier. In Melanesia 'agricultural produce is still often destroyed on death, and some small personal items as well, but cutters and launches are more lasting than canoes, and iron tools, unless they are buried or thrown to sea, are indestructible. The additional effort required for destruction makes people think twice about their action, and this, together with the teaching of the Churches, has a marked effect'.[2]

Thus, although there are serious obstacles to capital formation in under-developed countries stemming from sheer poverty, from political instability, or from certain institutional arrangements, there are often present reservoirs or potential sources of capital formation which are available once the process of development has begun.

§ 4. The International Demonstration Effect.

In recent years it has been widely suggested that in under-developed countries there operates an important and hitherto unsuspected obstacle to capital formation in a factor which has come to be termed the international demonstration effect. It has been argued by Professor Nurkse and others that modern communications and the spread of knowledge are so rapid and effective that the inhabitants of poor countries know all about the high standard of consumption enjoyed by most people in rich countries such as the United States, and that there is a strong desire

[1] Professor Ashton writes of eighteenth century England that 'the speeding up of production and distribution by the new machines and new means of transport made it possible to transmute circulating into fixed capital. The process is at the centre of what is called the industrial revolution.' *Op. cit.*, p. 112.

[2] C. S. Belshaw, *op. cit.*, p. 90.

and temptation to enjoy as much of this attractive way of living as incomes permit.   It follows that 'a high income and consumption level in an advanced country can do harm in that it tends to reduce the domestic means of capital formation in the under-developed countries; it puts extra pressure on countries with a relatively low income to spend a high proportion of it'.[1]   There are so many known and desired objects of consumption that, when income rises, little of the increase is saved; most or all of it is spent on items of food, clothing, household goods and gadgets made familiar in most corners of the earth by means of the cinema, the radio, the printed word and the activities of dispersed communities of foreigners.   Thus increases in personal expenditure on current goods and services more or less wipe out increases in income and the absolute amount of savings remains much the same as before.   Professor Nurkse, who introduced the demonstration effect into recent discussions of international economic problems and those of the under-developed areas in particular, concludes his discussion as follows: 'The vicious circle that keeps down the domestic supply of capital in low-income areas is bad enough by itself.[2]   My point is that it tends to be made even worse by the stresses that arise from relative as distinct from absolute poverty.'[3]

The possibility that the demonstration effect may inhibit saving in poor countries cannot be denied.   Past experience is not entirely relevant, because knowledge of living standards in the wealthier countries spreads more quickly and widely than ever before.   However, the importance of the demonstration effect acting *internationally* can easily be exaggerated.   In almost every country, rich or poor, there are wide differences in standards of living which can discourage saving by all but

[1] R. Nurkse, *op. cit.*, p. 68.

[2] This 'vicious circle' is examined in section 2 of this chapter.

[3] R. Nurkse, *ibid.*, p. 70.   It should be added that Professor Nurkse put forward his ideas as an 'hypothesis', that he did not wish to overemphasise the demonstration effect, and that its strength 'cannot be precisely determined; it is a matter of judgment and one that presumably varies from country to country'.

the very wealthiest if the demonstration effect is in fact potent.[1] It is difficult to see why knowledge of international disparities in level and range of consumption should have an especially powerful effect on the average person in poor countries.

A second omission from the usual analysis of the demonstration effect concerns the imitation of saving and investment habits. It is not obvious why the high standards of consumption in richer countries alone should arouse interest. Accumulation and investment as means to an improved standard of living may be imitated; or they may be imitated because of the prestige which may attach to ownership of productive assets. It is of interest, for example, that immigrants in rich countries not only gradually assimilate the local habits of consumption, but also that many of them save a very high proportion of their income in order to have greater security and also to raise later their own standard of living and that of their children. It is also of interest that many Africans, observing the superior economic productivity and social prestige of a professional or technical training, are investing a large part of their income in having their children educated and trained abroad.[2]

Moreover, the usual analysis of the international demonstration effect seems to leave out certain major considerations which are relevant to the economic problems of under-developed countries. We have already noted that information about a wider range of objects of expenditure and the accessibility of these objects have almost invariably provided strong inducements to productive effort, the transformation of a traditional subsistence economy into a money and exchange

---

[1] The international demonstration effect is derived as an hypothesis from the thesis of the interdependence of consumption functions of individuals within a community. In most poor countries there are wealthy people with prominently displayed spending habits.

[2] The desire for education is fairly widespread in the under-developed world, and many people are prepared to sacrifice present consumption for this end. For example, the resistance to sending children to school is weakening in Melanesia. 'Formerly their role as producers of immediate results was too important. Now it is felt that they should have the advantage of education which is considered to be such a panacea.' C. S. Belshaw, *op. cit.*, p. 90.

economy, and the exercise of initiative and enterprise. The prospect of a higher and more varied level of consumption serves to induce agricultural producers to produce for the market, whether in addition to subsistence production or in replacement of subsistence production. This process has served to establish or to enlarge the exchange economy throughout the under-developed world in much the same way as it has influenced development in the past in what are now more advanced countries. It generally involves the creation of capital through the extension and improvement of agricultural properties. By widening markets and promoting specialisation it conduces both to the growth of capital and to its more productive employment, which in turn facilitates further capital formation. It also promotes the growth of public services by creating sources of revenue. Similarly, the appearance of new consumer goods often induces people to accept wage-earning employment and thus to join the exchange economy.

In these circumstances consumption and investment are complementary: the higher level of consumption induces additional and more productive effort, which serves to generate incomes, and which in turn renders possible both increased consumption and increased accumulation of capital. It seems to have been overlooked in the international extension of the demonstration effect that the new types of consumer goods can be bought only if incomes are first earned to purchase them. The earning of higher incomes itself almost inevitably calls for the formation of some capital; and the consequential growth of the economy provides new opportunities for the employment of capital which, in turn, encourage saving for investment by enterprising members of the economy.

The thesis of the international demonstration effect implies that production for exchange has permeated the entire economy, so that material transfers of effort from the subsistence sector to the exchange sector are ruled out. But such shifts of activity are possible in many under-developed countries. The importance of new or improved consumer goods in inducing producers to join the exchange economy is implicit in the term

'inducement goods' often rightly applied to these commodities.[1]

There is one sphere of economic life where the international
demonstration effect does seem to apply. Governments,
politicians and government officials seem to be subject to this
effect in that they often seek to adopt technical, social and
educational standards which are inappropriate and wasteful in
under-developed countries. The same effect is seen in the
desire for conspicuous and spectacular investment and for
elaborate and spectacular schemes often undertaken to imitate
certain of the technical achievements of the more advanced
countries. This type of conspicuous expenditure is not confined
to public authorities (nor, of course, to under-developed countries), but it has been prominent in programmes of government
spending in many under-developed countries. The governments there are under strong pressures to emulate more
advanced countries; and the people subject to these pressures
do not spend their own resources in yielding to them.

Apart from the important exception just noted, the international demonstration effect does not seem to be a significant
factor retarding capital formation in under-developed countries. Indeed, in the private sector the prospect of a higher
level of consumption is more likely to promote than to hinder
capital formation and economic development generally. Contact with the more advanced economies not only stimulates
new wants and new activities to satisfy these, but often also
helps to provide the wherewithal to satisfy them; familiar
instances include the introduction of new crops, the transmission of improved techniques, and the opening up of new
markets.

It is paradoxical to suggest that the presence of economically
more advanced countries should retard the progress of the

[1] It will be noted that the view (considered on pp. 85–7, above) that
in some economies the people have a low ceiling to their wants is dia-
metrically opposite to the view that the international demonstration effect
raises consumption requirements so quickly that little or no saving out of
higher incomes is possible.

under-developed countries. It is possible to imagine such a relationship; though actual instances of its operation would be among the *curiosa* of economic development or economic history. The stimulating effects of international or inter-regional intercourse are a commonplace of economic history. At present in under-developed countries the more advanced sectors and areas are those which are in contact with the more developed countries. They would not have advanced so far without the stimulus of international contact.

§ 5. Foreign Capital in Under-developed Countries.   Foreign capital has contributed greatly towards the economic development of many countries, in much the same way as have foreign personnel, both entrepreneurs and others. International capital movements have added to the resources available for capital formation in developing economies or have eased balance of payments problems arising out of rapid growth. Sometimes the flow of foreign capital into a particular country has continued for decades, supporting and sustaining economic growth. In other cases foreign assistance has been concentrated in short periods when the domestic demand for resources for investment has been particularly heavy.

Though it is generally agreed that under-developed countries have in the main to rely upon their own resources, the important role of foreign capital in the progress of many parts of the now developed world is also generally recognised. The two halves of the preceding sentence are not contradictory, since the borrowing countries would not have made rapid progress if, among other things, domestic savings and investment had not also been substantial. Foreign capital has usually been complementary to local capital, and no less vital or valuable for not being the sole or major source of capital formation. Evidence of local enterprise and capital formation has also encouraged foreign lenders and investors, which again emphasises the complementarity of the two sources of supply. There are instances, of course, when foreign capital has been attracted to countries in which there was little trace of local enterprise or capital formation; the oases of highly-developed mining and oil-production activities in otherwise almost stagnant economies are examples of this. But pervasive growth has almost invariably depended greatly upon domestic savings and investment. Where foreign capital has been attracted into a country's external trade and industry, the process has almost always been the counterpart of capital formation in agricultural production for export.

Foreign capital may be supplied by international agencies, governments or private individuals or firms, and can be supplied to the public sector or the private sector. An important category is that known as direct investment, under which a foreign firm invests directly in its own undertaking in the local economy.

Direct investment is of special interest for several reasons. It is dictated almost exclusively by commercial considerations, so that its volume is a reliable index of independent opinions on the economic prospects of the local economy and on the productivity of capital in different employments in it. It differs in these respects from inter-governmental loans or grants, or loans or grants made by international agencies, which are often determined in part at least by political considerations. Moreover, direct investment tends to provide some safeguard against misuse of the capital made available. Care is taken in the selection of the project and the choice of its management, and the investing group provides the otherwise lacking co-operant resources which are necessary for the success of the venture. If the missing resources cannot be provided (because of impediments or cost), then the venture will not be undertaken. Mistakes are made; but those providing the capital have a continuing interest in minimising the chances of error and in taking remedial action when necessary. Their direct interest in the success of the investment and their power to control the use of their capital persist after the initial transfer of the capital has been made.

Obstacles and circumstances which discourage investment by local individuals and firms also discourage direct investment by foreign enterprises. There are often other deterrents to investment by foreigners. Some of these stem from the uncertainties of international political, economic and financial relationships. Further, in many under-developed countries measures are in force which discourage foreign investors and are indeed intended to penalise them. These include regulations which compel foreign enterprises to admit substantial participation by local capital and personnel in their operations, special taxes levied on foreign firms, discriminatory treatment in the allocation of import licenses and of foreign exchange, and immigration restrictions.

It is often argued that these restrictions on private capital from foreign sources reflect nationalist sentiment, especially the fear of political domination and of exploitation. Whilst this is a possible motive, other explanations are more probable. If grants or subsidised loans are obtainable from abroad, these will be preferred to borrowing on commercial terms. Again, the restrictions are often examples of restrictionism designed to raise the value of the services of particular groups, as is obvious when they are directed against people without political power; they often do not differ essentially from restrictions affecting members of the local population. Whatever the motives, the adverse effects of these restrictions on the prospects of development are plain. They restrict the supply of capital available to under-developed countries, and they obstruct the most effective deployment of the available supply.

There are various influences and factors which sometimes affect adversely the economic productivity of international governmental capital transfers. The lender or donor government or international agency often has little power, detailed knowledge or interest to ensure that the capital supplied is used efficiently. Indeed, any endeavour to ensure that it should be so used is likely to be embarrassing, and for this reason is not likely to be pressed. The receiving countries are apt to resent conditions attached to capital transfers; and the complaint of foreign interference is easily raised. However, since there are many under-developed countries asking for foreign aid, and since the total foreign capital available for this purpose is limited, the case for attaching safeguarding conditions to inter-government or similar loans has much merit.

Abstracting from political expediency which may dictate the direction of capital to some countries, there is much to be said for the view that international agencies and the leading lending countries should make capital available only to countries which agree to follow economic policies which are likely to conduce to the best use of the available capital, foreign or local. Opinions will differ about what is the right economic policy. But there will be fairly general agreement that certain measures are not consonant with the objective of economic development. In many under-developed countries legislation is in force specifically restricting the operations of private foreign capital. An interesting example may be cited from Syria, where in 1952 legislation was introduced to enforce a minimum of a two-thirds Syrian interest in all commercial enterprises. This resulted in the withdrawal of a number of foreign enterprises from Syria, including a large international trading and manufacturing enterprise which had operated there for a number of years. This measure was introduced at a time when the Syrian government asked for capital from various foreign governmental and international agencies.[1]

The use of capital, often obtained from abroad, in the improvement of communications also provides paradoxes. This form of capital expenditure is rightly regarded as of major importance in economic development. In many under-developed countries, however, where large sums are spent for these purposes, there is restrictive licensing in force for road transport which necessarily raises the cost of this service.

[1] Similarly, official policies in Ceylon, notably that of accelerated Ceylonisation, have discouraged the inflow of foreign private capital and encouraged disinvestment by established foreign firms. *Report of the Taxation Commission*, Ceylon, 1955, p. 83.

§ 6. Compulsory Saving—a Reference Forward.   In this chapter we have not said anything about the state as a source of capital formation.   This topic raises crucial issues of economic policy, and the discussion is left over to be considered in Part II which deals more specifically with some issues of development policy.

PART II

GOVERNMENT AND ECONOMIC DEVELOPMENT

CHAPTER XI

GENERAL APPRAISAL OF THE ROLE OF GOVERNMENT

§ 1. **An Interpretation of Economic Improvement.** In this second part of the book we are concerned primarily with the role of government in influencing economic development and growth. Discussion of official policy is more seriously affected by political (value) judgments than the description and analysis presented in the earlier chapters. But it does not follow that such a discussion should be merely a recital of personal opinions and preferences. There is an important place for objective analysis and empirical observation, though in the final stages of the argument recourse to value judgments is inevitable. It is therefore incumbent on us to indicate our political position since this influences our selection of topics for discussion, and also our assessment of the probable results and desirability of particular policies.

In a world in which there is a profusion of political labels and an absence of standardisation in their use it is difficult to find a suitable one to indicate our standpoint. Perhaps it would be more helpful if we state that in assessing policies we tend to use as a yardstick their probable effects on the range of alternative courses of action open to individuals, and that we prefer a society in which policy is directed towards widening the effective range of alternatives open to members of that society. It follows that we think it should be the function of the state to widen the range of opportunities and facilitate access to them, but that it is for the members of society to choose among the alternative opportunities open to them and develop them with the aid of their personal endowments and the property they own. We believe that the widening of the range of effective choice is the most valuable single objective of economic

149

development as well as the best single criterion of its attainment. We shall show that our approach does not confine the state to a passive and negligible role, but that on the contrary it envisages state action on a wide scale, on a scale, indeed, which is sufficient to tax the political and administrative resources of most governments in under-developed countries. Our political position influences the direction in which we prefer official policy to go; it does not postulate state inaction.

The deep-seated diversity in the under-developed world in the quality of the population, natural resources, level of development, rate of growth, and political and social institutions reduces the width of possible generalisation about specific policy measures. A low level of income and capital per head, the uniform characteristic of under-developed countries, is often an insufficient basis for general analytical conclusions, and even more so for generalised recommendations for policy. For this reason the same measure of policy may yield quite different results in different under-developed countries. For example, the quality of government administration and of the people attracted to its service varies greatly, and this affects the efficiency of particular measures of policy.

Suggestions or recommendations for development policy framed in general terms—not qualified, as it were, in time or space—are of limited use. Yet we shall adopt this approach, since it is the only one possible in a general study of the economics of under-developed countries. It makes it all the more necessary to emphasise that in devising and applying policy measures in practice a thorough and detailed study of the specific local conditions is essential. Such a study is beset with difficulties. For example, the economy may be in a process of change, and it is not always easy to recognise whether an observed state of affairs is a phase or stage in a continuing development rather than an equilibrium or final position of forces which have been at work. In the former case, primary concern is with the position likely to be reached when present forces have been at work longer, while in the second case it is with the likelihood of the appearance of new forces promoting development.

§ **2. Different Criteria of Economic Advance.** Our criterion for judging economic development is the widening of the range of alternatives open to people as consumers and as producers. The extent of the achievement of this goal is obviously not one which can be measured quantitatively. However, it corresponds broadly to an increase in the national income. Other things beings equal, an increase in the goods and services available for consumption or investment improves the range of choice and of opportunities in economic life.[1] But an increase in the national income as conventionally measured may occur because of a deliberate narrowing of the range of alternatives open to people. An unambiguous example is where the state raises the physical output of the economy by using forced labour.

An increase in the national income sets up a presumption of economic growth in the more fundamental sense, but it is one which can be overthrown. It is necessary to go behind the national income statistics to ascertain whether it can be confirmed. Thus some qualification is called for when taxes are levied, since their payment represents the compulsory transfer of resources from taxpayers to the government. This qualification is particularly relevant when the tax receipts are used for the purchase of goods and services which are not subjected to the test of the market, rather than for redistribution by means of transfer payments. These considerations are important when there is a marked change in the share of the national income taken in taxation, or in the composition of government expenditure.

---

[1] We have shown in Chapter II that the conventional definition and measurement of the national income is subject to important limitations even as an index of the volume of goods and services available for consumption and investment; an increase in the national income may be accompanied by a decrease in the value of services and incomes not included in the usual calculations, or by an increase in effort, hours of work or other real costs not reflected (as a deduction) in national income calculations.

We need also consider whether there is economic improvement when an increase in total national income is offset by an
increase in population so that the national income per head
remains unchanged. Our criterion operates unambiguously
when there is an effective choice between taking out an
increase in the national output in the form of higher individual
incomes or in the form of larger families; there is no presumption that one form is always to be preferred to the other.
Moreover, larger families brought about by lower death rates,
for example, may add to psychic income which is excluded
from conventional calculations of the national income. However, this general range of issues need not concern us further,
since the policy measures we shall consider affect the national
output, and it is rare for an increase in the national output to
be completely counter-balanced by an increase in population;
in general, total and average tend to move together, though
not necessarily at the same rate.

The statement of our criterion of development should not
obscure the fact that there are other possible criteria. These
include, among others, military power, the volume of industrial
production (in total or per capita) or even the volume of production of capital goods or particular kinds of capital goods.
This multiplicity of criteria, especially when a particular
criterion is implicit rather than explicit, or when there is an
unstated shift in criterion, is apt to confuse discussion, both of
the achievement of particular economies and of the potentialities of policy measures.[1]

§ 3. **Decentralised Decision-making.** As we see development
essentially as the widening of people's access to alternatives,
our inclination is towards economic systems in which decisions
about the composition of national output, including those
affecting the distribution of resources between consumption
and investment, are taken largely by the individuals partici-

[1] For example, reliance on industrial production, and especially production of iron and steel products, as an index of growth has probably
exaggerated the progress in the nineteenth century of Britain and Germany as compared with that of France.

pating in economic life, and against economic systems in which central direction and detailed economic decision-making by governmental bodies affect a large sector of economic activity. This is not to deny that state agencies are capable of bringing about impressive individual economic achievements. It reflects a facet of our criterion of economic improvement, in which it is implicit that the way in which development takes place essentially affects both the merits of the process and its results.

It is inherent in our concept and criterion of economic development that we attach significance to acts of choice and valuation made by individuals, including those which express individual time-preferences between present and future consumption. The role of the state is seen primarily as that of making it possible for individuals to have access to a wider range of alternatives and to more adequate knowledge of them. It is arguable, however, that individual preferences and valuations have little real significance and should not be placed in the forefront as the principal determinant of economic activities, including that of providing for the future. This line of reasoning may be advanced on the grounds that these preferences are essentially a function of a given social and economic environment, and that they are readily adjusted by individuals to changes in this environment; that is to say, they should be looked upon as products rather than as determinants of this environment. On this basis a government, or any group with sufficient power, can feel justified in setting targets for economic performance which may be partly or wholly unrelated to the current preferences of some or all of the individuals constituting the society. We specifically reject this interpretation that individual valuations and choices are irrelevant, though we cannot appeal to economic theory or analysis to support this essentially political premise.

Further, we favour private economic decision-making, and the diffusion of power which it implies, because they help to safeguard the individual in society, both generally and also in his capacity as an economic agent. They do this by enlarging the range of actual or potential alternatives open to individuals.

However, our preference for an economic system in which decision-making is widely diffused and co-ordinated by the market mechanism is not predicated solely on our criterion of development, nor on the political safeguards which the system provides. We consider that in general this system secures an efficient deployment of available resources, and also promotes the growth of resources. Its efficiency stems largely from two of its features: mobilisation of knowledge and provision of incentive.

Diffused knowledge of the availability of resources, production possibilities and economic opportunities is gathered together and made available for use in the economic system as a whole. We do not see how a central planning authority would be able to organise and make use of so large and diverse a flow of information as is available in the aggregate (though not in the mind of any one person or body) in a decentralised economic society. Our conclusion applies to knowledge both of present combinations and uses of resources and also of opportunities for growth. Decentralised decision-making in the sense used here links knowledge and opportunity to act; it conduces to 'maximum economic experimentation'[1] informed by local or particular knowledge.

Our general conclusion is independent of the issue of consumer sovereignty, though it is greatly strengthened where, as in our criterion, the sovereignty of the consumer is given a high place. It does not derive from consumer sovereignty, because even if the objectives of economic activity are prescribed centrally, knowledge can be utilised more effectively if decentralised decisions and the operation of the price mechanism are compatible with these objectives. For example, a defence programme, or a programme of heavy public investment, is likely to be cheapest in terms of real resources if the government expresses its demand in the form

---

[1] This term is used by J. Baster in *Kyklos*, Vol. IX, 1950, pp. 94–6.

of orders for the required products rather than in the form of instructions controlling such matters as the location, organisation and techniques of production.[1]

The provision of widely diffused incentives is the second feature of a system of decentralised decision-making likely to contribute to the efficient use and growth of resources. This means that there is a widely diffused but nevertheless direct pressure on the participants in economic life to use or transmit their particular knowledge of resources and opportunities.[2] Those who make erroneous decisions suffer losses. This in turn is likely to induce people to explore opportunities with care before committing their resources, whether labour, land or capital. Moreover, the waste resulting from mistaken decisions falls primarily on those who made the mistake: they have made losses and to that extent have smaller claims on resources. By way of contrast, wasteful decisions made by an official body involve a loss of resources which have been acquired compulsorily from the economy as a whole; the loss is in a real sense avoided by the decision-makers.

§ 4. Some General Considerations of Public Enterprise in Under-developed Countries.

Our general views are not incompatible with advocacy of a wide range of government activities of direct relevance to economic growth. But it is a corollary

---

[1] The discussion in the text does not derive from the proposition that a competitive market results in ideal output in the sense that market forces bring about an optimum distribution of resources. We are not concerned primarily with the propositions of welfare economics, which are, in effect, statements of formal conditions of optima with a given volume of resources. Our primary concern is with the quality and level of knowledge and with its transmission which activates resources and in fact makes them available.

The reader is referred to an instructive article by F. A. Hayek, 'The Use of Knowledge in Society', *American Economic Review*, September 1945.

[2] There are other incentives to economic activity, such as loyalty to family, group or nation, or the fear of the displeasure of superior authorities. However, the market mechanism has the peculiar advantage that pervasive incentive is linked with diffused knowledge. Moreover, other incentives are compatible with those of the market, and indeed usually operate concurrently.

of these views that in our scheme of things government has only a limited role as an active propulsive agent in economic development in the capacity of saver or entrepreneur, or as controller or director of the economic activities of others. The precise limits to be set to government's activities in this wide sphere are likely to vary from country to country; and different observers sharing our general approach may not reach quite the same conclusion of the admissible role of the state in any particular case. But it is central to our approach that the role is circumscribed.

We have indicated the basic reasons for our attitude and preferences. These may become still clearer if we examine a few propositions which appear to be advanced in support of the view which we reject. The first is that government action is likely to be disinterested while, on the other hand, private individuals and firms act in their own interest, and that, especially in under-developed countries, this tells in favour of official action. But this contrast is crude and misleading. Individuals, whether politicians, officials, farmers or businessmen, tend to act largely in their own interests as these are seen by themselves, and it is necessary to devise suitable institutional arrangements to ensure that selfish actions (conscious, or more likely unconscious) should not operate to the general disadvantage, and if possible should even be harnessed to serve the general interest. Although they do not work for private profit, politicians, civil servants or administrators of statutory organisations do not necessarily have interests identical with the interests of those they nominally serve, or with those of the community at large. Indeed, the cleavage of interest between organisers and administrators of large organisations and their members is a conspicuous feature of modern economic life; it can be found in large joint-stock companies, trade unions and co-operative societies.

Politicians, civil servants and administrators have their own interests in terms of power, prestige and position, as well as economic interests which may differ greatly from those of the rest of the community. Moreover, in under-developed countries public opinion is likely to be even less effective than in more advanced societies in controlling and checking their activities. Again, in under-developed countries administrators usually are members of the urban community, the interests of which, especially in the short run, often diverge from those of the rural population. This tends to weight the scales of official policy in favour of the urban community, quite apart from other factors which tend to give cities and towns a disproportionately large share of political influence in most under-developed countries.

There is an important and relevant difference between actions in the private and the public sectors of the economy. If an individual (or firm) acts in a fashion contrary to the interests of all (or some) of those he sets out to serve, there are in general elements of self-correction in the private sector in that buyers and sellers can withdraw their custom. The self-correcting tendencies, which set a curb to the divergence between private and general interests, may take time when there are elements of private monopoly. In the public sector there are no self-correcting influences when the public enterprise is endowed by statute with monopoly or when, as is generally the case, the decisions of public servants are supported by statutory powers. Even in countries with a long tradition of a critical press and a vigilant parliament it has been found that there is no close substitute for the pervasive disciplinary effect of competition, actual or potential, partial or complete. Again, governments, and administrators more particularly, are generally reluctant to admit mistakes and to change mistaken policies until much harm has been done. Indeed, they often attempt to shore up a weak position by extending state control and direction even further, so that the correcting forces can be stifled. This multiplication of controls and acts of intervention is quite distinct from the extension of controls and state undertakings for its own sake or as part of a process of administrative empire-building, tendencies which are less likely to be checked by public or political opinion in under-developed countries than in advanced countries. The analogy with a private monopolist attempting to prolong his monopoly by aggressive or forestalling action suggests itself. There is, however, the important difference that, even in the absence of official measures directed against private monopoly, the exercise of monopoly power unsupported by official action is always tempered by the fear of residual or potential competition and of state intervention.

It would also be unrealistic to ignore that in many under-developed countries public administration has not reached high standards of probity. The case against the enlargement of the economic role of the state is especially powerful where public servants are both able and willing to take advantage of their position for purposes of direct personal gain, though of course the case is not destroyed even if the civil servants are men of complete integrity.

It may be argued that, granted that the market mechanism is a technically efficient device for organising economic activity, in under-developed countries in particular its working is likely to be defective because the economic horizons of individuals and firms are too limited by inexperience or the crushing effect of a poor society to make the best use of available opportunities. *Prima facie* this line of argument may have its attraction; yet we do not attach much importance to it, and are not led to the conclusion that extended action of the state as an economic agent is the remedy. The fact that a particular arrangement or situation may not be perfect does not mean (as is often implied) that the alternative proposed is preferable. Moreover, we are impressed that in fact even in under-developed countries many individuals and firms are well able to recognise and take advantage of favourable market situations and developments,[1] and that their activities frequently have resulted in the establishment of very distant economic relationships and contacts in the search for profitable opportunities and mutually advan-

[1] The ability of even illiterate people to respond to changing market opportunities is considered and illustrated in Chapter VII, section 4, above.

tageous transactions; indeed, it is hard to believe that these latter would have come to be established if there had been no diffused private initiative but only central decision and direction.

We have already instanced the establishment and successful development of rubber-growing in Malaya and Sumatra, where the rubber tree is not indigenous, the soil not particularly rich, and where at the time of the establishment of the industry local supplies of both labour and capital were very sparse, so that these territories would hardly have been singled out *a priori* as suitable for rubber cultivation. We may also mention a small and more picturesque example. In the coastal areas of southern Nigeria, especially round Port Harcourt, large quantities of sun-dried fish are eaten. Almost the whole of the supply is derived from two sources: the arctic waters of northern Norway, and the inland lakes and rivers of the Bornu-Chad region on the southern fringes of the Sahara about 1,000 miles from Port Harcourt.[1] The first source supplies Norwegian stock fish (sun-dried cod or haddock), the second a variety of freshwater fish. The consumers have shown repeatedly a strong preference for these sources of supply, as has been found out to their cost by merchants who have tried alternative sources. The movement of dried fish over long distances to provide a suitable commodity for discriminating African consumers is an interesting example of the unexpected contacts which are established without central direction.

A limitation of economic horizons may also be said to take the form of a heavy discounting of the future. A low level of capital tends indeed to produce an intense preoccupation with the problems of the present. However, the extension by peasant producers of large acreages of tree-crops yielding a delayed income is evidence that many are prepared to take a long view and to postpone consumption for several years if the prizes are considered satisfactory. The state can provide information and advice so that the individuals are aware of what can be achieved by abstinence and investment and can

---

[1] The strong sun combined with the very dry atmosphere in these areas makes possible the production of sun-dried fish of high keeping quality.

make a more effective distribution of their efforts and consumption through time. The effective performance of this task by the state is likely to be highly productive of development both in terms of our wider criterion and in terms of the somewhat narrower criterion of a rising national income.[1]

There is a world of difference between ordering peasants to uproot old vines and replace them by higher-yielding ones (which will, however, be unproductive for five years), and instructing them with demonstrations that the new vines in fact have higher yields. The former method is likely to involve a compulsory over-riding of the time-preferences of the peasants, whereas the latter widens the range of alternatives open to them and enables them to undertake such adjustments as they think fit given their resources, opportunities and preferences.[2] This conclusion applies with particular force when producers are compelled to undertake investment or to adopt methods on which the return is long deferred and often uncertain.

The attraction of the spectacular, often combined with the pressures of political life, frequently leads to extravagant government expenditure whether on capital or income account. The international demonstration effect, which has already been mentioned,[3] seems to operate powerfully in the public sector both in the form of the inauguration of grandiose capital projects and of social services modelled on those current in richer countries. It is facile to suppose that governments always take a longer view than private individuals or firms, or that long-term large-scale projects initiated by governments are necessarily more productive than the less spectacular investments made in the private sector.

[1] The task fits into our minimum agenda of official policy measures in that agricultural extension work and advisory services are apt to produce benefits indiscriminately, so that private enterprise would not provide them at all or only on an insufficient scale; this is discussed further in Chapters XII and XIV, below. It would be impossible to prevent one farmer, who paid for advice, from passing it on to others free or at cut rates; moreover, secrets cannot easily be kept in outdoor activities.

[2] The case would be different in circumstances in which the old stock is diseased and might cause losses to other producers through infection.

[3] Chapter X, section 4, above.

We have already referred to the assumption, implicit in much discussion on under-developed countries, that because existing conditions are not perfect therefore the alternative proposed, usually in the form of government action, would be more nearly perfect. We may conclude this general discussion with a particular example of this inadmissible assumption. It is often argued that, because people in a particular country are devoid of the initiative and drive of entrepreneurship necessary for economic growth, state action is required to make good this deficiency. It is not at all clear why government or the public service should be able to muster the talents which, by hypothesis, are lacking in the population. There can be no general presumption that, in a country notable for its lack of entrepreneurs or organisers, the government, after performing a wide range of essential activities, should have at its disposal a surplus of talent for initiating and conducting a miscellaneous collection of economic enterprises.[1] In such countries or regions the dearth of a valuable type of resource is a serious barrier to economic growth; the barrier cannot be removed by assuming away the dearth.

§ 5. Economic Development by Soviet Methods.   The extreme of government intervention in economic life is to be found in systems such as those of the Soviet Union. We do not propose to examine the economics or political economy of a system in which central direction and state control and compulsion are so complete and pervasive. The interest of such an examination for our present purposes may seem to be largely in comparisons between the present rate of progress achieved under the Soviet system and that achieved under other systems.

[1] The public sector may sometimes have attracted an exceptionally large proportion of able and enterprising people; a possible example is that of nineteenth-century Japan. But a general lack of enterprise in a country does not in itself set up a presumption of such initiative in the public sector. Moreover, government measures designed to expand the public sector almost inevitably reduce the means and opportunities for enterprise in the private sector; individuals who are not attracted by government service but who have entrepreneurial qualities may therefore be unable to make their contribution towards economic growth.

But this would require detailed discussion of the conflicting claims about the comparative rates of progress in these economies, which would take us too far from our central themes.

The economic progress and position of the Soviet Union are matters of serious debate and disagreement among specialist scholars, and there is no agreement on key questions such as the rate of growth of the economy as a whole. The meaning of statistics of national income, industrial output and capital formation is also debatable in an economy when so large a part of output is not governed by consumers' choices in the market; the difficulties of interpretation are particularly obvious in connection with the huge capital expenditure undertaken by government without reference to the valuation of the output by consumers. It would not be possible within the compass of this book to examine, interpret and assess the statistics and their implications. We feel that, in addition to difficulties of this kind, comparisons would be meaningless between the performance of economic systems along Western lines, with their varying admixtures of public and private enterprise, and that of a system in which there is a high degree of direction of labour and in which decisions are essentially taken centrally. The widening of alternatives open to individuals, which to us is central to the process and purpose of economic development, is not high on the list of priorities in the Soviet system. This is not to deny, of course, that its material achievement in particular sectors of the economy may be impressive, though both its costs and the factors underlying its achievement are much disputed.

It will be readily agreed that a study of the Soviet system at work is of great interest and relevance to students of economics generally, and it is to be hoped that those responsible for the publication of this series of handbooks might consider the inclusion of such a work in their future plans. In the remainder of this volume, however, we shall be concerned with government action in economies in which state control and influence are not so complete and pervasive as in the Soviet system.

CHAPTER XII

FUNCTIONS OF GOVERNMENT

§ **1. Maintenance of Law and Order.** Certain tasks are practically everywhere performed by government or by other agencies closely controlled or supervised by government. The maintenance of law and order, national defence, the control of the issue and supply of fiduciary money, and the provision of minimum education and health services are leading examples. We do not propose to consider a list of these minimum government services in detail, not because they are unimportant or do not raise interesting issues, but because such discussion would take us too far from the central themes of the book. In fact, the adequate performance of these minimum tasks is of vital importance for economic growth and generally a necessary condition for such growth. At the same time the adequate performance even of such tasks as the maintenance of law and order [1] or the regulation of the supply of money cannot always be taken for granted. In some under-developed countries governments which cannot safeguard the lives or property of their citizens nevertheless engage in the most far-reaching and detailed regulation of economic life. Many instances could be drawn from some Latin-American countries, or from Burma and Indonesia since the Second World War. A small but characteristic example can be cited from West Africa. In August 1950 the government was unable to prevent physical maltreatment in the centre of Lagos of people who wanted to work during a partial strike; in some areas of Lagos the strikers even held courts where they sentenced those who had

---

[1] This concept is often ambiguous. We mean here the effective monopoly by government of the power of physical coercion and the use of this power in accordance with rules clearly laid down and generally applicable.

gone to work.   But while the administration was unable to maintain order on its door-step, at about the same time administrative time and effort was spent on extending the system of marketing by export monopolies to take in sunflower seed, a commodity of such trivial importance to Nigeria that it did not even figure separately in the official trade returns.

Failure to maintain law and order or to avoid monetary chaos may bring about conditions in which direct state participation in economic activity may seem desirable or even inevitable.   The exercise of business initiative and enterprise and the formation of capital by individuals and firms are likely to be seriously reduced or distorted by the failure of the state to perform its minimum tasks.   The failure of the private sector may then, spuriously, create the impression that the necessary ingredients for economic activity and growth have to be supplied by the state itself.

§ 2. **Expenditures yielding Indiscriminate Benefits.** Expenditure yielding all or much of its benefits indiscriminately devolves largely on government, since the individuals benefiting from it cannot (or cannot easily) be made to pay directly for these services.   The principle of state expenditure or of state enterprise in these circumstances (or of state control of private authorities which have, in effect, to be given taxing powers) is generally agreed, though there is scope for differences of interpretation in its application to particular situations.

It will be generally agreed that expenditure on locust control or the eradication of malaria or sleeping sickness, for example, yields its benefits indiscriminately; the benefits cannot be offered to the beneficiaries at a price in such a way that the individual who refuses to pay does not benefit from the scheme. This is to be distinguished from cases where a particular investment or expenditure yields separable benefits to many beneficiaries, or over a long period of time.   The development of an irrigation scheme or the opening of a new railway falls wholly or partly in this other category.   Here it is possible in principle for those undertaking the expenditure to charge for their services and, by and large, to deny the benefits of their improvement to those unwilling to pay the price.[1]   However, in many such cases there will be an element of monopoly which is likely to warrant some form of state control; and in practice there may be strong political pressure by the beneficiaries of the projects (or by their private sponsors, if they are undertaken privately) for state financial support or the conferment of powers for compulsory acquisition of property.   Nevertheless, it is helpful to distinguish the precise grounds for government intervention, since otherwise there may be a tendency to put too many kinds of expenditure into the category of expenditure yielding indiscriminate benefits, which in fact, is generally likely to be small in total.

It is possible to enlarge the scope of the argument that state intervention of some kind is indispensable because of indiscriminate benefits, on the ground that all economic activities are inter-related and inter-dependent.   Each participant by his action may confer some benefits on others in respect of which he cannot charge them, and conversely, cause disservices or disadvantages to others without having to compensate them.   A firm which pioneers factory production in an

---

[1] In the case of a railway undertaking, for example, there is no difficulty in making customers pay directly for the services which they require.   It is possible, however, that the opening of the railway confers benefits (e.g. in the form of higher land values) on people who do not directly use the services of the railway to a commensurate extent.   This does not call for government action if the receipts from direct charges are estimated to be large enough to induce the investment.   Again, even if these receipts are inadequate, it is conceivable that some or all of those who benefit indirectly from the investment could be induced to participate in the undertaking as investors or guarantors, provided they were satisfied of the reality of the benefits to come.   The case for government action arises on these grounds only when the project is economically justified (that is, if the value of the services rendered and of the indiscriminate benefits is expected to exceed the cost), and when the receipts from direct services are likely to be insufficient and the indirect beneficiaries for one reason or another are unable or unwilling to contribute adequately to the undertaking.   There is then a case for government assistance, with the proviso that government be empowered to recover its expenditure later by means of special taxation of those who in fact have gained from the indiscriminate benefits, though in practice it may not be easy to identify these beneficiaries and the extent of their gains.

under-developed area is diffusing some knowledge of factory life (for example, the need for regularity) and familiarity with industrial techniques; subsequent industrialists may benefit from this knowledge without having to pay for it. It is possible that the value of such spill-over effects, if it could accrue to the pioneer, might make all the difference between success or failure, and the impossibility of garnering this yield may deter economic developments. In these circumstances should the government not recompense the benefactor or even undertake the activity itself?

The answers to this and similar questions are matters of judgment. Those advancing such arguments rarely explain why this type of benefit should flow from one class of economic activity or from one industry rather than from another, so that the case for subsidising particular activities is not clearly established. There is also the difficulty of assessing the value of these benefits. In general, recognition in principle of a case for state intervention is not tantamount to a recommendation of policy measures, the implementation of which, even with the best will in the world, may easily deviate far from the theoretical ideal and then be wasteful. General statements or propositions about discrepancies between private and social costs and benefits, while formally correct, hardly serve as worthwhile guides to policy, and are indeed so vague that they could be invoked to justify practically any action.[1]

§ 3. **The State and the Distribution of Income and Wealth.** The proper role of the government in promoting greater equality of income and wealth is a controversial matter of great importance in political economy both for rich countries and for poor. In terms of our criterion, other things being equal, a more equal distribution of income and wealth is preferable to a less equal one in that a more effective access to a wider range of alternatives is secured for a larger part of the population. But a general statement of aims does not take us far.

[1] The relevance and application of these considerations to state assistance for the promotion of industrialisation is examined in Chapter XV.

Only a few of the complexities which arise when this is translated into practice can be mentioned here.   Identical degrees of
inequality at any given time may represent very different conditions if the composition of the different groups of income
receivers is stable or fluid; even a large measure of apparent
inequality is compatible with a largely equal distribution of
income if the composition of the wealthier groups changes
rapidly.   Again, the receivers of high incomes may or may
not perform valuable economic or social functions; and
whether or not they do is in some ways a political judgment.

Further—and this is of great importance—the introduction
of measures to secure a greater equality of income and wealth
may bring about inequalities of power greater than would
prevail in their absence.   If a greater equality in income and
wealth is brought about at the cost of greater inequality of
power, in particular at the cost of increasing the power of
some individuals and groups over others, there is an important
disadvantage to be set against any benefit from greater economic equality; and the cost may exceed the benefit.   Again,
diffusion of decision-making and the promotion of individual
initiative and responsibility can be affected adversely by some
measures for securing a greater equality of income and wealth.
These considerations bear particularly on measures involving
the enlargement or intensification of government activity in
economic life, or the conferment of monopoly powers on privileged groups or government bodies.   They do not apply to
greater equality effected by the widening of access to alternatives through the elimination of privileges or of barriers to
entry, or the wider provision of education.

The repercussions and implications of particular acts of redistribution are likely to differ in significance from one situation
to another, so that it is not possible to prescribe a general policy
of redistribution applicable to all economies.   This would be
true even if there were general agreement on the desirable
extent of economic equality and on the probable effects on
the growth of income of different measures of redistribution.

In practice there are major political disagreements both on the extent of equality which is considered desirable and on the methods of securing it.

Redistribution from the richer to the poorer members of a society is likely to strike at some of the most important sources of capital formation, and also to penalise, and hence inhibit, the exercise of special skills and initiative which are rare in all societies and particularly in under-developed ones.   On the other hand, the beneficiaries of the process of redistribution, quite apart from the direct advantages which may be derived from their enlarged incomes, may become more efficient participants in economic life, though this effect is likely to be deferred.   On balance, it would be rare for this favourable effect on the productivity of an economy to outweigh the more certain unfavourable effects.   Redistribution of income in favour of the poor is not likely to promote economic growth in the sense of greater output per head;[1] it may nevertheless be desirable up to a point for its own sake.

Although it is impossible to generalise meaningfully on the scope for redistribution, some observations are in point on the methods for its accomplishment.   Thus redistribution through the operations of public finance in the form of transfer payments to the selected classes of beneficiary is usually preferable to redistribution affected by pegging the prices of commodities or services bought by the people to be assisted.   The second method is likely to bring about certain adverse results which have to be set against any of its

---

[1] Redistribution of income and wealth may in some cases contribute to economic growth if it is accompanied by other changes.   For example, the removal of feudal or similar restrictions on the economic freedom of many people may be conducive to growth; in such cases the redistribution of wealth in favour of those previously handicapped may accelerate the process of growth.

Some advocates of accelerated economic growth in under-developed countries favour measures to bring about greater inequality of incomes on the grounds that the beneficiaries are likely to save a larger part of the income transferred to them and so add to capital formation.   Policies of inflation are sometimes espoused for this purpose; the role of inflation is considered in Chapter XIII, section 6, below.

benefits as a measure for redistribution. Its incidence is on the suppliers of the commodities and services in question and is therefore largely haphazard. Moreover, it does not re-allocate purchasing power; in particular it does not remove money from the richer section of the community, the members of which are therefore left with the purchasing power to out-bid the supposed beneficiaries of redistribution in the purchase of other commodities (other than those of which the prices are controlled), so that there may be no redistribution of real income at all.

A price fixed below the equilibrium level has other adverse effects. It encourages the wasteful use of the commodity, and, if the price is below the long-term supply price, it reduces the future level of supplies when productive resources can shift between different activities. When such factor movement is possible it enhances the likelihood (implicit in the fact that purchasing power has not been re-allocated) that there is no redistribution of real income between different income groups; even if there is some redistribution, neither its extent or even its direction can be assessed under these conditions. The diffi-culties of using price control as a means for redistributing income are increased in under-developed countries where effective consumer rationing is generally not possible. More-over, where price control is ineffective, and especially where it is of different degrees of effectiveness at the various stages in the distributive chain, its introduction may lead to consider-able political and administrative strain.

Some of these objections also apply to schemes for raising or maintaining the incomes of particular groups of producers or wage earners by raising or maintaining the prices of the goods or services they supply. The extent of the element of redistribution in the relevant transactions is unknown. The incidence of what is in fact a form of indirect taxation is hap-hazard. A large part of the incidence is on would-be pro-ducers of the commodity or service who are perforce excluded from its production, an exclusion made necessary by the measures to raise the price. The people thus excluded may be among the poorest members of the community.[1]   Moreover, the benefit of such measures may not accrue wholly to the intended beneficiaries but in part to other groups.   The last point can be illustrated with the example of various official measures, whether by raising prices or granting subsidies, which may be intended to help farmers but may principally increase the rent-incomes of land-owners.

The imposition of taxation also has various indirect repercussions, the incidence of which is often difficult to assess; and these repercussions of taxation obscure the precise nature and extent of the redistribution which is achieved.   However, the methods we have criticised have additional features which make them less acceptable as instruments for bringing about a measure of redistribution.

§ **4. Aid to Victims of Catastrophe.**   The granting of assistance and the organisation of relief to victims of natural catastrophes such as floods, earthquakes and the like are everywhere recognised as tasks for government.   In under-developed countries this task is likely to be both more important and urgent than in more advanced countries and also to pose greater difficulties.   It is more important in under-developed countries because they operate on a lower economic level, and have small accumulated reserves and limited access to the resources of distant regions.   For these reasons extreme distress stemming from natural calamity is characteristic of subsistence economies and not of advanced economies.   However, the resources of the government and of the community at large are scanty, and resources used for these purposes diminish those available for others such as, for example, the task of developing primary education.   Because of the low level of resources and income, expenditures which are taken almost for granted in rich countries raise serious problems of choice in poor ones.

There is also the question of drawing the line separating the

---

[1] Thus the maintenance of money wages in certain forms of employment may result in increasing the numbers of people who find themselves in overcrowded occupations such as agriculture or petty trading.

responsibilities of the state from those of its citizens. For instance, it is sometimes suggested that, when agricultural producers are heavily indebted, a fall in agricultural prices should be considered as being akin to a natural calamity, and that the resulting distress should be alleviated by government grants, with or without a mandatory scaling-down of agricultural debts.   Such measures may be unavoidable for political reasons. There are, however, certain relevant differences between the distress caused by a sharp fall in prices and that stemming from a natural calamity.   It is very difficult or even impossible to provide against the occurrence of natural disasters, which are usually also accompanied by destruction of capital and sometimes of natural resources.   A fall in prices does not destroy capital physically, and, in principle at any rate, the effects of the contraction of cash incomes which it implies can be partly provided for by setting aside reserves at times of higher prices and incomes.[1]   These issues are also relevant to the scaling down of debt, which raises other issues as well.   If relief of distress from this source is thought desirable its cost should be borne by the community as a whole, and not by a section whose members are in commercial contact with the afflicted group, or who happen to be politically unpopular.   They often represent the more enterprising and resourceful members of the community whose activities play an important part in promoting economic growth.   Also, once contracts have been repudiated at the instance of the state, it may be difficult to restore confidence, and this may react adversely on the interests of those gaining an advantage in the short run.[2]

§ 5. Government and the Institutional Framework.   There is another wide range of tasks which devolves on the government as the executive organ of a politically-organised society, tasks which devolve on the government even where it is not the

[1] Fluctuations in prices and incomes are discussed further in Chapter XIV, section 6, below.
[2] The mandatory alteration of the terms of contracts affecting agricultural producers is considered in more detail in Chapter XIV, section 1, below.

object to magnify its role in economic life. Whether the
direction and content of economic activity are determined
primarily by the market mechanism or by government directives, the functioning of the economic system is profoundly
influenced by the institutional framework within which it takes
place; and, in turn, the framework is necessarily affected by
government action. The establishment of institutions suitable
for the efficient operation of the economic system does not
necessarily emerge from the operation of the system itself.
For example, the market cannot be expected to bring about
a suitable law of property or the institution of limited liability.
Nor is the role of the state in this sphere a passive one once the
minimum services have been organised and an institutional
framework established. Changed conditions may render
obsolete existing institutions, and the economic endeavour of
individuals and firms may be frustrated unless the institutional
structure is consciously and appropriately reshaped.[1]

The reform of inheritance laws and of the system of land
tenure, the introduction of limited liability and the control
of its operation, and the removal or control of monopolies—
these are only a few of the changes in the legal framework
which cannot be affected by the action of individuals operating
through the market. However, it is in the field of religious
observances and tribal and social customs that certain institutional changes may have most far-reaching effects on the performance and growth of the economic system. But in this
sphere it is especially difficult to generalise about the economic
effects of the reshaping of institutions; and such generalisations

[1] The role of government in shaping institutions to promote economic
development was a familiar theme in earlier economic writings, such as
those of Adam Smith and Marshall. It has received little systematic
treatment in the recent literature on under-developed countries and their
development. The most valuable discussions include Y. Brozen, 'Entrepreneurship and Technological Change' in Williamson and Buttrick (eds.),
op. cit.; S. H. Frankel, op. cit., passim; H. D. Gideonse, 'Colonial Experience and the Social Context of Economic Development', in R. A. Solo
(ed.), Economics and the Public Interest, New Brunswick, 1955; W. A.
Lewis, The Theory of Economic Growth, London, 1955, passim; and W.
Röpke, 'Unentwickelte Länder', Ordo Jahrbuch, 1953.

as are possible are largely outside the scope of economics. Here, too, the assessment both of the desirability of reshaping the institutional structure and of the probable results of such action is particularly heavily influenced by political preferences and judgment. Certain attitudes, practices and beliefs such as the resistance to selective reduction of cattle populations over large areas in Africa, or to the slaughter of the sacred cow in India, greatly retard economic growth as this is generally understood. But there are differences of opinion which cannot be resolved by the economist on the extent to which these beliefs are held by the population at large or are enforced upon them by smaller groups, on the intensity of these beliefs, and on the repercussions of enforced reforms, and so on. Although we recognise the great importance of these matters, we have to leave them on one side because there is very little that economists can say about them in general terms.

There are certain problems of institutional change in connection with the use of land which are nearer to the central themes of this book and closer to the interests of economists. These institutional changes are likely to affect the interest and prospects of large numbers, since in most under-developed countries the bulk of the population have for many generations been engaged in agriculture or in economic activities closely associated with it. They are also likely to have an impact extending beyond the narrowly economic scene, because religious practices and social customs are often closely integrated with the use of the land and systems or methods of farming, and agricultural practice is interwoven into the way of life of the people. It is understandable that there often is strong resistance to changes in institutions affecting the use of land, or to the introduction of new methods of cultivation. Non-commercial considerations strengthen the familiar resistance to change; changes are looked upon not merely as innovations which may affect the economic prospects and security of many individuals, but as the beginning of upheavals which may threaten the accustomed fabric of society.

All this seriously complicates the framing and carrying-out of government policy.

§ 6. Reform of Land Tenure.   We have discussed the system of communal (as opposed to individual) rights in the use and disposal of land as an illustration of a type of institution which may be inimical to economic growth.[1]   The replacement of communal by individual tenure (whether by individual farmers, corporate bodies, co-operative societies or government departments) may become essential to ensure that sufficient is produced to support the community at its prevailing standard of living, and, *a fortiori*, to raise it.   This transformation of property rights is almost certain to call for some sort of government intervention, since the unaided attempts of the more far-sighted, independent or venturesome to establish individual tenure are likely to be frustrated, or at least held up, by those anxious to maintain traditional practices.   Even if such attempts meet with some success, they are affected by the uncertainty of individual tenure which may be challenged by the counter-assertion of customary communal rights until it is explicitly recognised by the government.   In these conditions an officially recognised procedure is necessary for securing individual title to particular pieces of land.

The encouragement of the institution of individual tenure of land imposes upon the government the concomitant duty of explaining to the people the nature and expected benefits of the change and of assisting those who are harmed by it. The timing of policy as well as the pace of change are important variables partly within the control of government.   A premature policy will arouse fears with little advantage; there is no economic merit *per se* in a change from communal to individual tenure, since the advantages depend on individuals willing and able to apply new methods.[2]   On the other hand, prolonged delay is likely to increase the resistance to change. Paradoxically, the more urgent the need for reform of land

---

[1] Chapter IV, section 4, above.
[2] However, it is possible that such a change may throw up latent talent.

tenure, the more anxious and vocal the opposition is likely to be. For example, when the land can no longer support a growing population with existing methods of organisation and production, many more people will be reluctant to give up their customary rights and their stake in the common wealth. Again, a very rapid rate of change is apt to exacerbate tensions and ill-feelings; it may also make it impossible for government to come to the aid of those who may be severely disadvantaged by the changing conditions. In short, there are a number of economic, social and political prerequisites for successful reforms of land-tenure systems.

Another aspect of the introduction of individual tenure may require government attention. Some property owners may use their new property rights unwisely and to their own detriment. The possessor of individual property rights has new opportunities not present in the communal system; he can borrow on the security of his land, or he can sell part or all of it. His lack of experience may induce him to take actions which he would have avoided if he were more experienced. The state could stand aside and let people gain experience the hard way. However, inaction may merely defer the difficulties since people who run into debt or dispose of their land too cheaply are apt to be troublesome. Moreover, the ensuing distribution of land may have little to commend it if many of the transfers reflect mistakes due to inexperience.

In principle, the imposition of educative restraints may be desirable in these conditions, especially when the emergence of individual rights in the land is the result in part of official encouragement.[1] Thus the new individual property rights might be circumscribed with limitations on the right to alienate or to mortgage; for instance it may be stipulated that such transactions concluded during a prescribed initial period are invalid or unenforceable, or that only part of a man's property can be disposed of freely by the owner. However, such a

---

[1] We have taken the term 'educative restraint' from W. H. Hutt, who discusses the scope for this type of government intervention in *Economists and the Public*, London, 1936, Chapter XVII.

policy raises difficulties. Since some owners will not make mistakes, restrictions on the use of their property may reduce the benefits expected to flow from a policy of conferring individual tenure. In the absence of a completely collectivised economy, property and credit transactions are important elements in economic development; they are, in fact, indispensable conditions for securing the major advantages of individual tenure. Thus, even if some of these transactions might be unwise, many or most would be beneficial; yet the legal restraints would apply to all the transactions. It is therefore desirable that the educative restraints should be imposed for a limited period only, that the restraints should not apply in respect of the whole of a man's property (otherwise there would be no transactions from which individuals and the community could gain experience), and that as far as it is possible land-owners should be informed of the risks attaching to the eventual exercise of their rights.[1]

How extensive is the scope for legitimate educative restraints in an economy starting from a low level and embarking, or being encouraged to embark, on a process of change and growth? We have given one example where we feel some restraint may be wise. But we are chary of advocating the more widespread application of the principle. Thus we would not suggest in the present context that the state should prescribe the exact utilisation of land for a probationary period after the establishment of individual tenure. It could be argued that mistakes in choice of crops or methods of cultivation can easily be made, since the change removes the customary restraints of a communal system and puts the new owners into a novel environment. However, in these matters we think it better for the authorities to spread information and to show by the example of model farms the possibilities of alternative courses of action rather than to prescribe the activities

---

[1] It may be possible in some situations for the exercise of individual rights to sell or mortgage to be made conditional on the approval of local authorities, or for individuals to be able to apply for exemption from the restraints. This involves great practical administrative difficulties.

of the new land-owners. The executive officers of the government cannot in any case be fully informed of the preferences, costs, resources and abilities of each land-owner and of the opportunities open to him; hence any general or particular restraints or directives are often likely to be inappropriate and wasteful. Mistakes in the use of land are not so irrevocable as those connected with sale or mortgage, and individual experience is gained more rapidly. The longer-term development of the individual person—the enlargement of his experience, the encouragement of initiative and the inculcation of a sense of responsibility—seems to us to be desirable generally as well as in the interests of economic growth, even if it is accompanied by some short-term waste and error. This general presumption or judgment can be reversed in special conditions only. These may indeed be present in real property transactions, chiefly because the transactions of an individual in this field are discontinuous and often of an irrevocable once-for-all character.

§ 7. **The Consolidation of Agricultural Holdings.** The familiar phenomenon of the fragmentation of agricultural holdings provides another useful illustration both of the scope for government action in remodelling the framework of economic institutions and of the attendant complications.

Where agricultural holdings are fragmented, the individual farmer owns several pieces of land scattered over an area. Fragmentation stems generally from inheritance laws and customs which not only provide for the sharing of the property among the heirs, but also secure to each heir the right to a portion of each of the different parts of the property so that all share in land of different qualities. When a previously undivided holding passes to heirs, each may receive his legacy in the form of half-a-dozen separated pieces; within a generation or two the holding may be fragmented into hundreds of scattered pieces, and this fragmentation may affect most holdings. The cultivation of fragmented holdings is often extremely wasteful of labour, of capital (especially in the form of storage facilities and transport equipment) and even of land as well. In these circumstances economy in the use of resources and a consequent increase in total output could be secured from the consolidation of holdings into contiguous properties. In other words, consolidation could raise output, and a division of the consolidated holdings is possible which in principle might improve the position of each cultivator.

At first sight it might seem that in an exchange economy the operation of market forces would bring about the required consolidation, either through exchanges among individual holders or through the action of larger owners, dealers or speculators buying up adjacent parcels of land, uniting them in individual holdings, and either cultivating these themselves or reselling or letting them at the (postulated) higher value, thus acting in a sense as property developers. One or other of these methods may indeed bring about the required solution; yet, for various reasons, neither solution may be available in practice.

Consolidation through voluntary exchanges may call not simply for a series of exchanges between pairs of owners but for a whole chain of multiple transactions. The difficulties of reconciling different valuations and individual preferences are likely to prove insurmountable, since in the circumstances there is no continuously operating market but only a series of isolated bilateral exchanges.[1] The other solution may be excluded for different reasons. The profit to be secured from the purchase of fragmented holdings and their subsequent utilisation as consolidated properties is liable to disappear if, towards the end of the process, the owners of some of the pieces ask very high prices for their plots based not on their value whilst still cultivated as fragments, nor even on their higher value as parts of eventual consolidated holdings, but on the bargaining power derived from a strategic advantage.

[1] In parts of India voluntary exchanges have worked quite well in regions in which the availability of a good irrigation system, for example, has made all pieces of land more or less homogeneous from the point of view of cultivation. In other regions where this favourable circumstance is absent schemes for exchanges have had little success.

This stems from the fact that these plots are required to secure a contiguous consolidated holding without which a large part of the anticipated increase in output would be lost. Thus much of the profit expected by the enterprising developers may be transferred to the owners of some of these plots without the exercise of any foresight or effort on their part. Awareness of this probable situation is likely to deter the developer from embarking on the project. The risk of political and social unpopularity often attaching to profitable transactions in real property may also act as a deterrent.

By compulsory purchase the government may overcome the difficulties, possibly without affecting adversely the interests of any single owner. The government may acquire compulsorily the scattered holdings, amalgamate them and resell them as consolidated properties. In view of the (postulated) higher productivity of the consolidated properties it is possible for the government to offer each owner of fragmented holdings a higher price than his properties would fetch in the absence of consolidation, and to resell the consolidated plots at a price no higher than their value based on the higher productivity, or at a lower price if this is thought desirable. The valuation of properties may present a problem, especially the valuation of fixed capital and other improvements, and compensation for the severance of sentimental associations.

There is a *prima facie* case for compulsion if it can be shown that all participants would be better off and that this result would not have emerged without compulsion. But whether or not it is regarded as desirable is dependent on such considerations as the estimate of the resulting increase in output, the presence or absence of sentimental attachments, the possibility and probability of equitable administration of the details of the scheme, and the likelihood of achieving consolidation by a voluntary process over a longer period. It is essentially a matter of political judgment how far a compulsory scheme is justified—how great an increase in output is required before it can be said to justify the application of compulsion is not a matter on which an unambiguous opinion can be expressed.   An appeal to the notion that with full knowledge people would do voluntarily what in an imperfect world has to be done by compulsion in their interests may seem relevant here.   On the formal level it is no doubt appropriate; but in practice much injustice may be perpetrated, wittingly as well as unwittingly, in the name of an acceptable general principle.

§ 8. **Problems of Resistance to Economic Change.**   The discussion of reforms of institutions affecting the use of land touched on an issue of wider importance.   All economic change creates advantageous opportunities for those who are adaptable or enterprising, and the possibility of loss, either absolutely or relatively to the position of others, for those who are not successful in reshaping their activities to suit a changing environment.   Change brings risk, and with it the chance of losses to some individuals even if the change itself is in the direction of economic growth.   Moreover, when change or growth is rapid, many people have to face a new environment or new set of problems for which past experience, collective or individual, may have little relevance; there is the risk of making mistakes out of ignorance, even for those who do not lack in enterprise and are willing and eager to change their mode of behaviour.

It may be said that economic growth brings a clash between security or stability and progress.   However, in practice it is usually not sensible to frame the issue simply as a clash between security and progress.   The security of the *status quo* may be largely or wholly illusory, and economic growth may provide the only real safeguard of prevailing standards of living, as well as the opportunity for greater security at improved standards of living.   The preservation of the *status quo* does not usually maintain security at the cost of the surrender of possible benefits of change.   More often it substitutes one set of risks for another set, while at the same time it forfeits the advantages of change.   For instance in under-developed countries where population is increasing, the problem is better seen as a race between population and productivity than as a conflict between security and progress.[1]

It is natural that there should be some resistance to change even when growth in the form of higher standards of living is thought of as a desirable goal. Those who fear the risks of change are apt to magnify the security provided by the *status quo*, and governments sometimes find it the path of least resistance to yield to the pressures of sectional interests. Indeed, it is not easy to generalise about the proper role of government in these matters. A preference for security over increasing opportunities is not irrational, though the choice is likely to be misdirected if the full implications of alternative policies are not understood. It would seem to be a general duty of government to acquaint itself with the probable consequences of the alternative policies of resisting change or of allowing it (or even stimulating it), and to disseminate information to counter the arguments advanced by sectional interests and allay the fears of those whose judgment is warped by exaggerated apprehensions. The scope of government action in this field may extend beyond the dissemination of information. The impact on individuals of rapid change may be cushioned and its adverse effects mitigated by devising institutional changes and official measures designed to prevent the hardship which may accompany rapid economic change, especially when the informal social security system of the extended family is disintegrating. Such measures may assist people in adapting themselves to changed conditions. However, their adoption often raises difficult issues, for the various devices for conditioning the course of change or for shielding individuals from its effects in turn introduce other risks which may be more serious. A failure to recognise these other risks aggravates their impact since it prevents the introduction of appropriate safeguards or counter-measures.

[1] This point is made in these terms by Sheila van der Horst in 'Equal Pay for Equal Work', *South African Journal of Economics*, June 1954. This article deals with some aspects of restrictionism in the labour market in multi-racial South Africa.

The emergence of a market or exchange economy in place of a subsistence economy is an essential condition of economic progress beyond a most primitive level.   In a subsistence or near-subsistence economy people consume very little beyond what they produce by primitive methods.   Production aims at meeting directly the wants of the producer, his family or some other narrowly defined and circumscribed group. Specialisation, an essential condition of efficient production, is severely limited.   Moreover, people have access only to the very restricted volume and variety of commodities produced by themselves or other members of the narrowly circumscribed group.   In an exchange economy, on the other hand, they can draw on the resources, reserves and ideas of different and distant people.   The promotion of the extension of an exchange economy is therefore a very important task of a government which wishes to advance economic development.

However, it is often thought that a near-subsistence economy, although operating on a lower level than a market economy, does at least offer greater security.   This is not so. Disaster such as famine or pestilence occurs in subsistence economies, not in exchange economies.   Exchange economies operate on a higher level, have much larger reserves, and in times of adversity can usually draw on outside resources.   But while the risks of a subsistence economy are far greater, they seem to be politically more acceptable.   This is partly because in a subsistence economy people are too poor to be much concerned with political activity and the expression of discontent. But more probably the reason why people accept these disasters with resignation is that their immediate causes in a subsistence economy are obvious, readily intelligible and apparently outside human control.   By contrast the causes of adversity in an exchange economy are not readily grasped; at the same time they are felt to stem from avoidable human causes, such as mismanagement or malice, because economic difficulties are reflected in such forms as the reduction of numbers employed by particular employing firms or lower prices paid by particular buyers.   For these reasons the political risks of discontent are greater in an exchange economy than in a subsistence economy.

This conclusion strengthens the case for political and economic education, and for such measures as the cushioning of the impact of rapid and discontinuous fluctuations. It also suggests that it is advisable to progress gradually in the development of the exchange economy. But it does not affect the fundamental conclusion that the growth of an exchange economy is a necessary requirement of economic advance beyond a low level and also of greater real security. It is also an essential condition of access to a wider range of alternatives in terms not only of goods and services but also in terms of occupations and activities, and beyond this, of human contacts and ideas.

Restrictive practices devised or supported by government for the benefit of particular groups or sectors may at times appear to be justified in the interests of security and stability; the argument is often put forward that such practices have this supposedly desirable effect. In practice, however, this is at best only one aspect of restrictionism; the income of other members of the society, both of those who are excluded from the particular activity and have therefore to find less preferred alternatives, and of those who purchase the services of the members of the protected group, are necessarily reduced, and almost always by more than the net benefits accruing to the favoured individuals. Moreover, any security achieved for the group is at the expense of the rest of the community; and if the restrictions become cumulative, as they tend to do, the adverse effects on growth may undermine the main source of security for the economy as a whole and for those groups whose position appears to be safeguarded.

§ 9. Government and Monopoly.

There are certain undesirable economic effects of monopoly: uneconomic allocation of resources, enhanced inequality of income and concentration of economic power. Concentration of economic power, in particular, has implications beyond those of the ability of monopolists to influence prices significantly, to keep out competitors or to engender a feeling of dependence. One of these wider implications is that the diffusion of decision-making is reduced. In certain special circumstances these adverse effects may be offset by counteracting advantages. But there is a presumption that the economic effects of monopoly, especially the concentration of economic power, are undesirable. On these grounds there is a *prima facie* case for official measures to prevent the emergence of monopoly.

The essence of monopoly is a high degree of dependence on the part of those who buy from or sell to the monopolist firm or concerted group of firms. This is an important aspect of the limited range of alternatives which is the characteristic feature of monopoly or quasi-monopoly situations; moreover, the high degree of dependence is present regardless of whether the monopolist actively or consciously attempts to make the most of the situation in which he is dominant.[1] An incidental but not unimportant result of this is that the population is apt to ascribe any adverse price change to the deliberate manipulation of the monopolist or quasi-monopolists.

There is scope for positive government action to promote more effective competition if there are reasonable grounds for believing that the reduction or elimination of monopoly power is practicable in particular concrete situations. This depends largely upon the reasons for the absence of sufficiently effective independent competitors to safeguard a satisfactory range of alternatives to those who deal with the monopolists; that is, it depends upon the nature and severity of the barriers to the entry and expansion of new competing firms.[2]

[1] It is sometimes thought that customers who are poor are in a weak bargaining position *vis-a-vis* traders who are rich. But this is not so where the traders, however rich they may be, compete effectively with one another. The availability of effective alternatives is the safeguard of the customer, be he rich or poor. This aspect of competition and monopoly is illustrated in our article 'Competition and Prices: A Study of Groundnut Buying in Nigeria', *Economica*, February 1952.

[2] The number of competitors and the shares of trade handled by each are imperfect measures of monopoly power. The conditions affecting the entry of new firms are not reflected in such statistics. Moreover, the

The obstacles to the entry and growth of new competing firms vary greatly in nature and severity from one situation to another. Three main types of restriction may be identified; the differences between them are crucial for public policy.

First, barriers to entry may be set up directly by legislation or indirectly as the intended or unintended results of official measures. The most effective monopolies are those created by statute, since no new competing firms may present customers with independent alternatives. The statutory monopoly is able to pursue policies which are against the interests of its customers without fear of the sanctions provided by competition. This type of barrier to entry is in principle the easiest to remove; the barriers are erected by government and can therefore be removed by government. In general they are responsible for the most serious monopoly situations in under-developed countries, and to that extent it is not difficult to frame a policy of promoting or restoring competition which, if applied, would be certain to have the desired effects.

Barriers to entry may also be set up by the action of the monopolists themselves. The dominant firm or group may be in a position to induce suppliers to refrain from supplying new firms, or to bind customers to refrain from supporting new competitors. The monopolist may thus have opportunities for extending or prolonging his monopoly power. But in practice immunity from competition is rarely complete or permanent, and it is almost invariably less complete or permanent than where it is provided by statute or by other official measures such as licensing or officially supported cartelisation. In principle, the second type of barrier can be dealt with by prohibiting the use by monopolists of the specified practices. In practice, there are likely to be difficulties of identifying and defining the practices and of enforcing the prohibition; further, the presence of the monopolist may in itself act as a deterrent

propensity of the established firms to compete is not the same in all situations, and this is sometimes as important as their number. These points are considered and illustrated in the article referred to in the preceding footnote.

to new entry by creating a fear of action specially designed to obstruct a new entrant. The precise action to be taken must depend largely upon local circumstances.

The third type of barrier refers to obstacles to entry which are not attributable to official measures or to the actions of established firms. Thus entry is difficult where economic operation requires a large initial investment (large in relation to the extent of the market) or a combination of rare skills, knowledge and experience. In these conditions it is difficult to promote competition if neither of the other two types of restriction is present. When the presence of monopoly stems from a low level of economically efficient resources, the situation is obviously much more difficult to remedy than when it derives from some contrived barriers to the entry of effective competitors.

Though details are likely to differ greatly from one country to another, it may be helpful to indicate the likelihood of monopoly in several of the main economic activities in under-developed countries generally. In passing we add some further observations on the scope for government action to promote competition.[1]

In the absence of official restrictions it is unlikely that there will be much effective monopoly in small-scale trade in under-developed countries. Entry into this important class of trade does not require much capital or expensive skills, so that there is generally no lack of suitable participants, particularly where alternative opportunities for employment are limited.[2] Customers tend to be mobile; the low incomes and the lack of other opportunities for the use of labour of at least some

---

[1] The principal barriers to entry into trade in tropical countries and especially in West Africa are discussed in some detail in P. T. Bauer, *op. cit.*, Part 3.

[2] Sometimes the traders in particular branches of retailing or produce buying are drawn largely from particular racial or national groups. It is often said that the particular group monopolises the trade. But this is not monopoly in the economic sense unless the members of the group act in concert in setting their prices or in adopting practices which tend to exclude traders from other racial or national groups.

members of the household make it worthwhile for time and care to be devoted to the search for the most profitable alternatives for buying or selling.   The farmer or the shopper is not restricted to the traders in his immediate neighbour-hood; these traders have to meet the competition of traders further afield but accessible to their customers, as well as that of itinerant traders, a feature of poor countries.   For this reason even the presence of only a few traders in a particular district does not indicate any effective monopoly power but rather the fact that the small turnover does not enable larger numbers to make a living.   In many under-developed coun-tries, however, there are official restrictions on the number of traders, the location of trading sites, the movement of traders and of goods, or the time and place of sales of produce; these measures reduce the range of alternatives which would other-wise be available to producers and consumers, and they create or encourage monopoly groups in a field of economic activity in which restraints on competition would otherwise be in-significant.   These restrictions are likely to be especially harmful in countries where the exchange sector of the economy is still growing so that highly adaptable methods of trading are necessary to encourage further production for the market.[1]

The market for small-scale loans, especially to peasant producers, is more likely to be subject to some degree of local monopoly.   Capital is at a low level so that even the actual or potential suppliers of small loans may be limited in number. Moreover, the mobility of both lenders and borrowers is limited relatively to that of buyers and sellers of goods.   The lender is unlikely to lend to a borrower of whom he knows little; the market for loans cannot be impersonal.   On the other hand, in early stages of economic development small-scale lending may attract the interests of many of the more

[1] Several of these types of official measures affecting marketing in under-developed countries are illustrated and examined in our article 'The Economics of Marketing Reform', *Journal of Poutical Economy*, June 1954.

industrious or successful producers who have accumulated some capital. The remedy for such monopoly elements as may be present lies in the growth of the economy, which increases the volume of available funds and the possible sources of supply. There may also be scope for voluntary co-operative enterprise on the part of potential borrowers. Government measures designed to deal with local monopoly by fixing maximum rates of interest on loans are likely to be unenforceable, and, if enforced, are likely to reduce the flow of funds to the disadvantage of the supposed beneficiaries.

The external trade of some under-developed countries is handled by a small number of large firms with extensive and variegated activities. In these conditions of oligopoly some individual firms may have appreciable power to influence prices; moreover, it may be easy for the firms to agree on concerted action. The high degree of concentration stems largely from the presence of heavy risks, and the requirement of a large capital and of administrative and commercial skill combined with local business experience. These tend to impede the entry of new firms. But the barriers are frequently overcome by new competitors, unless they are obstructed by official measures. These measures which by accident or design may serve to strengthen the position of established firms, especially of large firms, are to be found in such diverse fields of government activity as taxation, import licensing, price control, the licensing of trade and transport enterprises and immigration control.

Some measure of monopoly is likely to be present in manufacturing activities requiring expensive and specific capital investments and highly-trained personnel, particularly as the total market is likely to be limited. Restrictions on imports and on immigration strengthen the position of established firms, which will be strong even without them until the market has expanded sufficiently to support a number of competing firms.

Generally, the growth of the economy as a whole is perhaps the most effective solvent of the more intractable kinds of monopoly situations. It is therefore all the more necessary for government to deal with the less intractable types of monopoly by removing measures or practices which create or strengthen monopoly positions, which in turn are likely to retard economic growth.

CHAPTER XIII

ACCELERATED CAPITAL FORMATION

§ **1. Advocacy of Compulsory Saving.** The use of the proceeds of taxation to finance accelerated capital or investment expenditure is usually termed compulsory saving, or more properly taxation for development; it is a principal issue in contemporary discussions of development and of the economics of under-developed countries generally. The process can also be termed the socialisation of saving. Although the proceeds of compulsory saving could be lent to private entrepreneurs, nevertheless substantial compulsory saving generally involves heavy investment in public enterprises. But a large volume of public investment and enterprise is possible without compulsory saving when the government can borrow from private lenders.

The advocacy of compulsory saving is, as a rule, based on three propositions: economic growth as such is desirable; economic growth is in large measure a function of capital accumulation; and compulsory saving necessarily increases capital accumulation. These propositions do not have general or incontrovertible validity.

The first and third propositions underlying the advocacy of compulsory saving are examined in sections 2 to 4 of this chapter. We have already looked into the relationship between capital accumulation and the growth of national income, and concluded that there is no simple functional relationship.[1] Opportunities for profitable investment, the availability of the necessary co-operant resources and a favourable and adaptable political and social environment are among the

---

[1] Chapter X, section 1, above.

factors, besides the supply of capital, which are required to promote an increase in the national income.

§ 2. The Case for Compulsion. The role we have assigned to government in economic development (which is discussed in Chapters XI and XII) would require heavy government expenditures in any under-developed country even if the programme of its activities were restrictively interpreted. The advocacy of compulsory saving for development involves both a material extension of the list of government action and also a qualitative change in the role given to government. It follows that judgment of the fruits of the government activity made possible by taxation for development must be much affected by one's political standpoint. This range of issues does not lend itself to analytical treatment. As we have already stated our views on the scope for government action, there is no point in pursuing these important issues here. However, our discussion of the effects of taxation in section 3 of this chapter reinforces our general position. In particular, the heavier taxation implied in a programme of compulsory saving is likely to impinge markedly on the economy with adverse effects on productive effort, the growth of specialisation and exchange, private saving and investment, and on economic growth generally. Compulsory saving brought about by taxation does not necessarily accelerate economic growth even in terms of the conventional, but inadequate, index of growth, that is to say an increase in the national income.

It may be thought that the preceding observations, deriving as they do largely from a political standpoint rather than from positive economic propositions, are deficient in that they leave out an important *economic* consideration. We must consider briefly a possible objection to our treatment.

The argument may be put in this way. Private savings make possible a series of continuous and marginal economic adjustments and adaptations which are conducive to growth. These are the kinds of adjustments with which economic analysis has largely been concerned during the last half-century, and they can be left safely to individual and dispersed decision-making. But this approach is not sufficient for dealing with the initiation of growth itself or with other large, discontinuous strides forward. Large and discontinuous changes are sometimes necessary to overcome obstacles or humps in the way of further economic growth. The problem is one of surmounting an abrupt threshold, and not of making a continuous series of a large number of individually small adjustments to marginal changes in economic variables. To get over the threshold on to a higher plateau of economic activity and well-being calls for an especially large expenditure of capital either on a single indivisible project or on a number of projects which have to be undertaken in combination or not at all. Individual savers or investors cannot comprehend or assess the productivity of such discontinuous and indivisible increments of investment, and hence are unwilling to make savings available for these investments although the benefits to them of the changes would be greater (even in their estimation) than the benefits to be derived from private investments or from current consumption. Compulsion, that is taxation in this context, is necessary to maximise the desirable flow of resources. It is true that individual preferences are overridden, but this in time enables individuals to have a wider and more effective range of choice and an increased command over resources. In other words, the case for compulsion would then be essentially the case for an educative restraint on the disposal of personal incomes.

Arguments along these lines may be questioned on various points. No detailed account of a specific example of the situations postulated has to our knowledge been provided, and the frequency and extent of these situations have not been established.[1] Moreover, if such a situation should be present, it is not clear why government could not publicise the facts

---

[1] A further discussion of the case for state action to promote schemes of balanced growth in industry, which may seem to fall within the category of situations under review here, will be found in Chapter XV, section 5, below.

and urge the postulated high productivity of the investment, and in this way persuade domestic or foreign lenders to make the capital available. The argument for compulsion implies that the government has a better appreciation than the citizens of the productivity of the competing uses to which their funds can be put, and that for some reason its superior knowledge cannot be communicated persuasively to them or to foreign lenders. Thus even if the particular type of situation is present, the case for compulsion is based essentially on political, or possibly administrative, considerations.

It is doubtful, however, whether the presence of an obstacle or hurdle of the kind postulated can ever debar all forms of further economic growth. The removal of a particular barrier may be a prerequisite to particular kinds or directions of economic expansion but may have little or no effect on other kinds of change. The recognition that expansion can occur along a variety of routes itself minimises the importance to be attached to particular obstacles blocking some of them.

Those who advocate compulsory saving usually take a narrow view of economic growth, and identify it with particular forms or directions of change, for example rapid industrialisation. This strengthens the conclusion that we are dealing with questions of political objectives and not with self-contained problems of economic analysis. Recognition that economic change can take place at varying rates and along various routes, and that advocates of compulsory saving favour a rate of change (usually in particular sectors) greater than the current rate of change, points in the same direction. In the sphere of economic growth, as in other spheres of economic decision-making, there are problems of choice. These problems have economic aspects. But economics does not prescribe the choices which ought to be made. Advocates of compulsory saving prefer that important decisions be made by the government rather than by dispersed individuals, and that decisions go one way rather than another. Our own preference is for arrangements in which decision-making is dispersed and individual preferences are given full expression.

In our view, therefore, the clearest case for economic activity by the state is where this is indispensable, in one form or another, to secure a supply of a good or service for which there is a current demand, and of which the cost of production could be recovered if it were possible to charge individual beneficiaries. Expenditures or activities yielding benefits indiscriminately are analytically the least ambiguous examples. However, since the intensity of demand for such services cannot be measured or tested in the market, the volume of such services to be provided or sponsored by the state is a matter of judgment.

Compulsory saving for development generally encompasses activities other than those yielding benefits indiscriminately, for example programmes of accelerated industrialisation. Our disussion is also relevant for over-expanded schemes of expenditure on investments yielding benefits indiscriminately, though, as has been explained, it is a matter of judgment at which point such expenditures are considered to be over-expanded.

The general conclusion is that the assessment of compulsory saving for development is based largely on political grounds. We have stated our reasons for rejecting compulsory saving as an instrument of economic policy. However, certain aspects of taxation for development are amenable to economic analysis, and some of these are considered in sections 3 and 4.

§ 3. Some Effects of Taxation in Under-developed Countries. Taxation for compulsory saving (or for any other purpose) involves the transfer of funds from the private to the public sector; it is obviously not a simple addition to resources. An examination of taxation for compulsory saving therefore involves a discussion of the repercussions of the collection of the funds on the private sector of the economy.[1]

[1] It is often argued that analysis of the effects of the collection of taxes is not meaningful without considering also the effects of the expenditure of tax receipts. This, however, is irrelevant to the discussion in the text. Even if the funds are spent most effectively, it is still desirable to minimise the adverse effects of taxation on the supply of effort and saving in the

The effects of taxation on the supply of effort and of saving are likely to be complex even in an apparently simple economy. No firm generalisations can be put forward because analysis by itself can do no more than provide a long list of possible results depending upon the different weights which can be given to each of the possibly relevant variables; and in fact the appropriate weights will not be the same in all concrete situations. Here we can do no more than consider the likely effects of some variations in what appear to be the key factors, and suggest tentative conclusions which we believe to apply fairly widely. It is convenient to consider the effects of various tax arrangements first on the supply of effort and then on private saving.

A poll tax is virtually certain to increase the aggregate supply of effort. This is because a poll tax raises the marginal utility of income (compared to its previous level) while leaving the reward on marginal effort in both the subsistence and the money sectors unaltered; in the circumstances individuals adjust to the new position by sacrificing some leisure.[1] But even with a tax as simple as a poll tax it cannot be said certainly that the supply of effort to the money sector will necessarily rise. Nevertheless, we think this is very probable because the tax, having to be paid in money, creates an additional demand for money income and not for the income yielded by subsistence activity.[2]

private sector, and this requires analysis along the lines of the discussion in the text. The expenditure of the proceeds of taxation for development is not susceptible to general economic analysis. We have stated our position on this type of expenditure in the preceding section.

[1] An extreme case is conceivable where no leisure is sacrificed, and the tax is met out of a reduction in saving and/or spending. This improbable limiting case postulates a zero income elasticity of demand for leisure over the relevant range.

[2] In certain special (and probably uncommon) circumstances the supply of effort to the money sector may be reduced. The simplest case is that in which the poll tax is less than the money income and in which the money income is obtained by the production and sale of a commodity for which the income elasticity of the producers' demand is negative (i.e. the commodity is for them an inferior good). The impoverishment of the producers caused by the imposition of the tax may make it preferable for the producers to consume part of the output of the commodity that had

A poll tax affects the distribution between leisure and effort through the income effect only. All other taxes have both an income and a substitution effect. The income effect stems from the higher marginal utility of income resulting from the reduction in the tax-payer's real income, and it induces an increased supply of effort; the substitution effect stems from the change in the value at the margin of leisure (which is untaxed) relatively to reward for effort (which is taxed). The two effects work in opposite directions. The income effect is a function of changes in total income, and the substitution effect is a function of changes in marginal income. The imposition of a tax (other than a poll tax) affects simultaneously total income and marginal income. For this reason the net effect on the supply of effort can be in either direction, whereas if there were only one effect (as with a poll tax) the change in the supply of effort would be unambiguous. However, where a tax falls proportionately more heavily on marginal income than on total income, there is to that extent a presumption that the substitution effect outweighs the income effect. This presumption becomes a certainty where the tax takes the form of a 100 per cent tax on incomes above a certain amount. Thus progressive taxes are more inhibitive of effort than proportional taxes and, *a fortiori*, than regressive taxes (of which a poll tax is an example).

This analysis requires an important addition when applied to economies not yet fully permeated by specialisation of economic activities and exchange. The bulk of taxes in practice are levied on money incomes, or on expenditure in the money sector, or on the proceeds of sales in the money sector

previously been sold for money, part of which had been used to buy other goods which are preferred when incomes are higher.

Sago appears to be an example of an inferior good in some parts of Sarawak. According to H. S. Morris (*op. cit.*, p. 42) 'sago slumps are immediately reflected in an increase in the amount of sago biscuit eaten instead of rice'. The sago producers buy rice with the proceeds of their sales, particularly of sago, in the money sector. The imposition of a heavy poll tax would have an effect similar to the income effect associated with a fall in the price of sago (but without the substitution effect of the latter).

(or part of it, such as the export trade). Such taxes raise the value at the margin of effort in the subsistence sector (which is untaxed) relatively to that of effort in the money sector (which is taxed). With a given income effect, there will be a tendency to divert effort from the money sector to the subsistence sector.[1] The strength of this tendency will depend largely on two factors: first, the relative valuations placed on the commodities and services obtainable in the two sectors; and second, the relative efficiency of production (allowing for costs incurred) in the two sectors. Thus the shift to subsistence will be reduced to the extent that the taxpayer has a strong preference for, say, imported merchandise, and to the extent that his skills are specific to activities in the exchange sector. Where such preferences and differences in productivity are marked, the imposition of the tax may even in some cases increase the supply of effort to the money sector. The substitution effect then is weak, and the income effect, which induces additional effort, is directed primarily towards effort in the money sector.

In different under-developed countries there are often marked differences in the ability and readiness of producers to shift between production for subsistence and production for the market. The readiness and ability of producers in many under-developed countries to abandon or reduce subsistence production in favour of production for the market are well known; the willingness to do so indicates the desire to shift to more productive activities. This suggests that producers will tend to revert to subsistence production if net returns in the exchange sector decline relatively to those in the subsistence sector. It may be objected that the shift to production for exchange is irreversible since new tastes are acquired, specific skills developed and commitments made in the money sector, which reduce the relative attractiveness of

[1] For reasons indicated there will be an increase in the supply of total effort in those situations in which the income effect outweighs the substitution effect. The present point concerns the division of the total effort between the money and the subsistence sectors, regardless whether the total effort remains unchanged or is altered.

a return to subsistence production. There is an element of truth in this; but it is clearly not true that the supply of effort to the money sector is virtually inelastic in response to reward. The tastes and wants even of those who have entered the money economy are not irrevocably fixed, or unaffected by the terms on which goods and services are available; and the advantages of acquired skills and specific investments are not absolute. The substantial curtailment of rubber production by small-holders in Indonesia, British North Borneo and Sarawak in the early 1930's and the increased effort given to subsistence production provide only one example of many where changes in relative rewards induce a withdrawal of effort from the money sector.

But even if those who have been completely absorbed into the money sector would never revert to subsistence production, taxation may nevertheless affect the supply of effort to the money economy. Producers who have not completely shifted to the money sector will have less incentive to enlarge their interest in it; and, similarly, those who have not yet entered it will have less inducement to do so. Moreover, taxation in the form of levies on the sale of output (for example, export taxes) reduces net returns, so that some marginal production becomes extra-marginal and output is curtailed.

In the earlier stages of development the shift of activity from the money to the subsistence sector is likely to involve relatively few sacrifices, since involvement in the money economy will be less deep-rooted and less complete. Moreover, in these stages many people have not entered the money economy at all, or have done so only to a limited extent. It is then that taxes falling on the money sector are most likely to reduce materially the supply of effort to the money sector and so to retard its growth. These effects are likely to be particularly pronounced if the taxation takes the form of progressive income taxes, or of taxes on commodities with a high income elasticity of demand, or of taxes on the sale of output in general, or of taxes on the principal cash crops. And it is such taxes, and not poll taxes, which are usually proposed in under-developed countries, both for ordinary revenue and for compulsory saving.

It is therefore likely that in many under-developed countries taxation falling on activity in the money sector will reduce the supply of effort to that sector below what it would be otherwise. This reallocation of resources affects adversely total real income. The lower national income and the retardation of the spread of the exchange economy in turn impede long-term growth.

So far we have considered the effect of various kinds of taxes on the supply of effort; we now turn more briefly to the supply of private saving.

Any tax is bound to reduce the taxpayer's real income after tax (except in the unlikely limiting case where the tax is met completely by a reduction in leisure).[1] Generally one would expect that a reduction in income would reduce savings and generally reduce them proportionately more than consumption. This applies even where the supply of effort has been increased; it applies even more where the supply of effort has been reduced and, *a fortiori*, where the supply of effort to the money sector has been reduced. And we have suggested that this last contingency is likely in the earlier stages of economic growth. But even in more advanced economies some reduction in private saving is likely to result. This effect may be mitigated by special tax concessions such as the exemption of capital goods from import duties, or the preferential treatment of savings in the assessment of income subject to income taxes. But such measures are relatively unimportant in this context, especially in under-developed countries.

The proceeds of compulsory savings are not a simple addition to total saving. It is not even certain that total saving will be increased by the process. Even when savings are increased in the short run, the repercussions of the taxation may reduce the flow of savings in the long run by retarding the spread of the exchange economy and the growth of specialisation, though conversely, it must also be remembered that the expenditure

[1] Strictly, the sacrifice of leisure also reduces real income.

of the funds may have important beneficial effects promoting economic progress. Taxes which are easiest to collect and offer the highest yields in the short run are particularly likely to affect adversely saving and investment in the private sector and to retard the long term growth of the economy; heavy export taxes on agricultural produce are an example. These repercussions are obscured when the proceeds of compulsory saving are regarded as a simple net addition to resources, whereas in fact they are a transfer of resources from the private sector to government. Whatever the merits of such a transfer, they cannot be assessed rationally unless it is recognised that it is a transfer and not a net increase of resources. Similarly, unless this is appreciated, it is not possible so to frame the tax structure as to minimise the disincentive effects in the private sector or to ensure conformity with whatever standards of equity are accepted.[1]

If compulsory saving is thought desirable, it should be carried out by government through the medium of a budget surplus. Taxation for development can then be integrated with the rest of the tax structure. The adverse effects are likely to be far more serious if the funds for development are compulsorily gathered by statutory marketing boards or similar organisations, such as those in West Africa, Uganda and Burma, which control the sale of particular agricultural products and withhold part of the sales proceeds. Here the burden is concentrated on producers of export crops, with the maximum of disincentive effect and the almost complete disregard of considerations of equity.

[1] Often enough is known about the conditions of supply and demand of individual commodities to take advantage of differences between them in framing the structure of taxation. For example, the elasticity of long-period supply is likely to be relatively low (that is compared to that of other products) for commodities which require the expenditure of little effort or money for the establishment of capacity or for the securing of recurrent yields. Thus from this point of view in West Africa wild products (that is the produce of naturally occurring trees) such as palm oil and palm kernels are more suitable objects of taxation than groundnuts, cocoa or cotton. The same applies to rubber compared to cotton or coffee in Brazil.

There is a further set of considerations relevant both to the implementation of compulsory saving and to the assessment of the merits of compulsory saving as an instrument of policy. This stems from the distribution of the burdens and benefits of the policy. Those who advocate taxation for development are often not those called upon to pay for it; those who support the imposition of the burden of compulsory savings do not always share in bearing it, and quite often, in addition, are direct beneficiaries of the process. Moreover, the advocates are often so placed as not to suffer from the economic and social strains of economic change which are accentuated by the implementation of policies aimed at accelerating that process. The easy equation of compulsory saving for development with the interests of the people as a whole neglects the diversity of individual or group interests and the fact that any far-reaching policy affects the varying interests differently.

§ 4. Compulsory Saving and Private Enterprise. When compulsory saving reduces private saving, it is likely also to restrict the supply and effectiveness of local entrepreneurship. Individuals are more likely to establish themselves successfully in business if they or members of their family can provide them with some capital; a reduction in the supply of private saving will inhibit the establishment of local business undertakings and the development of entrepreneurial talent.

The growth of an economy usually requires a large number of small changes, each taking advantage of local opportunities and availability of resources and each in turn making further growth possible. Dispersal of savings and dispersal of entrepreneurship are important aspects of much economic development even in countries in which the state has played an important part as provider of capital or as manager of business enterprises. This conclusion is stressed by Professor Lockwood in his study of the economic development of Japan, where, as is well known, the role of the state was prominent.[1]

[1] W. W. Lockwood, *op. cit.*, especially pp. 107, 192–4, 198–9 and 212–3.

The adverse effects of compulsory saving on dispersed private enterprise can, in principle at least, be offset by making the savings available to entrepreneurs in the private sector. This raises interesting issues of policy. The available funds being limited, it will be necessary for the state to select from among a number of competing private applicants. The state has to make investment decisions of the kind made by investment bankers or finance houses. Wise investment decisions demand detailed knowledge of the prospects of each project and of the capabilities of the men who will be in charge of it. There are many difficulties in the way of establishing effective government machinery which will provide for the flow of the necessary information, its interpretation and its translation into particular decisions.

In some respects these difficulties may be greater in an under-developed economy than in an advanced economy, in which experience suggests they are difficult enough. Government personnel of the required training and experience are likely to be lacking, and statistical services are often deficient. Many relevant economic features of an under-developed economy are not reducible to statistical terms, so that the task of investigation and communication is made more difficult. Some of these features have been considered in Chapters II and III. The wide variation in economic conditions (for example, the availability of labour and other resources) between different localities within a country, the result largely of poor communications and narrow markets, also complicates the task of acquainting the central allocators with the resources, opportunities, costs and prospects of the different private applicants for the limited investible funds. Moreover, if official funds are made available to certain private undertakings there will be a strong temptation to deny funds to competing, but otherwise economically desirable, concerns. There will also be a real danger of pressure on officials and politicians. In general, then, there are serious difficulties in the way of using official funds for investment in private concerns; and it is often undesirable and almost always politically dangerous to use public funds to set up or assist private firms in business.[1]

Where official savings are a large part of total savings, they are likely to be used to finance state undertakings. This is probable even without ideological hostility to private enterprise, and it is of course much more probable when there is such hostility. The use of official funds to finance state enterprise avoids some of the difficulties we have considered. But it does not avoid the major difficulties, that is those of the discovery of the most productive uses for the savings. Moreover, it has other drawbacks. Vested interests are strengthened; socialisation of savings and state enterprise make it more difficult for new or small private firms to become serious competitors of established state or private firms, and in this way strengthen monopoly positions. Again, heavy additional responsibilities are imposed on public administrative resources, which in under-developed countries are usually severely strained. At the same time managerial and entrepreneurial talent in the rest of the economy may be deprived of funds which they could use profitably. There will naturally be a general bias in favour of enterprises and forms of activity which are considered appropriate for the state to own and manage. There may also be a tendency to put savings in the

---

[1] The difficulties of achieving the optimal allocation of state savings to private entrepreneurs are made clearer when the process is contrasted with that of allocating a raw material controlled by government. If a government is the sole importer of, say, cement, it need not concern itself with the details of the uses to which it will be put: it can sell the cement to the highest bidders. It is different where the state is the sole (or predominant) supplier of capital. Capital (i.e. investible funds) cannot be auctioned to the highest bidders, since in the nature of things the lender cannot insist on payment on the spot. The lender has to consider the credit-worthiness of the borrower and also the probable results of the loan on his prospects. The administrative process is quite different. Further, if an aspirant borrower is not given funds he has few other sources to which he can turn when there is a heavy programme of compulsory saving. The government is most unlikely to allow a borrower to re-lend to a previously rejected borrower, since this may upset the lender's original calculations. In the case of the distribution of cement this consideration is irrelevant, and a buyer can be allowed to re-sell his purchases to a user who develops a more urgent need of supplies.

more spectacular kinds of investment, particularly those which
produce political dividends.   One may also reasonably expect
a bias in favour of large-scale undertakings and units of production, and of more capital-intensive methods of production,
since these are apt to be considered as evidence of progressive-
ness.   The wasteful use of savings, whether this is deliberate
or accidental, is particularly onerous in economies in which
capital is, by definition, at a low level.[1]

Compulsory saving through budget surpluses encourages
another form of waste.   Economy in the organisation and
running of government departments is difficult to enforce
when it is well known that there is no stringency in the government's finances.   A portion of what was intended to be a
budget surplus may disappear in extravagant administration.
It is, of course, possible to earmark the proceeds of particular
taxes for development; but this is no lasting safeguard, and
the raiding of specially earmarked funds for general purposes
is a common occurrence in fiscal history.

§ 5. Inflation and Capital Formation.   In the preceding sections
we considered the use of budget surpluses (that is a policy of
having tax revenues in excess of government spending on
current account) to accelerate the rate of savings in under-
developed economies.   We turn now to the use of budget
deficits as a means of raising the rate of capital formation.   In
more general terms the question is whether inflationary financial
policies can contribute to economic development by directing
a larger share of real resources into productive investment.[2]

Budget deficits need not be inflationary; they are not neces-

[1] A. Sturmthal, *art. cit.*, p. 200, has suggested that the deliberate concentration of 'scant resources in capital and skilled manpower' may have
a demonstration effect favourable to capital formation and growth in an
economy as a whole; the successful results of conspicuous investment
projects may encourage investment elsewhere.   He points out, however,
that 'excessive concentration' of resources in a few sectors is likely to
discourage enterprise in other sectors.   It may be added that where the
concentration is the result of removing potential savings from the rest of
the economy, the demonstration effect is likely to be of little avail.

[2] An interesting discussion of inflation as a mechanism for promoting
development will be found in W. A. Lewis, *op. cit.*, Chapter V.

sarily inflationary if resources are set free by the private sector without these having to be bid away by the offer of higher prices. An important special case arises when unemployed resources are available in combinations appropriate for the increased output which is planned. However, the problem of accelerated development in under-developed economies is complicated in that, in general, essential resources for increasing output are not unemployed, that is they are not freely available with no social opportunity costs attaching to their use in the new undertakings. In these economies there is no problem of unemployed or under-employed equipment, machinery and stocks of circulating assets, or of idle entrepreneurs and managers. The situation is not altered basically even if, as in some under-developed countries, there are unemployed or under-employed unskilled workers, since the co-operant resources are lacking. In short, deficit finance in under-developed areas tends to be inflationary finance.

The process of inflation brings about a redistribution of real income unless all prices and incomes rise proportionately and at the same time. Those who derive their incomes from the sale of goods and services, the prices of which lag behind the rest in the general upward movement, become relatively poorer; conversely, others become relatively better off if the prices of the goods and services sold by them lead in the inflationary race. The volume of saving rises if the marginal rate of saving of the gainers is greater than that of the losers; this is true even if the real national income remains unchanged. The increase in saving brought about by inflation is sometimes termed forced saving. Advocates of deficit finance and controlled inflation argue that the beneficiaries of inflation include a large proportion of industrialists and traders who are assumed to have a propensity to save and to invest above the average for the community; and it is argued further that the government can also benefit from the process. Moreover, moderately rising prices are held to encourage industrial and commercial investment.

In principle it is indisputable that in appropriate circum-

stances the process of inflation, particularly if it is kept within
sober bounds, may bring about a redistribution of income in
favour of individuals and classes who are likely to save a larger
part of the income transferred. But this does not mean that
an inflationary financial policy is easily managed and controlled or a ready panacea for the low capital and productivity of
backward economies; its possibilities are readily exaggerated,
and its dangers and disadvantages minimised or neglected.
It is true, too, that in the past periods of credit expansion
and rising prices have sometimes been periods of business
expansion and large-scale investment;[1] but equally there are
instances where large-scale capital formation has occurred in
periods of stable prices.[2] Simple cause-and-effect relationships
are not likely to provide illuminating general explanations of
the complex facts of economic history.

Assessment of the merits of inflationary finance as a source
of capital in under-developed countries will depend partly
on one's political outlook, and also on the specific conditions of particular countries in such matters as the ability
of the social fabric to stand the strain of inflation, the productivity of the capital created by the process (including the time-

[1] A careful discussion of inflation and economic growth in pre-war
Japan will be found in W. W. Lockwood, *op. cit.* Summing up, the author
observes (pp. 300–1): 'Through these decades, in short, the demand for
funds for investment and war spending chronically exceeded the sums
made available from existing incomes through voluntary savings and taxation. Given the acquiescent attitude of the authorities toward credit
expansion, the result was a more or less persistent tendency to inflation,
which periodically got out of hand and culminated in a slump. On the
whole, however, the boom periods predominated. They were often
wasteful, producing speculative excesses and distortions. By chronically
inflating profit margins, moreover, they relieved producers of the incentive
otherwise present to improve methods and cut costs. Yet, looking at the
troubled experience of other countries in this field, one is inclined to
conclude that the monetary mechanism was employed fairly successfully
in pre-war Japan to speed the transition to industrialism, to build the
power of the State, and to accelerate the growth of real income and
productive capacity.'

[2] The example of England in the eighteenth century is discussed in
T. S. Ashton, *op. cit.*, pp. 199–200. The conclusion is reached that 'the
eighteenth century offers little in support of the thesis that forced savings
were a major influence in the rise of large-scale industry'.

lag before the larger volume of consumer goods becomes available), and the prospects of capital formation in the absence of inflation. Academic economists who belong to a class which is generally adversely affected by inflation may be apt to under-estimate the advantages of inflationary finance; and we realise that we may suffer from this bias. But allowing for this as best we can, we still think that the scope for inflationary finance as a source of capital formation in under-developed countries is severely limited. People with fixed money incomes—whether they are land-owners, rentiers or wage-earners—form a relatively small class in most of these countries. All other incomes are derived from the sale of goods and services, the prices of which are likely to change in harmony with general price movements. Inflation by itself therefore cannot achieve significant transfers of purchasing power to the government or to any group which is believed to have a special capacity for saving and investment. More-over, the urban wage-earners are likely to be politically influ-ential. If their wages or earnings lag appreciably behind the cost of living, there may be political trouble or tension; if their wages are adjusted promptly and frequently, the possi-bility of transferring real income is reduced further.[1]

The general economic and social disadvantages of inflation should be set against the limited benefits (in terms of capital

[1] Strong trade unions and organised machinery for collective bargaining may sometimes cause the upward adjustment of wage rates to lag behind the rise in the general level of prices in a period of inflation. The in-evitable delay in negotiations, or the fact that there necessarily are inter-vals between successive negotiations, may cause the wage rates to be some-what below market equilibrium rates. At the same time the organisation of employers for collective bargaining may have the effect of restraining individual firms from paying openly more than the negotiated wage rates. A time lag in the adjustment of wage rates is said to have been significant during the post-war inflation in Mexico; this is discussed by A. Sturmthal, *art. cit.*, p. 193.

During an inflation wages may rise more rapidly in the absence of effective machinery for collective bargaining. This influence is reflected in a letter from the secretary of the British Overseas Employers' Federa-tion in *The Times*, 6 April 1956, which refers to 'many instances of lack of co-operation between employers in the Caribbean forcing up wages and failing to bring about a responsible procedure for collective bargaining'.

formation) which are possible in ideal conditions and with wise management of the currency. The personal incidence of the transfer of resources tends to be haphazard and unrelated to capacity to bear the strain of forced saving, and it may give rise to social and political discontent. Inflation often also encourages the wasteful use of resources. Again, it discourages the taking of long views by individuals and firms by weakening the sense of continuity in economic life. It is also likely to cause difficulties in the balance of payments. Moreover, a policy which sets out to be a policy of controlled and limited inflation does not always remain so, especially because in under-developed countries political pressures and administrative weakness are likely to undermine the necessary restraint of the monetary authorities. A general loss of confidence in the stability of the currency may convert an apparently controlled inflation into a runaway process which may have destructive social, political and economic results.[1]

The control of the supply of money is an important function of government, and its management in the interests of economic development in under-developed countries seems to be sufficiently complex without imposing upon it the further hazardous task of raising the flow of national savings. In particular, efficient management of the monetary system may provide the most effective cushion against the impact of unsettling and disturbing influences such as violent changes in the flow of incomes (caused, for example, by changes in the volume and prices of exports), all of which make it more difficult to develop a sense of continuity in economic life.

[1] It may seem possible to modify or control some of the adverse effects of inflation by means of direct or physical controls, such as restrictions on imports, price control and rationing. But in general such controls are inefficient and administratively expensive in under-developed countries. Import controls strengthen the position of established traders in markets which often are already highly concentrated; they also give rise to riskless profits unless there is effective price control. Consumer rationing may not be possible when illiteracy is widespread; and even with many inspectors price controls may not be effective for most retail sales. When price control is effective for wholesale transactions, riskless profits accrue to subsequent intermediaries. Such situations may produce political and commercial tension.

CHAPTER XIV

SPECIFIC POLICY MEASURES AFFECTING AGRICULTURE

§ **1. Compulsory Revision of Contracts and Prescription of Contract Terms.** In many parts of the under-developed world there is heavy pressure of population on the land which, with existing techniques of production and low levels of capital, gives rise to low average real output and consumption per head. There are usually large numbers of cultivators working smallholdings, either as owners or as tenants, with low real returns. In such conditions the rents paid by tenant-cultivators tend to be high in relation to gross output or the tenants' net income, and many owner-occupiers farming on a small scale tend to be in debt, often incurring heavy interest charges. In these circumstances, government intervention is frequently proposed. Thus it is suggested, for example, that rents or debt charges should be scaled down, or that land should be transferred into the hands of the small-scale tenant cultivators.

These proposals seem to have two different aims: the redistribution of wealth, and increased efficiency in agricultural production. We are not concerned here with the former aim. If redistribution of wealth is thought desirable, this should be undertaken in accordance with some clearly defined principle and on criteria such as wealth or income rather than at the expense of politically unpopular but otherwise arbitrarily-selected groups such as land-owners or creditors; some land-owners and creditors have lower incomes than those who advocate their expropriation.

Closer examination and analysis are necessary before the merits of the proposed reforms can be assessed as instruments of agricultural improvement. But in general it is doubtful

209

whether they are likely to bring about significant net benefits, and they may even reduce agricultural output and efficiency. The proposed reforms concentrate on symptoms rather than on underlying influences and conditions, and hence are not likely to offer long-run benefits. The main reason for the low average incomes in the so-called over-populated areas is the abundance of unskilled or semi-skilled labour relative to the available land and capital, and often especially to land improved by the embodiment of capital. Improvement for the majority depends ultimately on increasing the volume of capital and skill, thus changing the ratio between the various classes of resources. The measures of reform now being examined merely alter the institutional framework without influencing the availability of resources, and therefore do not get to the root of the problem. The appropriateness of this diagnosis is confirmed by the fact that the reforms concern both landless tenants and small-scale landed proprietors: the institutional setting—tenancy or ownership—does not by itself modify the nature of the problem, but only the details of the reform reflecting the particular symptoms which come to light in it—high rents in one case, and indebtedness in the other.[1]

The basis of the suggestion that rents should be scaled down or land given to tenants appears to be that land-owners in the countries in question render no (or inadequate) services, but simply (or primarily) own land and collect rents; and that this is inequitable, reduces agricultural production by weakening or removing the incentive of the cultivator to improve his methods, and also makes him less able to afford improvements. Broadly similar arguments are advanced in support of the proposal to scale down debts, though in this connection it is usually conceded that the creditors have at one time made resources available to the debtors.

[1] Our general conclusion applies to an economy in which the participants have personal freedom, particularly in respect of contract and of movement. Other considerations are likely to apply where tenants or cultivators are subject to feudal restrictions or similar restraints.

It is possible that the reduction of rents may encourage tenants to greater effort and the exercise of initiative. The result in terms of increased output will depend partly upon how far tenants were previously discouraged by the level of rents and partly upon the availability of opportunities for additional productive effort. Clearly no generalisations can be made on these points. Thus the relationship between the level of rent and the tenant's effort and initiative is not as simple as the suggestions for compulsory reduction of rents imply. If the rent is expressed in the form of a fixed sum, revised from time to time, and if there is contractual provision requiring the landlord to compensate an outgoing tenant for unexpired improvements, a high level of rent has no necessary disincentive effect. The tenant has every reason to secure the highest net output from his land, since he then maximises his income net of rent. Against this it may be suggested that the landlord would raise the rent at the first opportunity should a tenant succeed in raising the productivity of the land. But this overlooks the fact that the level of rents is determined by the supply and demand conditions for land in general, and that this is the major factor determining the level of rent which could be demanded from any particular tenant for a particular piece of land. Hence the landlord will at best be able to secure only a small part of the higher annual product resulting from a particular tenant's efforts and improvements, the size of which is determined by the cost and inconvenience to the tenant of moving to another property.[1]

It may be argued, further, that the mere fact of a heavy payment of rent demoralises the tenant with adverse effects on his effort and exercise of his initiative. This possibility

[1] The position may appear to be different where the rent takes the form of a proportion of the output. Such arrangements have a disincentive effect, somewhat analogous to that of a proportional income tax as contrasted with a poll tax. This is a disadvantage of proportional rents. But it would seem that in the opinion of those concerned, both landlords and tenants, it is offset by the advantages of a flexible rent payment. In some cases it may also be a transitional form of economic relationship, transitional between feudal or similar relationships and contractual relationships in an individualistic society.

cannot be denied, but it would be difficult to establish its general importance. Moreover, the compulsory reduction of rents may even reduce output, especially in the short run; this would occur if tenants prefer to take out the windfall gain partly or wholly in the form of more leisure.

We have considered the possible favourable effects of a policy of scaling down rents. But there are disadvantages to be set against these. The compulsory reduction of rents (and the compulsory waiving of claims to arrears), if effective, penalises a particular way of using a resource. It discourages the division of labour between those who are more efficient in managing or improving land, and those who are more efficient as cultivators unburdened by problems of the ownership and management of land. It also discourages arrangements between those who have capital which would flow into agriculture in the acquisition and improvement of land provided they did not also have to cultivate their land, and others who are good cultivators but do not dispose of the capital to acquire or improve the land for their purposes. The compulsory reduction of rents, or the prospect of such a measure, inhibits economically efficient arrangements, and obstructs the best combination of land, labour, capital and administrative ability; in particular situations it will work against the long-run interests of many of the small-scale cultivators who are supposed to be helped. In practice, moreover, it is likely that a statutory reduction of rents would have to be coupled with considerable restrictions of the right of owners to evict tenants. Such restrictions give a partial or qualified freehold to the tenants. This reduces the mobility of cultivators, and makes it difficult, if not impossible, for landlords to make changes so as to put their land at the disposal of those best able to use it. At the same time the freehold is not complete, and the more ambitious or wealthy tenants may not feel sufficiently secure to sink their own efforts or capital into improving the land.

The outright expropriation of large land-owners in favour of their tenants also gives the beneficiaries a breathing-space

and easement which may yield higher output. But the disadvantages are likely to be even greater than those attaching
to the scaling-down or pegging of rents. In particular, the
disregard of property rights is likely to weaken confidence
throughout the economy at large, and to discourage capital
formation, notably in forms which cannot be readily concealed. It will discourage particularly capital investment in land,
except by owner-occupiers operating on a small scale.   Many
of these—particularly the beneficiaries of the expropriation—
will not have the resources for carrying out improvements; and,
in addition, the unit of land appropriate for certain improvements may be larger than the holding of the typical owner-
occupier.

These measures will affect agricultural output especially
unfavourably when many landlords are prepared to undertake
improvements and have the means for doing it, when the
individual tenants are poor, when highly-productive improvements may have to be effected on a large scale relative to the
average holding capable of being worked by a family, and when
many of the landlords also are cultivators (or have been cultivators) who have reinvested their savings in land and are particularly well-equipped to know in what way and by whom
their land will be used most advantageously.   It may be noted
that measures for transferring ownership of land or for reducing rent cannot be operated selectively by qualitative criteria,
either in respect of landlords or of tenants.[1]

Broadly similar conclusions apply to compulsory measures
for the reduction or elimination of debts, or for the reduction
of interest rates in current loan contracts.   These measures
may give debtors some respite and leave them with a larger
income for undertaking improvements.   But apart from considerations of equity and the general implications of officially-

[1] We deliberately exclude from consideration here certain institutional
changes sometimes discussed in the context of land reform, notably col-
lectivisation, whether to reduce inequality of wealth or to secure more
efficient large-scale operations.   Compulsory collective farming is an
aspect of Soviet economies, and for reasons already indicated we do not
discuss these in this volume.

sponsored repudiation of contracts, these measures discourage future lending by adding to the risks faced by the lender, and so reduce the supply of agricultural credit which is an essential ingredient of an agricultural economy which has developed beyond the stage of subsistence production. This reduction in the supply of capital inevitably curtails output.

The preceding conclusion applies also to the official prescription and enforcement of maximum interest charges in all new loans to agriculturalists.[1] This is so even when the lenders would otherwise secure a high rate of return on capital invested in such loans. The adverse effects will be absent only when the supply of credit to the agricultural sector is unresponsive to reductions in the rate of return over the relevant range. But since loan capital is generally non-specific, the lender almost invariably can put his capital to use elsewhere, so that the supply of capital to agriculture is likely to be elastic.

The supply of funds even from lenders with some effective monopoly power is likely to have an appreciable degree of elasticity. Even when lenders are exercising monopoly power the general prescription of lower interest charges, if it is enforced, curtails the volume of lending, and deprives some agriculturalists of credit which they would be willing to accept on terms more favourable to the lenders.[2] The degree of elasticity of supply reflects largely the accessibility and profit-

[1] There is, however, a difference between the effects of official revision of existing contracts and those of official regulation of the terms of new contracts. A party to an existing contract can be relieved of some present or contingent liability, and to that extent his position is improved. The regulation of the terms of new contracts does not have this effect.

[2] Some producers are still able to secure loans if the permitted maximum rate is higher than the rate at which lenders in a free market would be prepared to lend to them in particular; they are not affected by the measure. Those affected are the producers whose circumstances are such that no one would extend credit to them at the prescribed rate, though some lenders would be willing to do so at higher rates. It is conceivable that some of those who are deprived of credit would be willing to enter into contracts on terms appreciably more favourable to lenders than those officially prescribed; the demand for loans may be very inelastic because capital is urgently needed, possibly for highly productive purposes, or possibly to satisfy a pressing demand for consumer goods or services.

ability of alternative employments for the capital. Thus the supply of credit will be more elastic when the prescribed maximum affects only small-scale loans to agriculturalists than when it covers loans to all categories of borrower. But even in the latter situation the supply will be affected to the extent that the monopolist owners of the capital can use it profitably in their own enterprises or in investment in foreign countries, or that they prefer to consume it rather than invest it when loans are less remunerative.

However, the elasticity of supply of capital from a particular lender over the relevant range may be small, or even zero, when he exercises effective monopoly power and when the returns on small-scale loans to agriculturalists materially exceed those on the most profitable alternative investments; that is when his returns include a surplus (a rent) above the minimum returns which are necessary to elicit the supply of capital. It may seem that in these circumstances the enforcement of maximum interest charges could transfer the rent element from lender to borrower without affecting the volume of lending. This conclusion is formally correct. But the relevant situations are not likely to be frequent. Moreover, even if they were common, in practice the general enforcement of maximum interest charges would nevertheless affect adversely the supply of credit. This would be so because a general policy of prescribing interest rates could not allow for differences in the rent element in different transactions, that is for differences in the position of individual lenders and of individual borrowers. A prescribed rate might not reduce the supply of credit from a particular lender; but it would affect that from others with less effective monopoly power or with easier access to alternative investment opportunities. Similarly, even if all lenders were in the same position, a maximum interest charge which would not deprive a particular borrower of credit would nevertheless deprive others to whom no accessible lenders would be willing to lend at the prescribed rate, but whom they would be prepared to accommodate on more favourable terms.

It may be said that the transfer of some of the monopoly profits or rent elements in loan transactions from lender to borrower is desirable even when the volume of credit is reduced, and especially when the reduction is comparatively small. But the special conditions in which a general prescription of interest charges may secure material benefits to some borrowers without curtailing total credit appreciably are almost certainly rare in practice. Moreover, the redistribution of income effected by the prescription of interest rates is largely haphazard, and much of its incidence may fall on potential borrowers who are denied access to capital though they could use it productively. Our consideration of the difficulties of assisting the agricultural sector as a whole even when there is some effective monopoly in the supply of capital reinforces the general conclusion that improvement of the conditions of the rural population depends primarily on the growth of the economy and on favourable changes in the proportions of available resources; within this general framework the position of particular borrowers can best be improved by an increase in the number of independent sources of capital available to them.

Thus there is no general case for the official prescription of maximum interest charges. This conclusion applies also to the prescription of maximum rents or of other terms of contracts, such as that of the minimum length of tenancies or standard terms governing compensation for improvements made by tenants. Flexibility in contract terms is desirable to suit the particular needs and situations of different pairs of contracting parties, and they are best able to judge the appropriateness of the terms in each case in the light of all other opportunities available to them. The landlord has a continuing interest in seeing that his property is used to best advantage, and therefore in devising terms of contract which bring this about. For example, landlords tend to avoid short tenancies if these have the effect of creating uncertainty in the minds of tenants, and so lead to practices which reduce the net yield of the property and hence the rents to be expected from it. Similarly, a landlord and a tenant are likely to settle without difficulty the financial aspects of an improvement which both agree to be desirable.

Throughout this section it has been stated or implied that it is the availability of alternatives which safeguards the interests of tenants and rural borrowers. However, in practice some producers may through ignorance, immobility or lack of skill in negotiation fail to secure the return warranted by the underlying conditions of supply and demand. But broad measures such as the official prescription of maximum rents, rates of interest and contract terms generally are crude devices for preventing such occurrences; and indeed, as we have shown, they can seriously affect the level of output, its prospective growth and the position of many producers. One way to help those who might fail to make the most of their market environment is to improve their understanding of this environment and to make them aware of their opportunities and rights. This is an aspect of education, which, in the context of agriculture, is considered in the next section.

§ 2. Agricultural Extension Work. Agricultural extension work is often an important government measure for improving agricultural output and raising incomes. In many underdeveloped countries output could be increased with little or no additional capital expenditure by the use of new techniques which may be quite simple and would be adopted by many farmers or peasants if they knew about them. The use of disease-resisting or high-yielding strains, the control of the mating of domestic animals, the performance of simple veterinary tasks, bud-grafting and inexpensive conservation practices, are examples of methods which may result in economic increases in productivity. Nevertheless, though in many cases these methods may yield a rich return to the farmers, it may not pay private organisations to develop the techniques to a practicable stage and sell the knowledge to them. The costs of collecting fees are high where farming operations are on a small scale; moreover, much of the benefit of private demonstrations or sale of knowledge is likely to accrue to third parties who may not be willing to pay and with whom the suppliers of the services are not in a contractual relationship. Hence the major part of the work has to be provided by the state largely without specific charges and financed out of government revenues.

The content and scope of agricultural extension services do not lend themselves to formal analytical discussion, and we confine ourselves to one particular aspect of the subject. This is the danger of confusing standards of technical efficiency with those of economic efficiency. There is no point in recommending or demonstrating methods and techniques which may be efficient in terms of some technical standard but are wasteful in terms of the use of scarce resources and inappropriate at the level of technical achievement of the local population. The possibility of confusion is likely to be greater if the officers in charge of the work are more familiar with conditions and techniques in more advanced countries, or where large-scale farming (estate) operations are practised side by side with small-scale peasant production. In both situations there may be a tendency to apply inappropriately the lessons of one situation to another in which the availability of factors of production is quite different. Emphasis on unsuitable methods may result in wasteful farming and it also tends to discredit extension work as a whole.

It seems desirable to acquaint farmers with methods for raising the quality of their produce so that they may judge whether it is worth their while to incur the additional effort or expense to secure the higher value of better crops or livestock. Extension services can do much to widen the opportunities for production open to peasants, and improved quality of output may ensue without compulsion or restriction. In this it differs from the improvement in quality which can be brought about by such measures as the compulsory prohibition of the sale of certain grades of produce for which there is a market, or the prescription of grade differentials (in the prices paid to producers by statutory monopolies to whom they must sell) which are not related to market values. The former measure must raise, and the latter measure is very likely to raise, the average quality of marketed produce. But the improvement in quality is achieved at the expense of a wasteful misdirection of effort to the net disadvantage of producers and of the economy as a whole; the measures either encourage un-economic expenditures and efforts or discourage economic expenditures and efforts.[1] Where the restrictions on the sale of certain qualities relate to produce consumed in the country itself they may also deprive poor consumers of the opportunity of buying any of the produce at all.

§ **3. Conservation of Natural Resources.** Government authorities may influence the rate of utilisation of natural resources and their effective life by a variety of measures of conservation. They may regulate or control directly or indirectly (for example by tax provisions) the rate of utilisation of privately-owned resources, or they may withhold state-owned resources from development and exploitation by private users. Basically, the economic rationale for such intervention is that official views on future output, prices and costs differ from those of private users, and that it is thought that the official views are sounder.

As the appropriate or most productive rate of utilisation of a wasting asset is a matter of judgment, there are grounds for reasonable differences of opinion;[2] but there is at least a presumption that the private owners of exhaustible assets are likely to be particularly careful in the assessment of the factors on which the value of their assets depends. The case for government measures of enforced conservation is perhaps strongest where the owners of natural resources are not fully conversant with the necessary consequences of their decisions

---

[1] A detailed analysis is presented in our article 'The Economics of Marketing Reform', *Journal of Political Economy*, June 1954, which also reviews specific examples.

[2] These differences of opinion can be illustrated by the division of political opinion in Mexico between the view that exports of sulphur should be maintained as being a vital factor in currently securing foreign exchange, and the opposing view that Mexico should conserve its sulphur deposits because it is possible that sulphur will become more valuable when present sources elsewhere are exhausted.

concerning production and utilisation.[1]   Thus, if producers
are not aware of the dangers and losses to them of soil erosion
resulting from an over-intensive cultivation or stocking of their
land, it may be argued that restrictions on planting or control
of the frequency of planting or the number of head of stock
to be carried may be desirable in the interests of the producers:
they would have come to the same decisions themselves if they
had known all the circumstances.   But even here it can be
argued on the other side that the spreading of knowledge
would be as effective as compulsory conservation, and would
be more desirable on general grounds.   This counter-argu-
ment gains in force when it is remembered that the effects on
the land of some farming practices, particularly in under-
developed territories, are not scientifically established, and
that, moreover, the standards of the scientist are not final in
what is essentially an economic issue.

Government employees entrusted with the formulation and
implementation of conservation policy tend to have a vested
interest in the long life of the assets in their care, and this may
influence official policy.[2]   Again, officials concerned with
conservation policy often confuse technical or physical with
economic criteria.   This may stem partly from the fact that
the economic criteria cannot be reduced to simple formulae to
be applied objectively.   It is far easier to stipulate that no trees
should be felled for timber until they are x years old than to
regulate felling on the principle that no tree should be cut

[1] It is therefore perhaps most cogent when drastic changes in land tenure
are taking place.   The case for educative restraints in this type of situation
is considered in Chapter XII, section 6, above, and it may be applied to
conservation practices.

[2] Managers of private firms using wasting resources also tend to be
concerned with prolonging the life of the assets of which they are in charge,
and not solely with the maximisation of the value of the net returns to be
derived from them by their owners.   They may give undue weight to the
advantages of the postponement of the exploitation of the assets, and the
owners may have difficulty in seeing the desirability in their own interests
of altering the decisions suggested by their subordinates, since decisions
depend upon individual and subjective estimates or expectations of future
prices, costs and methods of production.   An uneconomic and socially
undesirable under-utilisation of resources may ensue.

down if the additional costs of prolonging its life are lower than the consequential addition to its value as timber.

There is no economic merit in conservation as such; its merit depends on particular economic circumstances. The fact that conservation is often treated as a problem almost outside the sphere of economics, and elevated to the status of an unchallengeable principle or objective in its own right, suggests that conservation in practice may lead to uneconomic use of natural resources.[1] No one would question that a mineral deposit should be exploited if this is profitable; the fact that the resource cannot be restored to its original form is rightly disregarded, and it is realised that by raising national output the use of the resource enables capital to be accumulated in other, different forms. Equally, there is no case for any requirement that users of land or forests should restore to their resources what they have removed. It is in the interests of the owners to conserve if the conservation of assets seems to be economic and profitable.[2] If it is not profitable or economic to do so, it is better that the capital should be transferred to more productive activities in other forms and perhaps in other sectors of the economy.[3] The term soil-mining is usually used

[1] The widespread bias in favour of compulsory conservation contrasts oddly with the generally strong feeling against the so-called speculator who buys land, does not cultivate it (or does not cultivate it fully), but holds it in the expectation that it will become more valuable later. The speculator conserves; his decision not to cultivate depends upon his judgment about the costs and proceeds of cultivation, and his wish to have his land available for sale or development when expedient.

In inflationary conditions speculation in land is likely to increase, and the speculator is often able to make quick money profits. This often provokes hostile criticism of speculators, which, however, should more sensibly be directed against the monetary authorities.

[2] Institutional arrangements in the ownership of land may have distorting effects. An example is discussed in Chapter IV, section 4, above.

[3] There is no moral or economic command that a person should maintain the real value of his capital or that he should enlarge it. A person may judge it better to convert part of his capital into resources for consumption. However, where the growth of the economy is regarded as an important aim of policy it may be necessary for the state to encourage attitudes favourable to capital formation. Our present point is that measures are likely to be misguided if they compel the maintenance or accumulation of capital in specific physical forms.

in a pejorative sense. The practice of soil-mining would be assessed more realistically if the analogy of the economics of the mining of mineral deposits were taken into account. Reliance on mining or extractive industries as a source of current income always raises serious problems of national economic policy, since in the nature of things wasting assets do not last for ever, so that an important source of government revenue is essentially temporary. But these problems cannot be treated rationally on the assumption that it is desirable to maintain physically certain resources.

The case for deliberate conservation is weakest in a period of rapid change in scientific and technological knowledge. The value of particular natural resources may be reduced by the development of competing materials or competing sources, so that the expected long-term security of income may prove to be illusory. Thus Chile would probably have been better off if its natural deposits of nitrates had been exploited more rapidly before the commercial development of synthetic nitrates reduced their high value. Moreover, where the conserving country supplies a large part of total world supplies, its policy, whether by design or not, tends to raise prices which itself encourages the search for substitutes or new sources of supply.

The argument for official intervention in the conservation of resources in private ownership does not rest solely upon differences in the estimates of the state and the owners on future prices, methods of production and so forth. It may also be argued that the owners do not necessarily take into account all the consequences of the exploitation of resources. A rapid rate of exploitation of a mine or forest based on commercial considerations may provide a higher current level of employment; but it may entail an earlier and more serious adjustment than would be necessary if a slower rate of extraction were adopted using a smaller average labour force. The costs of the adjustment need not fall on the owners, who would therefore tend to ignore or underrate them; but their incidence on the economy as a whole might be no less real. This is one example of the possible divergence between private and social costs and benefits, a divergence which may be adduced, at least in principle, to justify a wide measure of government intervention in many economic activities. We have already considered this general issue.[1] It should be remembered, however, that the deprivation of current income and employment consequent upon an official policy of conservation is certain, while the expected eventual benefit in the form of reduced social costs is often uncertain and contingent, and its extent may be exaggerated since it cannot be known or be estimated easily.

§ 4. Promotion of Co-operative Enterprise.

The promotion of co-operation is often suggested as a major branch of government activity designed to raise the level of the economy, to promote economic growth and also to improve the position of peasant producers. We shall therefore discuss briefly the role of co-operative societies in this sphere, and also consider official policies towards them, policies which in practice range from non-interference to massive support.

The co-operative society is essentially a form of business organisation in which the people who supply its capital and organise its activities are also its suppliers and/or its customers. For instance, a marketing co-operative is an undertaking financed and controlled by its members; it is also an undertaking which supplies marketing services to its members as its customers. The co-operative member is both a part-owner and a customer of his society. It is this duality of role which is typical of co-operatives and serves to differentiate them economically from joint-stock companies or partnerships.

In general, economic or commercial services provided by co-operative societies are essentially the same as those supplied by private firms. This is true, for example, of the services of credit, consumer, marketing, transport or tractor co-operatives. Without any official assistance such an organisation may be viable and successful, since its members may find it

[1] Chapter XII, section 2, above.

more advantageous to use their society to supply their requirements than to have these satisfied by independent private
undertakings.   The advantages may stem from a variety of
sources.   A society may be efficient, or it may have seized
upon a commercial opportunity overlooked by private undertakings.   It may enter a branch of activity in which competition among private undertakings is weak so that there is
a ready demand for the services of a new independent supplier.
Moreover, some co-operators may prefer to deal with a
co-operative society not solely because they find that its prices
and terms of trading are satisfactory, but also because they
derive satisfaction from supporting an undertaking in which
they have a stake as part-owners and in which they are associated with others sharing common interests, common problems and a common background.   But whatever the precise
reasons for the successful operation and trading record of a
society, the fact of its success is its economic justification,
provided that the success is achieved without favours, financial
support and privileges which are denied its private competitors.
The co-operative nature of a society engaged in business does
not guarantee its success or provide it with a special formula
for efficiency, as the history of co-operation in all countries
amply shows.   From the strictly economic point of view
there is no special merit in co-operation, which is merely one
form of business organisation.[1]

Simple tests of the economic success or viability of a co-
operative society no longer apply when government intervention and assistance become significant.   This assistance may
take various forms: outright financial contributions or subsidised loans, preferential treatment in the allocation of controlled commodities for distribution, the provision without
charge of the services of special government departments, or

_____

[1] It is sometimes argued that a principal advantage of rural co-operative
credit societies derives from the knowledge of the borrowers' credit
status which enables societies to lend cheaply while they in turn borrow
at reasonable rates from commercial banks.   But the same possibilities
are also open to village moneylenders, who also know the credit status
of the villagers and can also borrow from commercial banks.

the use of co-operative societies as the sole channels for the distribution of official loans or of other forms of assistance to farmers.[1] A double handicap is imposed on the competitors of the societies if the funds for the support of the co-operatives are derived from taxes paid by private business.

When co-operative societies enjoy substantial government support, their economic performance cannot be rationally assessed. This applies even if the amount of direct and indirect government assistance can be measured, for a most important advantage of a policy of official support is the knowledge that more help can be expected from the familiar source, and that the government will not be in a position to refuse help in case of need, even if it might wish to refrain from helping. A policy of large-scale government support of co-operative societies in general, or of certain societies in particular, creates for government a contingent liability to continue the support, and to come to the aid of those societies which run into financial difficulties. This liability is particularly onerous when government support has been directed in favour of particular societies which have acquired large numbers of members as a result of this support. A large proportion of the inhabitants of a particular area may become largely dependent upon a particular society, and the ability of the government to stand aloof from its difficulties is impaired.

It is often suggested that co-operative enterprises should not be judged solely or mainly on the basis of their achievements as business enterprises. It may be urged that co-operation is socially and politically desirable because it encourages producers, for example, to be self-reliant, thrifty and ready to submerge individual interests for the greater good of a community of producers. It may also be said that participation in co-operation is economically desirable because it acquaints producers with the problems of markets and of business organisation, and so enables them to see their problems as

[1] All these methods have been used, on a large scale in the aggregate, to build up the co-operative movement in Cyprus, and in some other British colonies.

producers more intelligently in the larger setting of economic life; it also may widen the range of alternatives open to them.

There is some validity in these views, and this may justify government assistance in the form of providing an advisory service and technical assistance; thus it could maintain a corps of auditors to serve as a safeguard against abuse in the early stages of development. But these considerations are irrelevant when government assistance assumes such proportions and forms that it is better described as government participation. Co-operation then ceases to be a spontaneous outgrowth of a community of interests or of a desire for independence. Government assistance, and the promise and expectation of further assistance, undermine the self-reliance of the co-operators. Membership of a society comes to be prized largely because the society enjoys privileges and support which can only be shared by joining it. In many parts of the world the continuance of co-operative credit societies depends almost entirely on the availability to them, alone, of official funds on subsidised terms. Substantial official support does not generally promote the qualities which are so highly regarded in the literature of the co-operative movement and in its philosophy. On the contrary these qualities become subordinated to others which are in many ways their opposites, especially the ability to secure political influence and administrative privileges.

The discussion has so far dealt with situations in which co-operative enterprise is an alternative to private enterprise. There is, however, a sphere of activity in which, in principle, co-operative societies may be able to perform desirable services which cannot be supplied by private firms or individuals. This concerns activities in which, in the nature of things, benefits are conferred indiscriminately over the members of a group (for example, the inhabitants of a valley), so that private firms or individuals may not be able to exact full payment for the services they supply, and therefore may be unwilling to undertake otherwise economic investments. An individual producer may be loath to spend money on pest control or soil conservation if part of the benefit accrues without charge to his neighbours, and even more so if his efforts are frustrated by their carelessness or neglect. These difficulties may conceivably be overcome by a co-operative society which embraces all the producers in the group, and the factors which inhibit expenditures and efforts by private firms or individuals may be dealt with effectively. In practice there are great difficulties in the way of establishing such societies. But it is relevant to the policy of government support for the co-operative movement that there is a wide area for co-operation in which co-operative endeavours do not restrict the activities of individual producers or private firms but complement them, and in which they can also serve as an alternative to direct government action in such matters as local pest control or soil improvement schemes which can be important for rural prosperity.[1]

§ 5. Compulsory Co-operation. Thus in our view the role of the state in fostering the co-operative movement should be limited. It need hardly be added that we consider a policy of so-called compulsory co-operation as undesirable and inimical to economic growth. In compulsory co-operation monopoly powers are conferred on a designated producers' co-operative society, so that producers of the controlled product have to join it.[2]

The granting of a statutory monopoly to any economic organisation amounts to a denial to its customers of access to alternatives. In activities such as marketing or simple processing of agricultural produce (for example in the operation

[1] The possibilities of voluntary co-operative action can be illustrated by that of cotton growers in California who 'themselves have agreed to a system whereby only varieties approved by the regional experiment station may be grown—for the very simple purpose of eliminating poor grades that might adversely affect output on adjoining fields of high-grade cotton'. V. Salera, 'The Free Economy and Economic Development', *Kyklos*, Vol. IX, 1956.

Other examples are provided by co-operative road-building and similar activities in rural areas in many under-developed countries.

[2] The conferment of privileges short of statutory monopoly powers affects membership in a similar way.

of abattoirs or cotton ginneries) there is not even the possibility of any advantage of economies of scale to set against the disadvantages of monopoly. The absence of competition removes a spur to efficiency and to the development of facilities to meet changing needs or the varying needs of different producers and consumers.   The variety, volume and distribution of services may be restricted.   This will be especially harmful in regions which are not fully permeated by the exchange economy, or in which the area of cultivation is extending.   Alternatively, the organisation may elaborate its services. This will raise its costs and its charges to customers, who may not be willing to pay them or may prefer to have less lavish but cheaper services.   The administrators of the monopoly may follow policies which are in the interests of the organisation as they see them, but not necessarily in the interests of the members; this is particularly likely in under-developed countries in which many producers are illiterate and easily overawed by authority.   The only way of expressing dissatisfaction with the quality or prices of the services is ruled out since there are no competing agencies.   Finally, as monopolists the organisations may be in a position to exploit consumers; this may be in the interests of the producers, but these cannot be identified with those of the economy as a whole.

These disadvantages apply also if the monopoly powers are given to a co-operative society. The special relationship between member and society is destroyed by the possession of monopoly powers, and the members' main method of control over policy is removed when competing firms or societies are eliminated.   A divergence of interests between co-operative management and co-operative members is as likely to emerge in large-scale co-operation as in any other type of organisation. Moreover, the interests of all producers of a particular product are not necessarily the same.   The producer-constituents of a marketing organisation are likely to have conflicting views on many matters.   These include the determination of prices for different grades of the same product; the question of whether each producer should bear his own transport costs or whether these costs should be averaged; the distribution of representation on the governing body; the timing of payments to producers; and the types of marketing service to be provided.   The specific policies adopted by an organisation are certain to affect some of its constituents less favourably than others; those who feel that their interests are adversely affected relative to those of their fellow-producers are unable to seek better treatment elsewhere.

§ 6. Price and Income Stabilisation.   Specialisation of economic activity and production for the market are major features or concomitants of economic growth.   More people become dependent upon conditions ruling in the particular markets for their specialised output, and they become exposed to market risks, a type of risk which is not present in a subsistence economy.   Price fluctuations in the markets in which their output is sold affect their incomes directly and create uncertainties. Wide and discontinuous fluctuations in the prices of cash crops tend to retard the development of a sense of continuity in economic life, which is desirable in the interests of sustained economic growth.   The adverse effects of price fluctuations are likely to be particularly serious where the impact of the money economy is sudden and rapid, a condition which even by itself raises difficulties, for example by aggravating the problem of replacing systems of communal land tenure by systems more appropriate to a money economy.

It does not follow from this that specialisation of productive effort to serve overseas or home markets should be resisted. It is likely that the risks peculiar to a more self-sufficient village, district, regional or national economy are more onerous than those attaching to specialised production for more or less distant markets; moreover, the higher productivity from specialisation not only raises standards of living and makes possible improved methods of production but also makes it possible to bear risks more easily.

The impact of price fluctuations on standards of living depends primarily on the ease with which the people in question can move their resources and activities out of or into a particular line of production. In general, individuals in less developed countries are less dependent upon particular markets than individuals in advanced economies because specialisation in skills and resources has not been taken so far; there is therefore a greater fluidity between production for subsistence and production for the market, between different lines of production or economic activities generally, and between the production of different cash crops.   The degree of dependence differs greatly for different groups of producers or types of output in the under-developed world.   It varies with such factors as the availability of alternatives, the cost of shifts in activity, and the institutional barriers, such as restrictive practices, impeding movements between activities.   But the degree of dependence cannot be inferred from such statistics as those of the relative importance of particular commodities in total national exports, or of the share of the proceeds of the sale of a particular crop in the incomes of the producers.

Nevertheless important benefits might accrue if it were found possible to even out the effects of wide and discontinuous fluctuations in prices and incomes in the agricultural sectors of under-developed countries without offsetting disadvantages.

Unfortunately, although stabilisation is often mentioned as an aim of agricultural policy and as an objective of marketing reform, the term has in fact become an omnibus expression with hardly any clear meaning or specific content.

Stabilisation may refer to prices or to incomes.   Variations in market prices often move inversely with the size of crops and may compensate (or may even over-compensate) for changes in output from year to year.   In these conditions producers' incomes may be destabilised if producer prices are stabilised, and may fluctuate more widely than if prices had not been stabilised.   Further, stabilisation of prices is meaningless unless the relation between the prices envisaged under stabilisation and the uncontrolled market prices is clearly indicated.   Quite obviously there is no difficulty in maintaining a producer price constantly and without variation at a point which is well below the market levels.   When a statutory monopoly controls the purchase of agricultural produce, the producers can be cut off from access to the market, and it is possible to divorce prices paid to producers from the prices obtaining in world markets and to keep them constant at a level below the lowest market price.   But whilst this is possible, it is hardly stabilisation in the interests of producers.

References to stabilisation often imply the maintenance of incomes at least at a certain level, that is the setting of a floor to incomes is envisaged; at other times the term is used to refer to the raising of incomes; and at yet other times stabilisation is used to mean the imposition of a ceiling to incomes, that is the prescription of a maximum level of prices or incomes.

The first requirement of price or income stabilisation is a clear definition of its meaning and objective which will make it possible to assess whether the objective itself is sensible (since not all conceivable objectives of stability are sensible) and subsequently to compare performance with promise.   In the past, schemes ostensibly devised to secure undefined stabilisation have developed into monopolistic devices for raising prices, or into instruments of taxation to the detriment of the producers whose interests were supposed to be advanced.

What is required is some arrangement for smoothing the prices or incomes received by producers which at the same time does not bring about greater disadvantages or produce more serious risks for the producers and the economy as a whole.   These risks and disadvantages are of various kinds. If the prices received by producers in one country are kept below world prices, the long-run position of the producers and the economy is jeopardised.[1]   Alternatively, if the stabilised

---

[1] The adverse effects are sometimes reduced by the profit-maximising tendencies of peasant producers.   They can smuggle the controlled crop into neighbouring territories where prices are not kept down.   This sort of smuggling, even of bulky products, has been common in West Africa and East Africa.

prices are kept above world levels, there is the risk of inducing an uneconomic maintenance or even expansion of output. Again, attempts at price stabilisation by restriction schemes are likely to encourage production in countries not parties to the agreement, as well as the search for substitute sources or products by consuming industries or governments. The so-called price stabilisation schemes operated by statutory marketing boards, for example in Africa and Burma, and also the pre-war international restriction schemes, for example in rubber and sugar, have had serious adverse long-run effects on the economies and producers without achieving any substantial measure of long-term price or income stabilisation.[1]

The smoothing of short-term fluctuations around the changing trend of market prices would seem a rational aim of stabilisation policy.[2] This would ensure that the price received by producers would not deviate significantly or very long from the world price, so that the appropriate adjustments to world market conditions in terms of expanding or contracting capacity and output could be made; at the same time there would be some averaging of prices over a short period of a few successive years. The difficulty of forecasting whether a change in world prices is a short term fluctuation or the beginning of a change in the direction of the trend is a principal practical difficulty of any scheme which gives discretionary powers to the stabilising authority. Loss of contact with the trend has serious adverse results in that subsequently it calls for wide discontinuous adjustments, while meantime the extension of capacity has been unnecessarily discouraged or encouraged. It therefore seems desirable that any stabilisation policy should be implemented in terms of a prescribed formula which reduces the area of discretion and also provides for the self-adjusting correction of any errors which may be made in the remaining area. This would also serve to

[1] Some of these schemes are described and analysed in P. T. Bauer, *op. cit.*, Part 5, and *The Rubber Industry*, London, 1948, *passim.*
[2] It may be preferable to smooth the income of producers received from the sale of a particular product; the principle is the same.

define the meaning of stabilisation in any particular instance
and to keep it distinct from other objectives of policy.[1]

It may be asked why the effects of fluctuating product prices
should not be dealt with by individual producers without the
intervention of compulsory statutory authorities. Why should
not the producer decide, when prices are high, how much he
should set aside as a reserve from which to draw when prices
are low? The answer must be given in two parts. It would
be highly desirable if each producer could be left to operate
his own stabilisation policy, if only because, first, it would
mean that decisions would then be taken in the light of individual circumstances, whereas an official policy of stabilisation
cannot take individual variations into account, and, second,
because producers would be aware at all times of price movements in the markets in which their products are sold. However, it is doubtful whether all producers, particularly in the
early stages of the development of the production of cash
crops, will have sufficient experience of the volatility of world
(or local) market prices to take into consideration the desirability of some measure of precautionary savings (in a readily
realisable form) in times of high prices. Unfortunate experiences may not only provoke exaggerated fears of production
for the market, but also require official action to alleviate the
distress of those who in ignorance were improvident. Hence
there is some case for official measures of price stabilisation as
a form of educative restraint. However, it would be more
in conformity with our general position if individual producers
were able to contract out of participation in official schemes of
price stabilisation so that the element of compulsion would be
absent. Some peasant producers do in effect operate their
own private income or consumption stabilisation plans without state assistance or compulsion.[2] But there are practical

[1] This is not the place to consider in detail how such a formula could
be devised. A formula is presented and examined in P. T. Bauer and
F. W. Paish, 'The Reduction of Fluctuations in the Incomes of Primary
Producers', *Economic Journal*, December 1952.
[2] The purchase in good years of additional quantities of textiles is an
example of this kind of stabilisation.

difficulties in the way of adding such flexibility to otherwise workable and useful schemes for short-term smoothing of prices and incomes.[1]

[1] A general criticism of the idea of compulsory stabilisation will be found in Milton Friedman, 'The Reduction of Fluctuations in the Incomes of Primary Producers', *Economic Journal*, December 1954.

CHAPTER XV

SPECIFIC POLICY MEASURES AFFECTING MANUFACTURING INDUSTRY

§ **1. Inter-relationships between Agriculture and Industry.** In the short run any government assistance given to one sector of the economy is at the expense of other sectors; in the short run each sector competes for limited resources against all others. In the long run the matter is not so clear-cut. The different sectors of an economy are inter-related, and growth in one sector may not only raise the level of resources available generally but may also more directly promote growth in other sectors. This is yet another example of a relationship which is competitive in the short run but complementary over a longer period; and it is the long run which is of prime importance when the objective is growth, particularly growth which in a sense can sustain itself.

In many countries in the past growth and improvement in agriculture have fostered and smoothed the way for the establishment and growth of industry. The leading industrialised countries of today were once predominantly agricultural, and economic historians have traced the various ways in which a prosperous and expanding agriculture formed the basis for the concurrent or subsequent establishment and expansion of manufacturing. The agricultural sector served in various roles. It provided a large part of the sustenance of the growing urban population. It also supplied a market for manufactured goods bought out of higher real incomes, a source of capital for industry (often through the medium of the capital accumulated by traders), and a source of foreign income to pay for imported capital goods for industry. In many of the present under-developed countries similar processes are at work today.[1] The role of agriculture in easing the way for manufacturing industry can also be illustrated by other effects of the expansion of cash crops in an economy previously at a subsistence or near-subsistence level. The extension of the production of cash crops has led to a growth of the exchange economy, acquainted large sections of the population with the ways of such an economy, given opportunities for those with entrepreneurial and administrative skills, and supplied government with substantial sources of revenue. All these developments are likely to promote the growth of manufacturing industry.

These considerations complicate the formulation of government policy, for, paradoxically, the best way for government to foster industrialisation may be for it to use more rather than less of its resources to encourage the enlargement of agricultural output and the improvement of agricultural techniques. No generalisation is possible in view of the diversity of conditions in under-developed countries and the differences in the level of development attained in each. However, it may be suggested with some confidence that in the earliest stages of development suitable assistance to agriculture may be the best safeguard for the establishment and growth of a viable industrial sector. The promotion of production for the market is likely to cause the least painful break with customary methods and habits and so to minimise social and political tension. Moreover, the additional technical skills necessary for manufacturing industry can be acquired more readily and with less disturbance when many people have become accustomed to the workings of an exchange economy, and latent entrepreneurial and administrative talents have been given time and opportunity for development.

[1] For example, in West Africa almost every successful manufacturing enterprise was started by merchants previously operating largely in the agricultural sector. In several under-developed countries rising incomes in agriculture have created a growing market for manufactured consumer goods and for tools and equipment, providing a basis for local manufacturing or servicing industries. This development is conspicuous in Malaya, for example.

§ 2. Advocacy of Industrialisation. In contemporary discussions of the problems of under-developed countries government-sponsored industrialisation is widely regarded as the key to economic development and the improvement of standards of living.

Much of the discussion is obfuscated by a prevailing *mystique* of industrialisation in terms of which manufacturing industry is regarded as a panacea for economic stagnation and poverty. In fact, manufacturing industry is simply one type of economic activity, and there is no special reason why this activity rather than some other activity should at any given time serve best to promote either the most efficient allocation of existing resources or the most rapid growth of resources. Moreover, especially in under-developed countries, sharp distinctions and contrasts between different occupations and branches of economic activity are often inappropriate. This applies especially when we consider processes through time rather than situations at any given time; we have already referred to the frequency with which traders enter manufacturing industry, and have also noted that growth in one sector may strengthen growth in another.

The advocacy of accelerated industrialisation is generally based on one or more of the following lines of argument. The more advanced countries generally have a significant proportion of their occupied population in manufacturing industry, while in under-developed countries the proportion so employed is comparatively small; relatively to their population the advanced countries produce a much larger proportion of the total output of world manufactures than do the under-developed countries. Within individual countries income per head generated in manufacturing production is generally higher than it is in agriculture. On the basis of this type of data it is argued that industrialisation will promote the development of under-developed countries. A second line of argument postulates that the growth of manufacturing industry is necessary in some countries to absorb the surplus population on the land and to put it to productive work. A further argument is that since at higher income levels people spend an increasing proportion of their income on non-agricultural products, development implies an increase in the proportion of people employed in occupations other than agriculture, and among these manufacturing is one of the most important.

These arguments do not stand up well to examination. But their critical examination does not imply that the development of manufacturing industry may not be at times an important element in economic development and even a necessity for it.

It cannot be inferred from the higher level of real income in more industrialised countries that they owe their advantage to the higher degree of industrialisation. It is quite possible, and is often obviously the case, that the higher level of real income and the higher degree of industrialisation are both results of the same set of causes or influences such as the possession of, or access to, cheap sources of power, rich mineral ores or some other natural resource, or of accumulated capital, skill, technical or managerial ability. In such circumstances the extent of manufacturing activity cannot be regarded as the cause of a high level of real income. Much the same applies to differences in the incomes of industrial and agricultural producers within the same country. The former may owe the higher level of real income to the possession of, or their access to, valuable resources, material or human. A statistical relationship alone does not establish a functional or causal relationship; still less does it indicate which is the cause and which the effect. A situation in which manufacturing plays a small part in the economy may be an inevitable stage in the process of economic growth in many countries, and may represent the best possible use at the time and for some time of available resources. It is absurd to judge the needs of an economy in a particular stage of development and with a particular collection of resources by reference to some of the characteristics of far wealthier, different and more mature economies.

The statistical relationship between real income or other

indices of development and the proportion of population engaged in manufacturing industry, moreover, is not as straightforward as is often suggested. For instance, in the United States only about a quarter of the occupied population is in manufacturing industry, a far smaller proportion than in the United Kingdom; yet real income per head in the United States is appreciably higher than in the United Kingdom. The United States, Canada, New Zealand and Sweden all have an appreciably larger proportion of their population in agriculture than the United Kingdom, and yet their real income per head is larger. In the United States it was not until towards the end of the nineteenth century that manufacturing industry became generally prominent in the economy; and not until 1910 did the size of the labour force employed in agriculture cease to increase. And it is especially noteworthy that it was not until 1941 that manufacturing employment exceeded agricultural employment in the United States, by which time it had for many decades been the richest or one of the richest countries in the world.

The presence of surplus population on the land is not conclusive evidence in favour of industrialisation. The distinction between cultivable and uncultivable land is not as clear as is often implied; we have already explained that official estimates of cultivable land are largely arbitrary, and that land classified as uncultivable is often unquestionably cultivable even with existing techniques. Moreover, land which is uncultivable in particular conditions can often be brought into cultivation with changes in technology or government policy, or with the expenditure of capital. Even in India, which is sometimes instanced as a country in which there is no remaining land suitable for cultivation, there are extensive areas described as cultivable waste which, in the opinion of some administrators, would be suitable for cultivation with modest capital expenditures. Thus it is possible that the surplus rural population could be absorbed more profitably and with less expenditure of capital in the extension of agriculture than in the establishment of new industries.

Again, it does not follow that the growth of industry is inevitable or desirable in every country even if it were true that at higher levels of real income people spend a smaller proportion of their incomes on agricultural products. In some circumstances it may be far easier and more economical for a country to procure for itself an increasing volume of manufactured goods by specialising on agriculture for export. No one who has advocated accelerated industrialisation has suggested that each district or region within a country should have its share of the enlarged industrial sector. Possibilities of profitable and productive specialisation and exchange are present in the international economy in the same way as they are present within a national economy.

Quite apart from these obvious considerations which stem from international exchange, even within a closed system the prospective pattern of economic activity cannot be inferred from the simple proposition that the income elasticity of demand for industrial products is higher than that for the products of agriculture. When applied to the whole economy, the concept of the income elasticity of demand raises problems of aggregation which affect any general proposition about changes in its average value with economic growth; and this applies particularly when relative factor prices and the distribution of incomes change. The proportion of the total national income spent on agricultural products is necessarily the average of the proportions of income spent by each member of the population as a whole. Even if the income elasticity of demand for these products of every member of the population is less than unity (which is by no means necessarily the case), so that each individual spends a smaller proportion of his income on these products as his income increases, the average proportion of income spent on these products may still increase if most of the increase in the national income accrues to people whose relative expenditure on these products is above the national average. Such a result is a likely contingency in under-developed countries where the income elasticity of demand for many of these products is still generally

high. There is no ground for assuming a unique relation between changes in national income and changes in the average
expenditure on agricultural products; still less between changes
in the national income and the proportions of the population
in agricultural and industrial occupations.

§ 3. **Terms of Trade and the Case for Industrialisation.** Considerations of international specialisation raise the question
of the terms of trade between agriculture and industry. Here
the advocates of accelerated industrialisation sometimes seek
support for their views in the contention that the terms of
trade are generally unfavourable to agriculture and that they
have shown a long-term tendency to deteriorate. However,
the former proposition is meaningless; terms of trade can be
favourable or unfavourable only by reference to the index
on a base period.[1] The second proposition (the secular
deterioration of the terms of trade of primary producers) has
been influential, but is also of little substance. Any conclusion
about the past movements of the terms of trade depends on the
choice of the base period; 1873, the year sometimes used, was
particularly favourable to primary producers. But the reasoning from statistics of changes in the terms of trade is open to
more fundamental objections.

Over any prolonged period such as, say, half a century or
more, the volume and composition of world trade are likely to
change so greatly that any particular base loses all significance.
This certainly has been the case over the period from the 1870's
to the 1930's, which is sometimes quoted. Moreover, within
that span of years the trend was not steady, and over considerable periods the direction of movement was opposite to that of
the change between the two terminal dates. Again, there were,
as there always are, great differences in the movement of the

[1] It might be said with some point that the terms of trade are generally
unfavourable to agriculture in the sense that industry lends itself more
readily to restriction of entry and of output then does agriculture, and that
this depresses incomes from agriculture compared to industry even for
the same degree of skill and risk. This possible effect on the terms of
trade raises issues different from those of the more widely canvassed aspects
discussed in the text.

prices of particular commodities; countries and producers are always interested in particular commodities and not in commodities in general. There were also far-reaching changes in the areas and methods of production, in the costs of production and transport, and in the quality of the products exchanged. When there are substantial reductions in input per unit of output, a deterioration in the commodity terms of trade is compatible with an improvement both in the factorial terms of trade and in the standard of living. To neglect this is to commit an error akin to that of confusing an index of the cost of living with an index of the standard of living.[1]

Even if the terms of trade had deteriorated in some meaningful sense over a specified period, it does not follow that this movement should be extrapolated into the future. In the absence of other information such a procedure is not logically justified. Statistics of levels and trends in the past are unsuitable as a basis for estimates of prospective movements in the terms of trade. There are some reasons for thinking that the terms of trade over the next few decades are more likely to move in favour of primary producers than to their disadvantage; but this is a conjecture.[2]

In short, statistics of the changing ratio of import and export prices provide a highly insecure basis for judging the wisdom of particular developments after the event; and even a deterioration in the relative prices of the relevant agricultural product(s) would not demonstrate that some alternative activity would have been more profitable in the circumstances. Again, an adverse trend in the terms of trade in the past does not establish that it will be profitable to transfer resources to other activities in the future.

[1] Professor P. T. Ellsworth has shown in an article in *Inter-American Economic Affairs*, Summer 1956, that much of the supposed deterioration in the terms of trade of primary producers between 1873 and 1937 (which is expressed in terms of the export prices of primary products against the export prices of manufactures) disappears when the reduction in transport costs is taken into account.

[2] The probable change in the terms of trade over the next twenty years is examined in H. G. Aubrey, *United States Imports and World Trade*, Oxford, 1957, Chapter 3.

§ 4. Some Economic Arguments for Assisted Industrialisation.

The arguments reviewed in sections 2 and 3 lack serious content. We now turn to more substantial arguments for government assistance to manufacturing industry.[1]

The classical argument against government assistance, in the form of tariff protection, direct subsidisation or guarantees, is that, *ceteris paribus*, this brings about a diversion of resources from more to less productive activities. An industry which cannot pay its way without assistance is *prima facie* less efficient or productive than other industries or activities which do not need support. The substantial case for state assistance to particular industries is based upon arguments which claim that in certain postulated conditions the diversion of resources brought about by government assistance is economically efficient but would not take place without assistance.

The infant industry argument for government assistance to particular industries is so well known that it does not need to be elaborated here. Its essence is that certain types of economic activity, especially industrial activity, may need government assistance in the early stages of their development, but that, when developed, they may be completely viable and require no continuing assistance. The logical validity of this argument is unassailable.[2] Unfortunately, it does not help in

---

[1] The difficulties of pioneering industrial development, especially the obstacles facing individual manufacturing enterprises in under-developed countries, and the implications of these for measures of policy, are major topics in the recent literature on under-developed countries. Useful discussions include the writings of W. Arthur Lewis, especially *The Theory of Economic Growth*, London, 1955, and his articles on industrialisation in the West Indies in *Caribbean Economic Review*, Vols. I and II; the writings of H. G. Aubrey, especially 'Deliberate Industrialisation', *Social Research*, June 1949, and 'Small Industry in Economic Development', *Social Research*, September 1951; and the *Report of the Committee of Enquiry into the Protection of Secondary Industries in Southern Rhodesia*. Salisbury, 1946.

[2] The fact that the assistance may never be withdrawn is no evidence that the infant industry argument has been misapplied. The infant industry may well have reached a stage where it could continue without such assistance, though naturally it would welcome the retention of the assistance and indeed press for it. It is also possible that while some parts of the industry or some firms in it would succumb if the assistance

identifying the particular economic activities or particular industries which merit assistance.

Another ground on which government assistance to industry may be advocated is essentially an extended version of the infant industry argument. It is suggested that assistance is necessary because of the absence in under-developed countries of common facilities such as developed transport and financial systems, a tradition of industrial skill, and other external economies which in developed countries are enjoyed even by new enterprises and those engaging in new lines of activity. For example, industrial establishments in many under-developed countries may have to use labour which is not used to conditions of regular work, but which nevertheless would after training and experience become accustomed to such conditions, with the result that labour costs might fall considerably. It may be objected, however, that the probable improvement in the labour force is a factor which the private industrialist can allow for in his calculations, and that the cost of training labour should be borne by him and not by the state; but the strength of this objection is impaired by the fact that the industrial employer cannot be certain of retaining the workers after they have been trained at his expense.

However, while the absence of external economies and the initial labour difficulties may not be in dispute, the argument based on them is not convincing. The argument simply expresses the fact that the economy is not highly developed, which is true *ex hypothesi*. But this does not imply that particular industries should be assisted; indeed, it does not provide any general guide to policy. In the circumstances government assistance involves the transfer of resources from other sectors

were withdrawn, other parts or firms could continue even without it though they might not have come into being without the original assistance.

On the other hand, the fact that a previously assisted industry continues after it has been deprived of assistance is not proof that the infant industry policy was economically sound. Assistance of infant industries involves costs, and, in a strict economic accounting, the policy is justified only if the industry on reaching manhood can, in effect, repay the state for the initial assistance and still be able to pay its way. Of course, in practice it may be difficult to ascertain the costs; but the principle is clear.

of the economy; and it needs to be established in each case that this is a movement from less productive to more productive uses, or that in some clearly-defined way it will promote the growth of resources more effectively. A general reference to some aspects of the existing low level of an economy, or to the desirability of promoting growth, or to the absence of external economies, provides no general justification for assistance to manufacturing industry; it does not even set up a general presumption in this direction since other sectors of the economy may likewise be hampered by obstacles to growth.

In some under-developed countries the wages of labour in industrial employment may exceed materially the social opportunity cost of the labour in question, that is the marginal product of labour in alternative uses. The combination of rural unemployment or under-employment and the extended family system may raise the supply price of labour in urban employments above the marginal product of labour in rural activities.[1] A policy of assisting urban industries to the estimated extent of this discrepancy may then be thought appropriate both to relieve the industries of charges which do not reflect the real measure of scarcity of labour, and also to provide viable opportunities for the employment of the surplus labour.[2] In principle such assistance would have to be reduced when the growth of the economy reduced the extent of the discrepancy.

The formal validity of this line of reasoning is not in question. But it cannot be taken as axiomatic that assistance to industry is the most economic way of handling the problem of rural unemployment; assistance to agriculture may in some circumstances yield better results.

The discrepancy between wage rates in industrial employment and social opportunity costs may arise in another way. It may result from minimum wage regulation or trade union action (approved or assisted by government) which raises

[1] Chapter VI, section 2, above.
[2] The classical objection to government assistance (stated on p. 243, above) does not apply here because the labour resources absorbed are assumed to have opportunity costs which are zero or at any rate less than their productivity in the assisted industries.

wage rates above the supply price of labour.[1]   It is, however, debatable how far this type of discrepancy should be regarded as an unalterable datum for other measures of government policy; in particular it is debatable whether this should serve as a ground for government assistance to industrial activities, even though the classical argument against such assistance does not apply here.   A policy of assistance, judiciously applied, could offset the excess of wage rates over supply price, which here measures the opportunity cost of the labour.[2]   There is therefore *prima facie* a case for government assistance in the interests of a more efficient allocation of resources.   However, the assistance required to sustain wage rates and employment would not be necessary if official policy had not raised wage rates in the first place.   There is a transfer of income from consumers or taxpayers to the favoured workers.[3]   This is a process of redistribution which may be undesigned or contrary to the avowed objectives of the general policy of redistribution; and, if the redistribution were both known and desired, it could be achieved more directly and efficiently

[1] Chapter VI, section 2, above.

[2] In practice the supply price itself may exceed the opportunity cost, for the reason indicated in the two preceding paragraphs.   But the two situations differ analytically and are kept apart in the discussion.

[3] It may seem that the case for government assistance stated in the two preceding paragraphs is weakened on the same grounds.   But there is a significant difference in that the reduction in the number of rural unemployed reduces the burden on the agricultural community by an amount which in the aggregate cannot be less than the aggregate burden of higher prices or increased taxes which, in the main, would be borne by the agricultural community.   (It will be recalled that the supply price of the unemployed rural workers is governed largely by their consumption as members of rural households.)   Of course, this compensation occurs only in the aggregate and not necessarily for each individual producer. But, in so far as the urban population is affected as consumers or taxpayers, there is a net gain to the agricultural sector and a net loss to the urban; in effect part of the cost of maintaining the rural unemployed is transferred to the urban population.

In the case discussed in the text, above, even if there is rural unemployment there is for the reason given a net loss to the agricultural community, since they have to pay more, whether as consumers or as taxpayers, to sustain employment than the costs of maintaining the affected workers idle or semi-idle on the land.   This follows from the condition that wage rates exceed the supply price of labour.

without operating through the fixing of wage rates. Government assistance to industry to achieve redistribution is undesirable both because it is often difficult to assess its incidence, and also because in practice it is difficult to judge the extent of assistance required for any particular purpose.

§ 5. Industrialisation and 'Balanced Growth'.

In section 4 we considered the case for government assistance to individual industries to achieve a more efficient use of resources or to industry generally to offset obstacles to the economic use of resources. In the present section we examine a rather different case, that in favour of official measures to achieve economically desirable balanced growth, in the sense of the simultaneous promotion of a group of selected inter-related branches of manufacturing industry.

This argument runs along the following lines.[1] In an unindustrialised economy there is little or no demand for manufactured goods. The market for a particular class of manufactured goods is inadequate to take the minimum output of an efficient manufacturing plant, and the workers in the plant itself are not likely to make good the deficiency because they would want to spend their incomes on a variety of goods and services and not only or mainly on the products of their plant. Therefore the plant will be uneconomic and will not be established. However, if several manufacturing plants producing a range of different goods are established together, the market for the products of each is enlarged and, in appropriate cases (that is where the plants and products are appropriately balanced), the demands of the workers in the group of plants would provide the missing market for the products of each of the plants. The co-ordinated investment in a balanced group of manufacturing activities is profitable whereas the isolated investment in any one establishment alone is unprofitable.

In some of the expositions of this argument it is assumed or

[1] The idea of balanced industrialisation is considered, for example, by P. N. Rosenstein-Rodan, 'Problems of Industrialization of Eastern and South-Eastern Europe', *Economic Journal*, June–September 1943; R. Nurkse, *op. cit.*, Chapter I; and W. W. Lockwood, *op. cit.*, p. 227.

stated that the labour to be employed in the new complex of industries would otherwise be unemployed. However, the argument is distinct from that of the case for assistance based on discrepancies between the supply price of labour and its social opportunity costs which was considered in the preceding section. The discrepancy between supply price and opportunity costs merely raises a presumption in favour of subsidising appropriately employment in all those activities in which employers have to meet the postulated higher supply price. It does not strengthen the case for selective assistance to the particular industries constituting a postulated balanced group.

Though the type of situation which is the essence of the argument for balanced growth is not inherently impossible, it is difficult to see why it should be important in practice. The economic benefits even in appropriate situations are likely to be limited. In the first place, it assumes a fairly elastic supply of output (especially of food) from non-industrial activities to meet the increasing demand in the enlarged industrial sector; and this is unlikely to be the case unless the industries absorb previously unemployed people on the land.[1] The establishment of the balanced group of industries is likely to raise both money and real costs, and so to reduce the economic possibilities of the scheme. Second, any industry which is able to compete in the export market would be established independently of schemes of balanced industrialisation; the case for balanced growth is predicated on narrow domestic markets. Therefore the only relevant situations concern industries which cannot export but which, when established as a group, can hold their own on the domestic market against competing imports. Moreover, in these situations the econ-

---

[1] This qualification is necessary because, to the extent that the labour force in the industrial sector consists of people who had previously been unemployed consumers in the rural areas, there need be no additional demand for food. This in turn has to be qualified, because there may nevertheless be an additional demand for food if the rural communities, relieved of the burden of supporting the unemployed, decide to consume more.

omies are limited to the costs of transport which are avoided when home production replaces imports.[1]

In view of the limited benefits likely to flow from the establishment of balanced groups of industries, and the heavy costs and risks of such schemes, the case for government intervention to encourage balanced growth could be justified only in very special circumstances and not simply by reference to a theoretical possibility which may be no more than a *curiosum*.

If in a particular country there is a situation in which a programme of balanced growth is likely to be economic, it nevertheless does not postulate planned public investment or government assistance to one or more of the constituent industries. The government could inform industrialists of the potentialities of the situation, and negotiate for the simultaneous establishment of each industry without direct participation, guarantees or assistance. On the postulated assumptions that the combined group of activities would be economic and that the government is aware of this, there is a presumption that the industries would in fact be established if the information is made available and is encouraging. Moreover, firms operating in under-developed countries or interested in them keep themselves and each other informed of emerging opportunities and frequently participate in joint or complementary ventures. If industrialists do not respond favourably to the case for co-ordinated industrialisation put before them, it is likely that the market possibilities have been overestimated and the costs and risks under-estimated. This presumption is strengthened by the known readiness of private undertakings to supply their own ancillary services and social capital where this is necessary for the development of profitable opportunities. The activities of the international oil-producing, mining and plantation companies are the more spectacular examples of a widespread phenomenon; the establishment of roads, harbours, transport services, generating plant, housing

---

[1] This is apart from advantages of the absorption of rural unemployed or the encouragement of infant industries, which, where present, raise other issues and do not require programmes of balanced growth.

estates, hospitals and schools by private business firms in many under-developed countries indicates that these firms, either singly or in groups, are quite willing to make large-scale conglomerate investments where market prospects are promising.

Support for the idea of balanced industrialisation derives in part from the belief that without it industrialisation (and development generally) in under-developed countries will not occur or will occur only slowly. But this is not borne out by the experience of most countries now industrialised, nor of countries such as Malaya, Hong Kong, South Africa and Brazil in which industries are growing rapidly without schemes to assist supposedly balanced groups of industries and, in some instances, without any significant assistance at all.

§ 6. **Industrialisation and Economic Diversification.** The dependence of certain economies on the production and export of very few agricultural or mining products is often adduced as a ground for government assistance to manufacturing industries. It may be argued that such dependence is precarious because adverse changes in the world market for one or a few commodities may undermine the economic position of the country, and some measure of diversification of economic activity and of exports may seem to be desirable. Encouragement of selected manufacturing industries may be part of a programme of deliberate diversification. The formal grounds for assistance would be the divergence between private and social benefits: the advantages claimed for diversification do not accrue so much to the manufacturers as to the economy as a whole, and desirable enlargement of manufacturing industry would not take place without assistance, which is here, in effect, a communal payment for real but diffused and unmarketable services.

This argument is distinct from that which suggests official action to promote balanced growth. In the latter situation the balanced growth is supposed to make the constituent activities profitable; in the present case the activities are deemed to be desirable even though they are unprofitable in the sense that their costs exceed the value of their direct output.

This approach to diversification by way of assisted industrialisation may seem plausible, but on closer examination its deficiencies become evident. As we have already indicated, it is not correct to infer the degree of dependence of producers on particular products from statistics of production or of exports.[1] The problem of dependence of predominantly agricultural countries on one or a few products is certainly less widespread and serious than simple statistics might suggest. But even where the problem is present, the encouragement by direct subsidy or tariff protection of otherwise uneconomic industrial activities does little, if anything, to deal with it successfully. In the circumstances the assisted industries can only cater for the home market, of which the rural population and those connected with the distribution of the principal crops form a material part; hence their sales and output would tend to suffer a contraction at the same time as their main customers experience a decline in their incomes. The presence of such largely dependent industries can have little stabilising effect. Again, these industries obviously would not be able to export their products, so that they could not in any way offset the fluctuations in the foreign earnings accruing from the staple exports. When the assisted industries use imported raw materials or equipment, this adds to the difficulties of achieving equilibrium in the balance of payments.

It would be more sensible for government to deal with the problem of dependence and fluctuating incomes more directly. Schemes for the stabilisation of agricultural prices or of producers' incomes could be introduced. It is also possible for a government to deal directly with fluctuations in foreign exchange resources which arise from price movements in export markets, so that the impact of these changes is cushioned. The room for manoeuvre may be small in economies which are dependent in the sense that a large part of their foreign exchange earnings is derived from the export of

1 Chapter XIV, section 6, above.

one or two commodities, and that these account for a large part of the national income. Nevertheless, in so far as these risky and fluctuating activities over a period yield a higher income than do alternative activities, it should be possible in principle for the government to build up larger reserves of foreign exchange or of other resources than it could do otherwise. Similarly, it should be possible to raise larger government revenues and to spend more freely on the provision of basic services, especially on the improvement of communications, than would be the case otherwise, and these services can both strengthen the economy and facilitate shifts between activities should these become necessary. Such measures, though they have their difficulties, are *prima facie* preferable to the subsidisation of uneconomic activities which must put a direct or indirect burden on some of the main income-generating activities in the economy.

§ 7. **Small-scale Industry.** It is not possible to generalise about the types of industry, industrial techniques or types of organisation which on economic grounds are to be singled out for assistance should a government decide to embark upon a policy of encouraging industrialisation. It may seem sound to suggest that labour-intensive industries are likely to be more appropriate than capital-intensive ones; but in fact this is not helpful since labour is not homogeneous, and access to markets is obviously an important consideration. Again it may seem sound to suggest that industries using local raw materials are likely to be more appropriate than others using imported raw materials; but the proximity of supplies of raw materials is only one of many factors bearing on the economic location of processing industries.[1] Nevertheless, it is in point to elaborate the case for placing special emphasis on assistance to industries organised on the basis of relatively

[1] Similarly, the presence of processing industries within a country does not necessarily enhance the value of its agricultural resources; the value of these resources depends upon the intensity and accessibility of the demand for their products, and not on the location of the later stages of production.

small-scale industrial establishments, because the advantages are apt to be overlooked and it is common to equate large-scale operations with economic efficiency.

Government assistance to small firms need not take the usual forms of fiscal assistance through tariff protection, remission of taxation or the granting of direct subsidies. It can take the form of the performance by government of services akin to those provided in agricultural extension work. For example, the spreading of technical knowledge can be assisted, possibly with the aid of foreign technicians recruited by government. There may also be a case for the establishment by government of factory capacity which can be rented to small-scale enterprises. Institutions for mobilising scattered capital may not be available or effective, so that it may be difficult for local entrepreneurs to finance the acquisition of expensive items of fixed capital such as buildings.

The case for assisting small-scale industrial enterprise is not based on sentimental or political considerations.[1] Rather, it is based on advantages of small-scale operation in under-developed countries, advantages which in our view are important except in those industries where large-scale technical units are clearly more efficient. In the conditions prevailing in many under-developed countries the development of small industry may be the most economic form of industrialisation; it may be more economic than either large-scale organised industry or cottage industry. It avoids the heavy costs which often result from agglomeration of large labour forces; the overhead capital costs stemming from such agglomerations are often high, and do not directly increase productivity. In small industrial units administration presents less of a problem and makes less claim on administrative resources; small units also provide a more suitable training ground for administrative responsibility than larger units. Small-scale industry can be spread geographically to serve predominantly

[1] The case has been argued in various writings of H. G. Aubrey, especially in 'Small Industry in Economic Development', *Social Research*, September 1951.

agricultural areas; the market for its products may stem
largely from the cultivation of cash crops, and proximity to
the market may be helpful in conditions of a poorly-developed
transport system.   Small industry represents much less of a
break with previously established modes of living and therefore represents less of a strain than industrialisation in the
form of large units.   It may also avoid some political problems associated with larger industrial units (especially when
owned and managed by foreigners or strangers), notably the
sense of dependence felt by their customers and workers, and
also some of the social and technical problems created by the
agglomeration of large labour forces.

§ 8. Official Measures retarding Industrialisation.   Whilst
some policy measures purport to smooth the way for the
development of manufacturing industries, other measures have
effects which retard the growth of otherwise economic and
viable industry.   The withdrawal or relaxation of such measures promotes industrialisation.   The widespread restrictions
on immigration in under-developed countries are an example.
These prevent the entry of people who could contribute to
industrialisation by increasing the supply of skills and capital.
The restrictions obstruct the growth of industry even when
they are designed more specifically to prevent or control the
establishment or growth of foreign firms in trading activities,
or to exclude foreigners who have little or no capital.   Successful manufacturing enterprises in under-developed countries
have often been established by individuals and companies who
had gained experience of local conditions through previous
trading activities.

Foreign firms are less likely to invest capital in establishing
manufacturing branches in an under-developed country if they
cannot be assured of a supply of foreign managers and
technicians.   The inflow of foreign capital and enterprise is
also likely to be restricted by political instability and by uncertainty of property rights.   Official policies in under-
developed countries substantially influence these factors.

Trade union and government action inflating labour costs tend to inhibit the growth of industry. It is immaterial whether such measures reflect the pressure of sectional interests to maintain or to raise their incomes or whether they are motivated by a desire to alleviate poverty:[1] they raise the money costs of labour in industrial production above the supply price of labour.[2] Cheap labour may be among the more important factors offsetting the lack of other resources, and the inflation of costs can seriously retard industrial development in under-developed countries.[3]

Effective trade union action and factory, labour and social security legislation became important in Western Europe only after these countries had experienced a long period of economic and industrial expansion. In a sense they were then better able to afford such measures which directly or indirectly raise particular incomes by raising money costs of production. A country in which industrialisation has hardly started is not in this fortunate position, and policies which raise costs seriously inhibit industrialisation.[4] An international demonstration

[1] In fact such measures often aggravate rather than mitigate poverty both by retarding economic advance and by increasing the overcrowding in activities into which people are forced because they are excluded from more preferred activities.

[2] Where employers exercise monopsony power, up to a point the raising of wages by government or trade union action need not reduce the numbers employed. This type of situation is considered in Chapter VI, section 3, and is excluded from the discussion in the text, above.

[3] Firms and industries in more advanced countries are understandably concerned with the costs of their competitors in under-developed countries; this concern often is expressed in recommendations for official measures which would have the effect of raising these costs. In the closing decades of the nineteenth century, when factory production of textiles began to assume importance in India, British cotton and jute manufacturers agitated for the regulation of minimum wages and maximum hours in India; and this was regarded by Indian industrialists as a device to undermine their competitive position.

[4] It is sometimes argued that the raising of labour costs enforces the use of more capital-intensive methods and that this promotes growth. This argument is open to various objections, of which the most obvious are that it induces uneconomic mechanisation, raises costs and prices, reduces the employment of labour in the industries in question, and, by crowding labour in other branches of activity (including other branches of industry), discourages otherwise economic mechanisation. Contrary

effect, leading to premature attempts to introduce so-called advanced labour and social welfare legislation, may be at work, with the result that the growth of industry is retarded.

The control of the charges or profits of public utilities is a further example of a type of a policy measure which retards industrialisation and economic growth generally. In various parts of Latin America, for example, the rates which may be charged by railways or electricity supply undertakings have been officially fixed in such a manner that the enterprises have secured returns which have been inadequate to maintain their existing scale of operations, let alone to extend their activities. This has been most marked during the period of rising prices during and after the Second World War. The inadequacy of the transport system of several Latin-American countries is traceable partly to this policy, and this in its turn has retarded economic growth including industrialisation.

The promotion of any uneconomic activity retards the development of economic activities, including economic branches of manufacturing industry. Resources are diverted from uses which are productive on both short and long term considerations. Thus the fostering of uneconomic branches of agriculture and the introduction of policies which raise the prices of farm products hamper otherwise economic industrial (and agricultural) activities. For example, in Southern Rhodesia before the Second World War official regulation of the production of maize, whilst giving the maize-milling industry full protection against foreign competition, rendered 'the manufacture of such items as glucose, starch and cornflour . . . unprofitable because of the high price which the manufacturer was compelled to pay for maize'.[1]

The study of economics furnishes no generally valid formula which enables a government to distinguish in advance the

to what often seems to be implied, it does not follow that measures which result in uneconomic allocation of existing resources will in some mysterious way conduce to the growth of resources.

[1] *Report of the Committee of Enquiry into the Protection of Secondary Industries in Southern Rhodesia*, Salisbury, 1946, p. 33.

economic from the uneconomic activities. Economics does not provide a blueprint in terms of ideal patterns of economic growth and changing economic structure which can be applied directly to specific situations. There is no substitute for the careful examination of the circumstances and potentialities of each case. The economist has an important contribution to make here; for he can ask relevant questions, indicate problems and implications which may otherwise go undetected, and point to the necessary or probable consequences of particular policies.

consider. How the mechanism would... Economists that
not provide a framework in which an ideal pattern of economic
forces are guiding concrete situations which can be analyzed
through to a specific situation. There is no substitute for the
careful analysis of the given resources and circumstances
of each case. The economist has an important contribution
to make in... a great... general questions, various
problems, and policies upon which... decisions so will
protected and point to the necessary or probable consequences
of particular policies.

INDEX

INDEX

ACCESSIBILITY of natural resources, 43–57

Accra, 50, 104 n.

Accumulation, *see* Capital formation

Afghanistan, 113

Africa, 28, 30, 35, 62, 74, 232

Africa, East, 31, 51, 100, 114, 231 n.

Africa, South, 67 n., 81, 104 n., 106, 118–9

Africa, West, 19, 39, 72–3, 97–8, 114, 200 n., 231 n., 236 n.

Agriculture, and manufacturing industry, 235–6; nomadic, 5; policy measures affecting, 209–34; subsidies to, 170; wages in, 79

Agricultural credit, 213–7, 223–5

Agricultural exports, 29, 134, 229–33, 235–6, 250–2

Agricultural extension work, 217–9

Agricultural holdings, consolidation of, 178–80; establishment and improvement of, 29–31, 114, 132, 136, 140, 210–3, 216–7; fragmentation of, 177–8, 209

Agricultural rent, 55–6, 170, 209–13, 216–7

Airports, 46

Alcohol, 86 n., 93, 99

Alienation of land, *see* Land

Allocation and growth of resources, and industrialisation policies, 237; and inflationary policy, 205–8; and monopoly, 183–9; and taxation, 199; inter-relation of, 12, 235, 243–5, 255 n.;

treatment of, in economic theory, 10

America, South, 50, 74, 256

Antigua, 99

Argentine, 28

Ashton, T. S., 41 n., 129 n., 133 n., 137 n., 206 n.

Asia, 59

Asia, South-East, 30, 31

Aubrey, H. G., 242 n., 243 n., 253 n.

Autarky, 48

BALANCE of payments, 142, 208

Barlow, E. R., 41 n., 70 n., 104 n.

Baster, J., 154 n.

Bauer, P. T., 37 n., 40 n., 73 n., 98 n., 184 n., 186 n., 187 n., 219 n., 232 n., 233 n.

Bechuanaland, 86 n.

Beggary, 20

Belshaw, C. S., 82 n., 137 n., 139 n.

Bicycles, 27, 39, 86 n., 119

Biesanz, J. and M., 110 n.

Birmingham, 27 n.

Board of Trade, 86 n., 94

Booker, H. S., 116 n.

Brazil, 7, 113, 200 n.

British Guiana, 53

British North Borneo, 198

Brozen, Y., 172 n.

Budget deficits, *see* Deficit Finance

Budget surpluses, 200–4

Burma, 232

Buttrick, J. A., 59 n., 172 n.

Byzantium, 40 n.

261